LITTLE

BITTERN

A NOVEL BY R.E. BUCKHURST

Published by New Generation Publishing in 2016

Copyright © Jonathan Hyam & Sons 2016

First Edition

The author asserts the moral right under the Copyright, Designs and Patents Act 1988 to be identified as the author of this work.

All Rights reserved. No part of this publication may be reproduced, stored in a retrieval system or transmitted, in any form or by any means without the prior consent of the author, nor be otherwise circulated in any form of binding or cover other than that which it is published and without a similar condition being imposed on the subsequent purchaser.

www.newgeneration-publishing.com

 New Generation Publishing

Contents

Chapter 1 A bridge Tutu far

Sunday Morning 29th April 1973

"Gosh I'm cold!" Jim shivered under the tartan blanket, trying in vain to cover his whole body with the bright red and green material. He looked down at his feet and wondered why he was wearing ladies shoes. More importantly where was he? "Oh heck"! , It came back to him in a flash, he was in the car, He and Betty were at a party, they'd had a row and he'd stormed out.

It was late April, and although the morning was light, it was cold and heavy dew had settled on the windows of the blue Marina Estate. The condensation on the inside was just starting to form into rivulets, as Jim smeared his hand across the driver's side window. "Oh I'm bursting for a wee." He said out loud, as if speaking to some unseen friend.

He looked out to see if the coast was clear. The public loos weren't far away, but he had to negotiate half of the small village car park, dodging between the few parked cars, go up a steep grass bank and over a three foot hedge if he were to avoid being seen by the early rising tourists cooking breakfast on their inadequate hire craft stoves. His car was tucked up against the wall of the Robins House which served as the local Bakery and Village Store.

He was hemmed in at the front by the bottle bank and paper skip. He had no option. He had to go for it. A thirty yard dash, quickly up the bank, vault the hedge and he'd be in. No problem! Only difficulty? getting back still unseen. "Never mind" he thought; "cross that bridge when I come to it. Flipping heck I'm bursting!" He opened the door, looked again and made a dash for it. Ten yards!

"How do women run in these bloody things?" Twenty yards, he looked around "yeah I'm doing fine".

Thirty yards, over the hedge and towards the door. He grabbed the handle with his right hand, twisted his body and pushed with his shoulder. "Sugar!" he snarled as he was violently jarred backwards by his weight rebounding off the locked door. "Oh No!! Jessie you lazy cow"! he cursed

Jessie Chase had the job of opening both the Public loos and the bus shelter each morning, but if the night before she had been lucky enough to "tap" up a few tourists for a drink or two with her tales of the Norfolk Broads, she was apt to oversleep. This was one such morning! James was stuck there; He knew then, that he should have thought twice about arguing with Betty at a fancy dress party. His 6 '2' frame dressed in a pink tutu, white tights and ladies shoes that pinched like hell, was not a pretty sight first thing in the morning.

He should have waited, bided his time, before diving in, opening his mouth and saying what was in his heart. "I've got to go" one thought interrupting the other, "loo or no loo I've got to go." He opted to pee against the three foot hedge that he had just vaulted. It separated the car park from the loos and the river, as it ran along the top of the flood bank. With his back to the toilet block and facing the car park, he started to roll down the white tights past his large male bottom and on to his hips. He put his knees together, while moving his feet apart to aid the process.

With relief, he started to go against the hedge. "Ah!" He sighed loudly. 'EEEK!' He heard a scream, and registered it was that of a girl or young boy somewhere behind him.

He stepped forward like an ostrich with its knees locked together trying to hide as best he could. EEK!! The scream continued as if one long shout.

Another Step, through the hedge – Crash! Bash! His body jerked back as his feet went away. In an instant James found himself sliding, feet out, his bottom bouncing down the eight foot slope towards the car park below. He landed, still holding his manhood, and in the middle of performing the feat he had originally intended. Looking all the world like the famous Manneken Pis fountain in Brussels.

He tried to stand but fell backwards bashing his back against the steep bank, his knees still clamped together, pinned by the white tights. His bright pink tutu all ruffled up at the back and he was still peeing. Behind him, he could distinctly hear the Robin's girls screaming uncontrollably.

Just at that moment, as he thought it couldn't get any worse, two cars pulled in to the car park each full of tourists probably arriving early to collect their boats. Astonishment turned to laughter and then disbelief, as they were greeted by the sight of Jim Daily dressed in a pink tutu, his knees fastened in a pair of ladies tights now torn, trying to run while hiding his manhood stooping forward with every other pace as he attempted to vainly pull up the lingerie. "How do women ever wear this gear?" he again wondered as the screams around him turned to laughter. He reached the sanctuary of the car and dived in. The laughter increased, and he realised the sight of him viewed from the rear, bare bottom in the air, and legs flailing made an even worse spectacle than before. He rolled on to his back, somehow managing to flick the door closed with his foot losing a shoe in the process. Raising his head, he could see some clever wag from the first car standing in the car park, clapping while others joined in with laughter and pointing fingers.

"I hope to Christ those girls didn't recognise me", he muttered as he pulled the car rug over his head.

KNOCK! KNOCK! Someone was tapping on the window. "May be they'll go away" KNOCK! KNOCK! Louder this time. He'd have to look. Rolling the rug back and looking through the steamed up window he could just make out the figure of Jessie Chase using a size 9 ladies high heeled shoe to tap on the window.

"You want the toilets opened now then?" Enquired Jessie loudly through the closed window, in her unmistakeable Norfolk dialect. She had lived in Hornham all her life and you could trace her Norfolk family roots back for generations – even beyond the Doomsday book, or so she'd tell you. Especially if you happened to buy her a half a pint of Yare at the Wherry. She was a good old sort though, meaning no harm to anybody and working for very little money on behalf of the village.

"Yes please Jess, I need to clean up and regain some dignity".

You in't got that long" came back the old lady. Age may have changed her features but it hadn't blunted her wit.

"Jess, what the heck am I gonna do? I've left Betty last night after an argument; I have no clothes, nowhere to stay and no money on me.

"Best you get on and get you cleaned up fust. I'll get you some of them there clothes from Mr Browning's Charity shop". Jess was as good as her word by the time James had negotiated the car nearer to the toilets run the gauntlet of cat calls from the few people still there and cleaned himself up in the public loos, Jess was there with some clothes. There were no underpants or socks but a pair of ill-fitting black trousers, a striped Van Heusen shirt from the early 1960's and a dog tooth sports jacket like your geography teacher would wear.

It certainly framed a better picture than before. The brown brogues would have looked more at home on the golf course, but beggars can't be choosers, and at least they fitted!

"Thanks Jess how much do I owe you?"

"a favour or 2 that's all boyee" she replied with a nod and a grin that told James he could be paying his debt for some time.

"You an Betty split permanent or just a falling out? None of my business mind, but I bin havin a mardle"

"Split permanent Jess I think. She's been having a fling with old Salter's son. It came to a head last night and enough's enough. I don't think he's the first, I just can't give her the excitement she needs". Strange he thought, here he was telling Jess an acquaintance he'd known for only a few years, things that were personal and private and that he wouldn't even tell his own parents. It seemed to help and her slow purposeful nods, told him that she understood. "Peter could do with a hand you know!'

"Peter?"

"Peter Mason. He's got that place on the Loke, he's been trying to do it up for years, but he's passed it. Young man like you. You'd be able to give him a hand and I'm sure he'd let you live in."

"Thanks Jess, but I don't think I'm that desperate yet." Peter Mason was in his 60's and had inherited the house when his mother died four years earlier. It had no running water; no heating and the roof consisted of a blue tarpaulin spread over a few cracked pan tiles and held down by guy ropes. Peter was a nice old boy, but had little or no money to do the property up and no airs or social graces with which to persuade any one to help. Jim knew him well, and had even given him an old bike when Peter's disappeared. There was talk that the Gypsies had it, but most of the evidence pointed to it, being boat people (tourists). Occasionally things would go missing from the village in the height of summer, they'd even been known to pinch chairs from the Pub, and at one time, the landlord lost the doormat. Who would use it with "Welcome to the Wherry" on it was a mystery.

"He's a good sort really you know and he could do with a hand" said Jessie, interrupting his daydream. "...Sorry Jessie, yes I know, but I'm sure I'll sort something. Thanks for the clothes; I'll see you right." With that he was off.

As his car turned out of the car park towards Wroxham, Jessie gave a sigh and mused to herself. "That Betty dun't know when she is well off. He's wurth a hundret of them other boyees!"

Jim drove through the country lanes to Salhouse. A small pretty little Broadland village consisting of a main road, with a few smaller roads off it. The housing was predominantly early sixties style, red brick houses squeezed in between 1920's farm workers cottages. There was a pub at one end and a Post Office at the other. The main attraction was the access to the Norfolk Broads three quarters of a mile along a foot path winding down a long narrow track. Jim's parents owned a small property on the street. They'd moved to Norfolk when Thomas, James's first son was born six years ago. Jim hated asking them for anything, as he knew they would give it to him even though they could ill afford it. But now he had to.

His father John, a short well covered man with balding grey hair and brown-rimmed glasses, had suffered for the past 20 years with a bad back, and had been unable to continue working in the Engineering industry where he had been since the age of 15. His wife was a jolly, red-faced little lady, who also wore glasses, which she always perched on her silver grey curly hair, if she was reading or sewing. Living now on the meagre state pension, they struggled to make ends meet, but their bungalow was always clean and tidy. More importantly to them, it was theirs. Bought outright when they sold their home in Essex and moved up to be near their only son and his boys.

"I won't say I told you so," said Dad in a manner that meant I told you so, "No need for that" rebuked Mrs Daily Senior as she liked to introduce herself to those she didn't know. "Jim's had enough hardship already today, you telling him that we were right all along won't help matters. You ought to be more sensitive; isn't that right Jim?"

"Look Mum, Dad, I just popped in to tell you both before you heard it from anyone else. I don't know where I go from here, or what I'll do, but I will keep you in the picture."

"What about the boys? We could have the boys." Said Jim's mother hurriedly without really thinking what she had said.

"Don't be silly Elizabeth," John's interruption was quick, "How would we cope with a 4 year old and a 6 year old? We can hardly cope with my walking sticks and me, let alone 2 small boys who can't keep still for 5 minutes. They're welcome anytime you know that, but not permanent. Good heavens, it would be like stepping back 30 years"

"But they were happy times, think of the fun we had"

"Yes woman, I had me health and you had your teeth. They all went west 20 years ago. We've now got two good legs and one set of dentures between us. What with that and your piles, we make a right pair"

"All right! There's no need to be crude. Jim doesn't need to know I've.."

"WHOA!" Jim, raising his hands and stepping back as if it were all directed at him. "I only came round to let you know what's what. I didn't come round to start World War Three."

"All right Son, we understand. What do you want – you alright for money by the way?"

Yes Dad, I will be ok, but a tenner would be good, if you could lend it to me."

"Hang on Jimmy;" his mother spoke over her shoulder, as she reached into the kitchen cupboard. Opening an old tea caddy, she produced 3 ten-pound notes, and handed them to Jim, claiming they were for a rainy day, and the weather looked pretty bleak from where she was standing.

Turning out of their driveway on to the main road, Jim thought how lucky he was to have his parents nearby. Now armed with £30.00, a pair of his Dads old socks, and a borrowed set of clothes he felt ready to face Betty. His main worry was what the boys would say…. but this time it sank home. James felt the jealousy of his wife's affair, the frustration of being unable to simply resolve the issue and anger at the fact that the most important people, the boys, were already beginning to be impacted by his impulsiveness

"I'll punch his lights out, he comes round here. You wait and see if I don't. I'll punch his lights out."

William Salter was a hard talking angry young man in his late 20's with a liking for the ladies. His family owned the local abattoir and raised cattle on the marsh land from Acle across towards Reedham, some 12 miles away. He didn't really need to work and spent much of his time in the local pubs playing pool, talking tough and looking for his next conquest. He was a swarthy skinned man of about 5ft 9" with a bit of a beer gut and few people could understand what women saw in him but when he wanted to he could turn on the charm, that and an abundance of money, usually won the day and often as not, the night!

He was standing now in the kitchen of the 2 up, 2 down chalet bungalow that until last night, James had called home. Betty was busying herself making him a cup of tea. She put three sugars in, thinking after last night he would need the energy.

"Don't you worry Bill, he's not coming round here, he's cleared off'. I told him last night that you and I were lovers and he wasn't none too happy so he's cleared off and as far as I'm concerned he's not coming back."

"Good job too coz 1 would you know I would; I'd punch his lights out."

'Mummy, mummy,' Betty turned and sighed at the interruption,

"I told you to go and play"

'But Daddy's here! And Matthew and me want to see him.' The two excited boys were bouncing on the cushions of the brown draylon settee holding on to the back as they strained to look out of the front window.

The main door was at the side and opened out on to a shared driveway. As James walked down the short concrete drive he heard the tapping on the window and smiled at his boys. "At least someone's pleased to see me" he thought nearing the brown and white porch way doors. The door opened quickly even before he had reached it. The large frosted glass panels rattling with the unusual force.

'What do you want? And where did you get those ridiculous clothes?' Snapped Betty standing in the small alcove which formed the porch, her elbows out, her hands formed into fists nesting on the waist of her green print dress.

"I'm here for two reasons. One to see my boys and the other is to talk, can I come in?" said rhetorically as he pushed his way past her. Entering the small open plan lounge with the stairs leading to an upper floor he looked around, there was no one else to be seen, only the 'little monsters' as he affectionately called them. "Hi ya gang he called as the boys ran towards him. He picked them up, first one then the other. Resting them one on each hip supported by his arm, under their bottoms and their hand clasped around his neck. "You're getting too old for this" he said hoarsely, trying to breath. "No we are not!" they screeched almost in unison. "Are we going out somewhere daddy?", it is Sunday. And we're bored." "Yes it is Sunday and we're bored" repeated Matthew. The little lad seemed to have mastered the art of repeating the last or most important line that his brother had said which gave the appearance of intelligence beyond his actual age. Not too many people had noticed that nearly all his comments lacked original thought. All they could see was bright little blond haired boy with beautiful hazel brown eyes and a wide smile. His brother was the same in almost every respect save that his eyes were a pale blue like the sky on a summer's day. If it wasn't for the age and size difference you would think they were twins.

"We'll have to ask your mum. She might have other plans". "You take em if you want but I want 'em back by four" boomed the voice of Betty from the adjacent kitchen as she poured an over sweetened tea into the sink.

"Ok but we need to talk Betty!" He replied while resigning himself to the fact that the discussion would have to wait.

"Talk?, I think the first thing you need to do is change out of those ridiculous clothes. You look like a cross between Bring Crosby and Oliver Twist." He gave a wry smile and thought how accurate the analysis was.

"Dad are we going yet?" Shall we get in the car? Shall I get my bucket and spade?" The questions came so fast without even a pause for a breath. "Yes quick you two get your things and I'll get changed. We'll go to Happisburgh," A favourite spot of the boys. There was a car park on top of the cliff with an ice cream van which parked near to the toilets, a lifeboat station and a long slope leading down to a never ending sandy beach where they could paddle safely in pools along by the break water. They had spent many a happy hour on the beach as a family and deep inside Jim hoped that it would stir some emotion in Betty, but it didn't seem to work. She just pressed on with readying the boys for a beach trip. James went upstairs, changed and was down in minutes but to Matthew and Thomas it seemed like hours. He would have taken longer but on seeing the unmade bed where two people had clearly been lying and sleeping as man and wife he suddenly remembered why he was there. "We'll talk later then, when I return eh! It might be helpful if lover boys not about". James leaned into the kitchen as he was passing on his way out and called "it's ok Bill you can come out now, I'm going". The door slammed and they were gone.

"How'd he know that? How'd he know that?," 'know what Billy love?' Enquired a puzzled Betty,

"Know I was here of course. You tell him? I could have punched his lights out if not for you and the kids". The threat somehow didn't have the same ring to it this time and was ignored. Betty preferred to make another cup of tea.

James and the boys enjoyed the day on the beach as they often did on a Sunday. Over the past few years it had become very much their day as Betty needed a break to allow her to do the household chores that she seemed to enjoy and to have time to herself. Perhaps a little too much time James thought. Maybe if he'd been home more and had paid Betty more attention…… "Can I share your sandcastle mister?" Children have a nasty habit of bringing you back to reality. It was a child's voice, a young girl of five or six. "Yea of course you can, but only if you help me make it." 'Can I decorate it? Please mister, can I decorate it?!' She spoke so fast Jim knew this was her goal to decorate a castle in fine splendour with sea shells and stones and maybe even a flag. "No problem but you'll have to pat it down first."

The next two hours were spent with Thomas, Matthew and Emma as they discovered her name was, decorating the castle making an outer wall and then an even bigger outer wall which protected the raised inner castle area. As the size of the castle grew so did the helpers. Emma's cousin Mickey, a freckly ginger haired lad with glasses and big ears aged five and half. The half was very important. Emily's brother Christopher, two boys from Ireland, a girl named Julia and her mother, all gave a hand in the construction. By the time it was built the tide was returning and all the children stood in the inner area protected from the waves by a strong wall of sand. The first wave made hardly a dent, the water just filling the outer moat. A big cheer went up from the children led by Julia's mum and Jim as the wave receded. The next however was slightly larger and more powerful. The walls were not breached but the water did get all round the moat and washed away much of the walls. Three waves later and the group of some six children and Jim. Julia's Mum having left as soon as she had seen she might get her suede boots wet, clung to each other in the small but beautifully decorated inner castle. "Women and children first!" shouted Jim as the waves breached the walls. He picked up Emma and Matthew and beat a hasty retreat higher up the beach at first followed and then overtaken, by the boys, all except Mickey. Determined to stay till the end, giving up only as the sea soaked over his trousers whilst at the same time washing away the back wall of the once magnificent castle. "Oh no! what are we going to do said Jim laughingly as the remnants of two hours hard labour was washed away.

'Build another one' Emma's voice was quiet but none the less emphatic.

'Yea! let's build another one!" the cry went up and it seemed they all wanted to build another. 'Build another castle, build another castle.' As the chant grew James stood up hands held high in classic surrender position. "Woa! Hold on, hold on". In the moment of silence that followed he lowered his hands and sinking to his knees to be at their level he suggested to the children, "The tides full in now there is no way we can make another today. Why don't we agree to meet same time next weekend and do another?"

'Yes! Good idea, please, please'. "Seems like you've got a date then" Hearing an adult female voice James, still kneeling, shuffled around on his knees and looked up to see a lady of about 30 something looking down at him with an approving smile on her face. "I take it you're the pied piper of Happisburgh!?"

"Ha ha, you could say that, but more the sand piper than the pied piper. I think." 'Well you kept my three charges amused for a couple of hours. I've been watching from over there behind the safety of a good book. I have finished three chapters. They've had a good time, so thank you'

"Which are yours?"

'Emma, Chris, and Mickey'

"Oh yes!, seashells and freckles."

'Hey!' she said looking at James sternly straight in the eye. 'Don't let them hear you say that' there was a pause, 'she hates to be called seashells.'

James laughed out loud realising that Mrs. 30 something was pulling his leg but with a sense of humour was making a valid point. 'Thanks for looking after the children; maybe we will see you next time.' With that and a wave she was gone. Julia's mum collected her and as the beach began to empty Jim took the boys home. The journey from Happisburgh to the main A149 was silent, helped by an ice cream from the Dairy Crest man who kindly parked between the toilets and car park where you couldn't miss him. All very well when you have got money but a real pain if you haven't. Just as the car drove over Wroxham Bridge the one question James had been dreading was raised. "Dad you are coming home tonight aren't you?" 'Yes you are coming home tonight aren't you?' His heart sank, how do you tell your kids that you love them and want to be with them but their mother's found someone else who she'd rather be with. "Listen boys, I'd love to be home with you but I can't tonight. Mummy will be there and I'll see you tomorrow.

"We want you to read us our story" Matthew was only four and didn't say much but this time it sank home like a knife as James felt the jealousy of his wife's affair and the knife turned as the frustration of being unable to resolve the issue turned to anger at the fact that the most important people, their boys, were already being impacted by his impulsive decision to leave the marital home.

"Listen boys I'm sorry but I can't be there tonight; I'll try and see you tomorrow. Looking in the rear view mirror Jim could see that this hadn't gone down well. He thought about pulling over to have a proper discussion but as he passed the Wroxham Veterinary surgery on his left and the Masonic Hall on his right he knew he was too near home for a detailed chat with a six year old and his younger brother. He thought the best thing to do was to say little and try to mend fences in the morning. Talking of morning, where was he to sleep tonight? The boys were safely delivered back home. Jim didn't want to stay and chat, Betty had finished her ironing and was in to her Sunday routine of cleaning but made it clear that as far as she was concerned Jim had left the home and no longer lived there. Bill wasn't to be seen, probably still at the pub from lunch time.

Oh Heck! What do I do now? Sunday night, nowhere to go, no money and no one to turn to. Jim had various friends and neighbours that he could call on but these he'd use as a last resort. He was a proud man and before telling anyone what had happened he wanted to get himself settled.

What was it Jessie Chase had said about Peter Mason? Needed someone to give him a hand and living in? Maybe it's worth a try.

"Peter!"

'Helloo boyee. N' how ya bin?' A statement of greeting rather than a direct question. "could be better Peter" Jim replied as he walked across the deal planks which had been laid to allow a crossing from the shingle over the mud track to the front entrance of the half ruined brick and flint cottage. Peter had been slowly working on the cottage for years but it seemed that as fast as he did it up something else fell into disrepair. The story was that he was a gypsy and his family had settled in Hornham some years ago claiming the property as their own when no other owner could be found. Peter made a meagre living from selling vegetables at Acle market which he grew on an adjoining marsh that he had drained to create a field. What with that, chickens, rabbits and repairing the odd wooden boat he eked out his living. All spare cash went to buying materials to rebuild the cottage. A never ending battle that he was clearly losing having been reduced to one room for sleeping and one other for everything else. There was no proper roof to speak of. Only a blue tarpaulin stretched over the half built walls which formed the gable ends and housed what was left of the upper bedrooms. While these were almost intact there were no window frames or internal timber work.

That had long since gone for fire wood. He cooked downstairs on the old cast iron range which dated back to the early 1900s. The toilet was an outside brick built privy and a bucket of water. For some reason this was better preserved than the rest of the property but still showed its age.

"Hair ya had a bit of trouble baw?!

"You're right there. I suppose it's all round the village. You can't trust Jessie with anything."

'She only got our interests at heart, she be a good gal rairly.'

"Yes I know, I can't complain".

'Times like this boy you need a friend like Jessie," Peter spoke in a broad Norfolk accent slow and purposeful which some people felt made him appear simple, not realising it hid an inner knowing and a dry sense of humour.

"Well that mutual friend of ours suggested I come and have word with you. I need somewhere to bed down for a few weeks until I sort myself out." Peter said nothing, just turned his head slightly to one side and gave a knowing smile. James continued "it's Betty and me see, we had words and I stormed out. I haven't got the money for a hotel, most of them are full anyway. My parents will put me up for a few nights but I couldn't stop there long they're both getting on and I would be more a burden and worry than they could cope with."

'Oh!, n' I could I suppose?

"Well, yes I think you could."

'What's in it for me then?'

"I'll pay you of course. Or I could help you with your renovation of this place." James looked around at the remnants of what was once two thatched cottages and wondered if he had said the right thing.

'I have always liked you son, your old man's bin good to me, always stops to pass the time at Thursday's market, always buys veg and eggs even when he don't need them. I reckon if he can't support you right now, I probably can.' James breathed a sigh of relief and just as he began to smile Peter followed with 'but you got t' work mind. I in't giving nothing for free. You earn good money and are fitter than me so its cash and work I want. You can stay with your parents tonight and move in tomorrow. I wants rent up front though.' A slight glimmer of a smile showed on the old man's unshaved face as he saw Jim looked downhearted 'Not cash!. Twenty lengths of 4 be 2, 10ft long. That'll do for starters.'

Jim was taken aback by the aggressive attitude of this normally placid old man.

'n I needs it hair by noon tomarra!,

"Why? Won't it wait until later in the week?"

'Not if you wants a roof over ya head it won't. If you are staying, looks like I will ha ta make the scullery habitable unless his lordship wants the west wing, with the view of the night sky.'

"Thanks Peter". said with a large sigh of relief.

'Don't thank me yet boyee thank me when works done.'

James smiled wondering to himself what you had to do to satisfy this grumpy old codger and as he did so he turned slightly and his foot slipped off the deal board and sank 12 inches into the thick black Norfolk mud. His other foot still on the board, he was unbalanced and put out his left hand to steady himself. "Oh bugger!," his hand followed his foot and the world seemed to go into slow motion as he rolled forward onto his elbow, his knee, and his shoulder, he felt the mud oozing through his outstretched fingers, squidging up his sleeve, his other knee followed his foot. He narrowly avoided sitting in it. He prized himself out of the mud soaked ditch and just as he thought it was all over the smell hit him, something between that of a dead sheep and two tons of rotting vegetables.

'N that's another thing, you need round here, good balance boyee! Ha! Ha!'

It was the first time he had seen the old boy's face crack. The white stubble of his chin catching the last of the day's spring sunshine. His teeth, what there was left of them, showing themselves a greeny-yellow. They laughed together as Peter put out a hand to help him up. As they gripped hands and shook they both knew then that the other was someone to trust.

That night time was spent by James at his parents place. His mother had made him change in the garage not wanting the smell in the house. His father had lectured him about getting into scrapes and coming in covered in mud. As he settled in for the night he thought It's just like the old times!

Chapter 2 Work! Who needs it?

Monday Morning 30th April

James rose early the next day; breakfast was a cup of tea and a slice of toast. His mother had wanted to spoil him and cook a full English of sausage, bacon, eggs and tomato, his favourite, but he didn't have time. He wanted to see the boys. Thomas into school and Matthew into playschool. Betty normally took and collected them but occasionally when she had been poorly or she was on holiday he had done it. It was less than a mile from their home to the school and a pleasant walk through the strawberry fields past the Memorial Hall and along a little unmade road to the main street. It would make him late for work but what the hell. Family came first. It was 9.45 when he turned the car out of Edward Gardens towards Norwich. His mind was replaying the events of the last hour. Betty had been none too pleased to see him at first, then as it dawned on her that she wouldn't have to walk all that way through the village and back, her mood changed.

'You gonna collect 'em too?' she sneered as he returned the pushchair and collected his car. "Don't think I can, I have to work. But I'll be over at about six."

'Don't you come over at six, I'm doing Bill's tea then.'

"Christ!" Snapped Jim, "Didn't take him long to get his feet under the table. I'll be round at six to see my boys in my house and if Bill doesn't like it I suggest he goes somewhere else."

'What!' She rounded on him in an instant, 'they're my boys and it's my house, ask a solicitor.' her eyes narrowed while her top lip curled as she spat the words out. 'You walked out on us, so I have every right to say what goes and what doesn't.' His face reddened as his temper got the better of him.

"Bloody hell Betty" he retorted, "I only walked out because you told me to; remember? I'm not sure how long this has been going on but it seems to me like you've got it all planned out."

'Months and yes I have' Her nostrils flailed and her upper lip rose again above her teeth as she continued to spit the words at him. 'Bills twice what you are. He's a real man and his family have got money.'

"So that's what it's all about is it? Money! I should have known. Well don't go spending it yet coz I'm not finished. I'll be back at six. I'll collect my things and see the boys." With that he turned walked the few paces to the car, got in quickly and drove off before Betty could have the satisfaction of having the last word.

Damn! Why didn't I see it coming? As far as I knew things were fine, sure she'd gone off sex but that had been gradual hadn't it? The nights out with the girls. They'd become more and more regular. Phone calls when there was no one there, when he answered it. The calls from her sister, the late nights out babysitting. "I've been a naive fool". All the clues he had missed started to build in his mind. It was racing ten times faster than usual. "Who else knew,? Linda did, I'm sure. I never did trust her ever since she made a play for me at the New Year's party. Bollocks I've been a bloody fool. When did it start? Why did it start? Where did they do it. In my bed? In my house. Bastard Bill! You slimy little so and so" Temper turned to anger, anger to fury and then to utter frustration. He turned off the ring road by the Hotel Norwich and on to the trading estate where his works was situated opposite May and Bakers fertilizer and earth enrichment products plant. He'd been driving on auto pilot and could remember nothing. It wasn't until he stopped that he realized tears were running down his face on to another of his Father's white shirts.

'Where you bin? Don't you know what time it is? I've told you before, we can't have your London ways round here.' Kelvin Dickson was a failed salesman who had risen by default to be branch manager of Wilson's Wire

Works. The main company made wire products in the outskirts of London and when they bought out a small Norwich agent who had run into financial difficulties they inherited Kelvin. A little man who was said to be very evenly balanced as he had a chip on both shoulders. He seemed to hate anyone or anything from outside of Norfolk, in particular anyone with a London accent and anyone taller than him. All three categories Jim fell into. If Jim had not been recruited by the London Directors he knows he would not have got the job. In the past Jim had taken the easy road and avoided confrontation but today he was not in the mood. He breathed in filling his chest and raising his shoulders he moved a pace toward Kelvin and looked down at the little man beneath him like a cat above a mouse. He put one hand on his shoulder and gripped it hard. "I've had a bad day already and I don't intend to make it any worse by discussing it with you. I like to keep my affairs private." Dickson was taken aback. He was not used to being intimidated Jim's emphasis was on the My affairs and he wasn't sure how much Jim knew about his relationship with the Saturday cleaner. He quickly backed down 'Ok I'm just saying that we expected you in earlier that's al!' "Well I'm here now and I'll make the time up if I need to; You know that. I'll deal with my calls I have to deal with and I'll get out on the road"

Monday was paperwork day when the rounds for the week were organized and the appointments made. Jim busied himself until lunch time but couldn't concentrate. His mind kept returning to the argument with Betty and how she seemed to have been calculating it all. He suddenly remembered the 20 lengths of 4 x 2 for Peter.

He ran down the small flight of stairs from the upper office pausing at the little glass sliding window for just enough time to pass over his call sheet for the day. "I'm off out. Jewsons, Looses, Roys. If I get time I'll do Brundall Pet and Hardware on my way back".

'Jim, you all right? Only you've hardly said a word since you came in.' As she spoke the words Mills poked her head through the opening of the sliding window turning it to the left to watch Jim as he passed through the entrance door on the car park. "Sorry Mills, tell you later…" As he said it the part glazed entrance door automatically closed behind him and he was gone.

Tuesday Morning 1st May

It was Tuesday morning the week hadn't started well and Jim wasn't looking forward to the weekly sales meeting with Kelvin Dickson the "poison dwarf", Jim saw him as a little ginger haired excuse for a man who seemed to have a huge inferiority complex especially when standing next to someone tall like Jim. To make matters worse he was an ex-football referee and a close friend of old man Salter who had been a customer of Wilson's Wire Works for years

"You want a cup of tea?"

'Please Mills, I'd love one if I've got time.'

"Oh! you'll have time alright, He'll keep you waiting just to show you how important he is."

"Mills, that's not like you; You would normally have nothing said against him. What's changed?"

"Nothing, that's what" came the curt reply. From the speed with which she said it and the tone of her voice Jim knew something was not quite right. Jim stood behind her as she made the tea in the little kitchen just off the corridor, which separated the offices and showroom from reception.

He didn't like to see anyone upset especially Mills who was usually very happy go lucky and the life and soul of the office. Jim had taken to Mills as soon as he met her. She reminded him of his favourite aunt who lived in Bristol. It was Mills who answered the phone and people often called just to listen to her funny little Norfolk accent.

"Hellooo, Wilkinsons Wire Works." She'd say, blissfully unaware that people from outside the county found it amusing. When they asked to speak to one of the reps she'd reply "He's now coming" and hold the line please was always "hold you hard"

'Come on, Mills What's the problem? Maybe I can help'

"You got enough problems of your hone, you dun't want nun a mine as well."

'Go on try me, what's up?'

"Ooh, it's just Kelvin. Brenda comes in on Saturdee morning to clean the hoffices and I does it when she's on Holiday. My Harry's bin laid off from Laurence's and I asked if me an' Brenda couldn't do it one week about and Kelvin's having none of it. Says it wun't suit him and he wouldn't have the flexibility as I lives out at Helsdon and Brenda's just over the rood. I mean, I needs the money and she dun't, wot with her old man working at Bacton gas Works."

"Mills I can't promise anything but I'll have a word with Kelvin if you wish and I'll see what we can do."

"James! Come" a wood panelled door had been flicked open just enough so the command could be shouted through. By the time Jim entered the office the poison dwarf was seated back behind his desk.

"Sit!"

Jim did as instructed and sat with his back straight, raised his hands up to the middle of his chest, held his head high and looked left and right like a dog begging for a biscuit. The humour was lost on Dickson and Jim thought it best not to labour the point, as the little man was obviously in a worse temper than usual. Jim knew things were not good as the chair he was sitting on was lowered right down and Dickson's was raised so high that his feet didn't actually touch the ground. This made it that Dickson was an inch or two higher than the person opposite and as far as Dickson was concerned, "superior".

'I have had reports that you have been sleeping rough in the company car, picking fights and been drunk. Worse than that you have been abusive to one of our most important customers. We can't tolerate such behaviour. The reputation of this company is more important than anything,,,'

"B,b,but Hang on. I, I.."

'Hang on Nothing!' Dickson was refusing to be interrupted. He was in referee mode and nothing was going to stop him.' You can have your say when I have had mine.

You've brought this company into disrepute. You were not a good rep when you were at your best but the final straw is you insulting and threatening our customers. That's gross misconduct and as far as I'm concerned that's a red card'

"Bloody Hell" thought Jim, He's even using football phrases now!

'And as of now you are dismissed. Your P45 and what's owing to you will be forwarded to your home address. Mills!' He barked, into the small intercom and phone system taking his first breath for what seemed like five minutes, 'James Daily is leaving us. Please make his cards and wages out.' Turning to James with the intercom still on, 'Leave your car keys here with me'.

"What my car keys?" came the worried Norfolk response through the crackle of the intercom.

'Not your car keys Mills, I was talking to Daily.

"OOH!, Sorry'

James was stunned. He'd never expected in a million years that his boss would dismiss him especially for something he hadn't done. "Look you can't just dismiss me. You haven't heard my side of it yet and I haven't done anything."

'As far as I am concerned you have. I have spoken with your wife and our customers and I believe what they tell me. You are a liability and I don't need you. If you don't like it you know what you can do.' He paused and raised himself as far as he could without falling over. 'Leave your keys on the desk and go.'

Pushing his chair back Jim stood up and moved towards the desk, Dickson shrank back and pushed himself away with the palms of his hands on the edge of the desk as his feet couldn't quite touch the ground to give any purchase. Leaning right over the desk Jim looked down at the little man saying "I'll clear my things out first. Then I'll go, but what you're doing is wrong. You are just a weak little man with no backbone. And it won't rest here."

'You can't talk to me like that!' He squealed his face reddening and going towards purple at the thought of someone telling him the truth.

"What are you going to do then shorthouse? Fire me?"

Dickson looked down to avoid the eye contact as Jim turned and walked towards the door.

"I'm ever so sorry Jim, I dun't think he'd take it that bad. I should never ha let you get involved." Gloria Mills was almost crying. "Wot if I goo tell him I dun't need to work Satdees afterall?"

Jim couldn't help laughing, although filled with irony it did lighten the moment.

"Mills'y don't you worry my love, I don't think your working Saturday's will have any effect on this."

With the contents of the glove box, his maps an old flask and that trusty tartan travel rug placed in a black bin bag he stepped back into the reception.

Stretching slightly he raised his right hand to push up a ceiling tile. He let it fall back into place trapping the leather thong of his car keys in the process.

Your car keys are here Kelvin, Want to come and get them while we all watch?

The question was purely rhetorical. The cowardly little man was nowhere to be seen.

Mick Mates one of the other reps, came in just as this scene was ending and realizing what was happening offered to run Jim home.

The journey was a verbal re-run of the day's events with each of the salesmen puzzling at why Jim had been dismissed and what had been said by the "Customers"

Was it the abattoir? They were a regular customer but certainly not the biggest. Depending on which time of year that was probably Roy's or Looses or even Coopers on the coast. But all of these were good companies and wouldn't get involved with the dismissal of a suppliers representative. There must be more to it.

"I'm up the other end of Hornham village now" Jim said having almost forgotten that Mike didn't know he had moved out. They turned into the muddy path.

Jim was pleased that Mike had agreed to keep in touch and find out more if he could, about why Jim had been sacked. As he drove away Jim looked across as Mike waved his right hand out of the window and didn't look back.

'God!!' he thought, "what a difference two weeks makes, from top sales rep with a loving family, good job, good house nice car and great prospects; to this, Run down, beaten up verbally at least, no home; no job no car and no family. What a way to go. And I wonder who's going to take over my customers."

"You're back early. You got my timber and bits I need?" George was putting in joist hangers and working on the joists that Jim had got earlier

'Peter, The only thing I have got is the sack.'

'You're jookin! What did you do steal the wood?'

'No,,'Jim shook his head slowly breathed a sigh of desperation "oh! I don't know. I don't know what I did. That's the problem." and as the anger built within him his eyes screwed and through gritted teeth he went on "All I know is that the ginger haired little twat raised himself up to his full height of three foot eight and flipping well sacked me. Evil little peasant. As if I didn't have enough trouble."

'Don't you hold back son, let your true feelings shoo.'
The sarcasms hit home and James resolved to tone down
his feelings, in public any way.

"Two things I need now then, A job and a car."

'Noo! You need a pint boy, Lets goo see if the beer is
still ok. Come on we'll have 2 pints of Yare at the Wherry
and work out what we're gonna do.'

The Wherry was not full but it was busy enough for a
Tuesday. There were a few locals, some playing cards and
others talking loudly, each trying to outdo the other with
tales about river craft of yesteryear. There were also the
holiday makers with small children who had tied up their
boats to the moorings outside. Most of them wanting a
meal from the limited range that hadn't changed in 10
years, "yes but it's what they like and it draws them in"
Barry would say. And as the landlord it was his decision.
The sign hadn't changed for years either. 'The chefs
special' it proudly announced underneath which, someone
had written "The wife's not bad either". It caused people
to look twice so Barry and his wife Ann had left it there. It
also gave customers a false hope that he had a sense of
humour. "You can't afford a sense of humour in
business." He would explain "My customers are a joke,
what more do you want?" It was a funny old pub full of
brick a brac. A divers helmet, sheep dip fencing on the
ceiling and lots of things about boats from days gone by
called Wherry's that had a shallow draft and a real sail
that must have spanned 20ft or more, over the side of the
boat decapitating any unlucky fisherman on the bank if
they were not looking.

Everything in the early 1900's came by boat and
Hornham was a major boat building area. "What you
thinking?" Peter's voice interrupted Jims thought pattern
with a bump as he laid down 2 pints of 'Yare'. "Well
actually I was wondering who would ever have thought of
putting sheep fencing on the ceiling?".

'Well that was Mark Diamond's idea. He don't come in anymore; He was barred. He tried to make a ewe turn in the car park.' Jim missed the pun, his thoughts having moved on or perhaps back, to his own situation. 'So wot you gonna do boyee?'

"I don't know Pete. I'm ok for a month or so but it's after that I'm worried about. I'll have to sign on obviously and, look for another reps job but I want to stay local so I can see the kids and hopefully sort things out with Betty".

'You reckon there's a future?'

"Who knows? I hope so. I know I'm not the greatest catch in the world but we have been together for eight years and that's got to count for something. Trouble is I'm not rich, I'm not ambitious and I'm obviously not good in bed."

"Well you're living with me presently and the good news is I don't need your money, it's just your muscles I need. And as for being good in bed, you int moy type boyee soo it dun't matter too much in that department. Another pint?"

Two pints later and Jim had a plan. He would sign on in the morning and see what jobs were about. He had no car, no job, very little money, no home and no one to share his daily life with except a funny old man he hardly knew and two ageing parents. He did have the boys though and tomorrow first thing he would collect them from Betty and drop them off at school. That's if she'd let him. "Better make a phone call". It was quick. A few terse words and an aggressive attitude from Betty which only softened when she realized she wouldn't have to take the boys to school. "Well I'm fixed for the morning Peter. I drop the boys off at school and catch the 9.15 bus to Norwich. Let's go and have a look at them 4 be 2's and see if we can't make a start on the flooring joists."

They left the pub with Jim feeling much better than he had when they'd entered it and were now ready to crack on with the renovations.

Wednesday 2nd May

"Hair ya goo boyee". Jim was half awake, half asleep almost not wanting to open his eyes, hoping the past few days had been a dream. No such luck. As he reluctantly lifted his eyelids he was greeted with the sight of an unshaven unwashed grey haired old man thrusting a mug of tea at him.

"Are you usin the ablutions furst or am I?"

'You can Peter, I'm still coming round.' The facilities were sparse. An outside loo which flushed occasionally if you pulled the string that disappeared somewhere into the cistern, if not it was a bucket of cold water. There was a wash hand basin with running cold water that was pumped by hand from the well. There was a stand pipe but that was outside in the field and on a meter so was chargeable. Hot was an optional extra if you were prepared to heat it on the stove, and a mirror that was only ok if you didn't want to use the edges where the paint had lifted. But who cares, thought Jim. It was home and he had to get up and take the children to school.

"Peter!" there was a pause while the old man turned round. "Is there any chance I can use your bike to get to home and back? I won't be long." 'As you say boyee, I'll need her later though, I've got to pick up some nails and things so I can carry on where we left off'

The cycle ride through the village didn't take long. It would have been quicker if he hadn't met Jessie. She was collecting cans and picking up litter.

'Hat a do moi bit for the village ya noo.' She really was a gem, always on the go and thinking of others first. If only there were more like her thought Jim as he discussed his new board and lodgings. "I said he'd be royt din't I".

'You did Jess and thank you.'

"plenty time for that, you know what I drink.'

A food wrapper fluttered past in the wind and she was gone chasing it down the road as she spoke. Jim turned into the drive of his real home and propped the bike against the wall beneath the kitchen window. Rap, rap, a noise behind him made him jump. "You can't leave that there I need to get my car out. Mr. Holingsworth was a miserable old man. Jim was glad they'd only ever had to share a drive with him. Things were fine until Jim got a car and wanted to use the drive. The old devil changed overnight claiming the drive as his because of his infirm wife and a perceived need to rush her to hospital. In no mood for an argument Jim moved the bike further down to where the driveway parted, each to their own garage. Holingsworth scoured at Jim through his kitchen window. In return Jim gave a cheery wave and a broad smile saying "up yours too old man" loud enough for Jim to hear but quiet enough for the deaf octogenarian not to know. The front door of number 33 opened. "You're gonna have to get a move on. The words were hardly out of her mouth when Betty bundled the two boys out of the house. "Hi gang!" Jim choosing to ignore the grumpy greeting he had received from his wife. The boys were obviously pleased to see him, they didn't stop talking until they got Thomas to school. "Can you pick us up Dad? Can you?" 'Yes can you Dad? Please?' "I don't know, I can't promise, I'll see what I can do." He desperately wanted to but couldn't see how he could manage it. He loved his time with the boys just as much as they did. He'd always wanted more but Betty would have none of it. "Come on Matt we've got to run if we are going to make it to play school. You ready?" With that he beat a hasty retreat up the slight incline from the school to the street.

"Who's leading who?".

"Oh hi ya Julie. I'm not sure; Matt's in charge of me but your guess is as good as mine."

Julie and Tommy her husband, were friends and neighbours of both him and Betty but not on such terms as Jim felt he could or even should, involve them in his present predicament.

"Betty ok is she? We saw you both at the do. Hah!" a nervous but perhaps genuine laugh, "I thought you looked good in that ballerina's thing but we never saw you go, did you enjoy it?" Jim couldn't escape; he and Julie were both taking their children to the same playschool. His mind raced what should he say? Did she already know? Was she prying for answers to the gossip? If she knew, who else knew? It was only a ten minute walk along the street past the Spar turn right past the DIY store and poodle parlour and you're there, but this was going to be a very difficult ten minutes. They had to know sometime, maybe now was the right time. May be not, his mind was a blur. Does he let it all out or just a little. "I've left home Julie. I'm staying with Peter Mason until I can find somewhere."

"Oh Gord! You found out then?"

'What? You mean about Salter, who else knew?"

"Well I'm not saying we knew but..." There was an embarrassed pause, "Well I mean it was Joe really. He suspected something had been going on but didn't want to get involved you know because.."

"I understand" he interrupted sensing and hearing the embarrassment in Julie's voice, after all they were friends of both of them and shouldn't have to take sides. "But if you knew, how many others knew and never said?"

"I don't know it's just, you know.,, she shrugged her shoulders lost for the right words to say. They crossed the road at the Spar and completed their journey in silence. The children deposited at playschool they met again as they collected their respective buggies. "I'm sorry about what I said, about Betty n'that but if there's anything we can do. Have the kids or whatever, while you sort things out, you know, let us know". "Thanks Julie, I may well call on you for that but now I've got to get myself into Norwich to get another job." Julie was puzzled but didn't think that now was the time for more questions. Jim headed down the park to his former home. Leaving Julie to wonder. He rang the bell,

"one buggy!"

She was still in her dressing gown and wearing the makeup from the night before. The vision of an old prostitute flashed through Jim's mind but just as quickly he dismissed it as uncharitable. "You got time to talk? He asked. "On the door step yes but inside no." 'Hey I still own the flipping house don't forget.'

"No you don't I do. The house will soon be mine and you'll pay a quarter of what you earn to me and half to the boys. So as far as I'm concerned this is mine." She stood firm, her arms folded over her bosom, shoulders forward standing on the small step blocking the entrance to Jim's old home. He wanted to do as he had the other day and push past but felt it wouldn't achieve anything. "You're a smart arse cow, I'll give you that, that's part of the reason I married you, but I'll find out where I stand legally and I'll be back to claim what's mine." He turned, grabbed the old bike and rode off fuming. He hated to lose especially to her. "Christ that evil woman". How quickly it had come to this. On Friday they were, to all intents and purposes, a happily married couple with a bright secure future and less than a week on they hated each other with a passion and were heading for divorce. How come it had happened so quickly? Had he been blind or just stupid? The question he would keep asking himself. Pedalling back to Peters these things were going around and around in his head. I should have said this…., I should have said that. She'd have replied this or that and I'd have said so and so. Around and around the whole scenario went in his mind, getting nowhere just churning away. He wished he could turn it off but he couldn't. He'd wave to someone he knew give a false smile, think about them but as soon as his attention lapsed he was back to thinking about Betty, the boys, Salter and himself. What a mess. How could he resolve it, how could he win her back? Did he want to?

Chapter 3 A UB40 and a new CV

"Well done Son, if you hurry you'll catch the ten o five. Jim dispirited but at the same time determined, dashed in across the by now familiar scaffold plank and changed into some smart trousers and jacket. As he'd put on his only one remaining clean white shirt the thought suddenly struck him, he needed to do some washing. These thoughts came back to him as he sat on the single decker bus that went from Hornham into Norwich. Peter certainly didn't have a washing machine and there wasn't a launderette in the village. The nearest was at the Heartsease on the outskirts of Norwich. The other option was his mum. Maybe she could help out. She'd be pleased to do it. Bit of a way though, through Wroxham to the bridge then change buses to Salhouse. That would take ages and he wore a clean shirt every day for work. Two a day at weekends and few each week in the evenings. Flipping heck that's 12 shirts or T shirts and when you add up the socks, pants and jeans, that's a couple of black bin bags full and when you do find time to iron all that lot? The logistics of single living were beginning to hit home. The fact that Jim had no car in an area where buses were few and far between. No money coming in and no job made things even worse. As his mind flitted from one problem to the next, people began to stand and queue ready to get off. He hadn't really noticed any of them, they were just a queue of people yet he had a feeling he was being stared at, talked about. He didn't know, he couldn't remember any one calling his name but he just had a feeling. He daren't turn round, afraid that he'd have to get into conversation. Just sit where you are he told himself, stare at your knees. Don't make eye contact. His eyes darted from one knee to the other and across to the legs of the people to his right as they filed off. "S'cuse me young man, you getting off?" He'd been unaware of the old lady next to him. His mind in such a turmoil he hadn't given her a second thought. "Oh! Yes sorry." He rose and followed behind the other passengers leaving her to squeeze herself between the seats to the side. Stepping down into the bright sunshine of a spring day in Norwich he was momentarily blinded as he turned right towards the offices and studios of Anglia Television. That area of Norwich was often in shadow between the old Norman Castle set high on its mound and the three story building of offices with shops below but at this time in the morning the sun shone right down it as if a torch light in a tunnel. "Hello! Thought it was you." A female voice, cheerful, high pitched and happy with a hint of Essex. Jim was desperately trying to remember where he'd heard it before. His eyes blinking as he tried to adjust to the light and recognize the lady at the same time. "I said to Pauline that's Mr. Sandcastle. I'll have to introduce you, There was a bit of a pregnant pause until – "You don't recognize me do you? We met on the beach at Happisburgh. You built sandcastles for the children. Oh I feel such a fool. I shouldn't have said anything except the kids haven't stopped talking about it and when I saw you I thought….Oh! I am sorry. I feel such a fool," she started to blush. Jim could see it welling up from just above her bosom right to her forehead. Her ears turning a bright blush pink, redder than the rest and set amongst the back drop of her tumbling blond hair. She was right he hadn't recognized her, his mind was on other things. "Oh! Yes you're wots-is-names mum and thing. Where are they?"

"Uncle Earnest and Aunt Hilda's got them at the moment so as we could come shopping to Norwich. Where's your lot,?"

"back at school thank heavens. Ours must go back earlier than yours in the South" He noticed the redness starting to fade. "This is Pauline" she said quickly trying to ensure there were no more pregnant pauses, "Pauline, this is Mr. Sandcastles." She grabbed her reluctant sister by the elbow and dragged her forward. "It's Jim actually" he said offering a hand for the reticent Pauline to shake.

She took it and smiled at him as she did so. It was a warm smile of trust and friendship which took Jim aback somewhat as this was their first meeting but he was put at his ease rather than on his guard. "Hi ya Jim I've heard quite a bit about you over the past day or so. My Simon keeps being pestered to build sandcastles like you did."

"Gosh, I'm sorry it's the only way I know to keep the boys amused without it costing me a fortune. I hope I haven't caused any....."

"No I'm only kidding. It'll do him good. It's about time he realized there was more to life than sport on the telly." Ten minutes later having made polite excuses to rush off, Jim was heading down Davy's steps towards the market place along the close narrow streets which were crammed full of odd little shops that you don't see everywhere else. 'Shouldn't have stopped so long. Nice ladies but I've got things to do.' down the alley, first right, turn left at Jarrolds Department Store, Shire Hall on the left and on the right Citizens Advice Bureau. He'd remembered the instructions from some time ago when he'd accidentally run into the back of another car who was loitering at a junction. Names and addresses were exchanged, no damage, other than dented pride but the driver in front later wanted to claim for a broken mirror, musical instruments and scientific equipment which he claimed he was carrying in the boot. Luckily the insurance company settled it and Jim hadn't needed to seek further advice, but now it was different. This was a matter of life. Jim's life with his boys. May be even his life with Betty.

"Mrs Lamb will see you in about 20 minutes if you can wait". Not what he had wanted to hear but it would do. Mrs Lamb turned out to be a very attractive lady in her early 40s with a bright broad smile and knowing eyes that lit up as she looked at you. She was five foot nothing but gave an air of superiority that demanded recognition. She listened intently to Jim's pleading and then offered her view. "I'm sorry Jim, the law doesn't look at blame in a relationship. It looks first at the children and their needs and then at what's left over. The law generally sides with the mother and disregards the father's views or desires. In your case I would suggest that you should expect your wife to claim three quarters of your earnings. Fifty per cent for the children and twenty five percent for her to provide a home in which they can grow up" "Hold on, what about me; Don't I have some rights?"

'You do but they are limited and at the end of the day she will claim you walked out. Effectively abandoning her and the children. The judge won't be interested in your reasons, they'll only be interested in the boy's welfare.' As the conversation wore on Jim felt more and more despair. Finally, "so where do we go now?"

'I'll write to your wife on your behalf and see if we can't get a dialogue going. The most important thing for you is to still keep seeing the boys and continue to pay whatever commitments you have, mortgage etc.' "But I'm not living there!"

'I know but as far as the court is concerned it's still your responsibility and it is the family home.' Jim was devastated. He couldn't get his head around it. She had had an affair, she'd slung him out, she'd moved the boyfriend in and he was still having to pay. That's not fair, that's not justice, that's the world gone bonkers. He started to think of all the questions he should have asked Mrs. Lamb; What if he has no money? What if the boyfriends living there, how much should he pay? If Jim continues paying who owns the house? 'My golly! What a mess.' It was too late now. He was out in the street sitting underneath the trees by the taxi rank. Time in the citizens Advice Bureau is free but it's also limited. He looked down at the appointment card. Two weeks today. That would have to do but would another 20 minutes be enough? The sweet Mrs. Lamb hoped to refer him to a solicitors firm under the legal aid system but it was dependent upon the response from Betty.

'Big issue'?!

Too right it is, thought Jim but instead just said 'no thanks' as he realized there was always someone worse off.

The sun was still shining, Norwich was busy and bustling. For Jim the City always held a magical air. The bright coloured market stalls which stretched from the shops up to City Hall. The tight little lanes where you could buy anything from a Chinese imported toothpick to a locally produced double bore shotgun. Not to mention the jewellery, clothing and new age interest shops which seemed to be on every lane. Yes Jim thought; Norwich is a fine city and while Norwich market can still boast a hoover bag stall you know the world is in safe hands. However now was not the time to reflect on the merits of Norwich. The job in hand was to get employment. It was also to sign on. A thing Jim hadn't done ever before and he was not looking forward to now. Jim wasn't a snob or had ever considered himself such. He did however have standards and he now found himself between them standing in line with those people who he had always pitied. He'd never had to sign on before and wasn't sure what to do. "Name, address, proof of ID, when did you last sign on.?"

"Daily."

"We pay weekly or fortnightly by cheque, we don't pay daily."

"No, No, you've got it wrong, I'm Daily."

"We pay weekly or fortnightly, we don't pay daily." She spoke the words back so fast she was like a machine on auto response not even bothering to look up from her papers. Jim was reminded of school where such conversations took place every time he changed year tutor. "I'm James Daily. I've never signed on before and my address has just changed. I have a driving license as proof of ID, what more do I need to do?"

"When did you last work? Have you filled in your F7 and UB40?"

"I haven't filled in anything. I was only sacked yesterday and I was hoping you could give me some advice and direction as to what I should do."

"Oh yes, plenty of advice and direction but what most people want and we can't give them it, is money." Kay, or so the name badge said, looked up at this point and gave a broad special smile, so quick if you'd blinked you would have missed it. She was a slim lady with a fake tan, brown short cut hair and highlights. She dressed and looked at first glance, about 30 but her hands and neck showed her age as much older. "You'll need your employer's details an F7 and a UB40 filled in. You get them over there. Bring it all back here with your proof of ID and we will enter you on the system."

Jim did as instructed struggling only at the bit where it said address. He wasn't sure where he lived. Yes he was currently living with Peter but that wasn't his home or at least he didn't consider it as such. If he put his real home down any money would go there and Betty would grab it first. He could put down his parents address probably the easiest, occasionally he had junk mail sent there to him so he could probably 'prove it' was his house if he needed to.

Forms filled out and registered under his parent's address he hurried to the Employment Agency across the road.

'That's the first bit done. Now for a job, Rule one, have a good CV'.

"But I haven't got one".

'You will have as we fill this form out on the computer. The CV drops out the bottom'

Jim wasn't computer literate. He could type a bit having learned at school. He and his friend Paul Hatton were thrown out of woodwork and metal work as punishment for messing around. Their penance was to join the girls in typing and domestic science. The punishment back fired somewhat as both boys enjoyed the experience immensely ending up with more street credibility and more girlfriends than any of their peers.

"I'm sorry but I'm not any good with computers. The girls at work do my stuff on their word processors so I don't have to use them."

'Don't worry, I ask the questions, you provide the answers. I type them in and the machine does the rest. Simple.' And it was, in less than half an hour Jim had a CV. Malcolm the pleasant young man with a broad smile in a rounded face, was very personable and Jim could see why he had chosen this job. In less than 20 minutes he had explored Jim's previous employment, discussed his present situation and selected 4 positions that may suit him. Jim was impressed. "I'll make some phone calls and come back to you. Where can I best contact you? You can't really; I'm not on the phone at the moment. We're waiting for it to be connected" And we'll be waiting some time thought Jim. Shortly after they deliver the new roof and fit the central heating, that's probably about 2 years. "I'll call you if that's ok? I'm off for some lunch just after this so I'll pop back about two or ring later, ok.?

'Fine, yeh.'

"Can I take a copy of the CV? I'd like to show it to my mate who I'm meeting for lunch. He'll be impressed."

'No problem, I'll give you my card, I'll stick it on the top.'

Armed with the CV, he set off down Prince of Wales Road towards the copy print shop. Within 20 minutes Jim had his own bunch of CV's and was ready to do battle with the local Situations Vacant.

There were no end of sales jobs, but mainly for food, double glazing and insurance. The industries that Norwich was built upon. Wire work is a bit specialist thought Jim as he trawled his way through the Eastern Daily Press trying to fold the large broad sheet newspaper neatly without drawing too much attention to himself.

The EDP had resisted the temptation to go tabloid in an effort to be different., all very well but it was causing Jim difficulties, performing like a policeman on traffic duty with bits of newspaper flying everywhere with Jim after them, trying desperately to hold both his composure and the paper as a breezes blew in gusts through Cathedral Close and along the park bench where he had set up office.

Just as he thought he had it under control 2 pages billowed up on the blustery wind and went sailing across the grass towards the Cathedral cloisters." Crikey!" Bundling up the remainder of the paper he launched himself from his bench and set about chasing the loose sheets across the close, breathing a large sigh of relief as they fluttered to the ground caught in the lee of Nelsons statue. Within an instant he had one trapped beneath his foot and was reaching for the other when the wind had other ideas. Off he chased again "saved!" this time by a passerby trapping it beneath a pretty shoe and well-turned ankle. He grabbed the paper with the tips of his fingers and his thumb his eyes followed the ankle up the leg and towards its owner. Where they met those of, Mrs, Thirty something with the blond hair smiling back down at him.

"Thank you for that" an embarrassed smile crossed his face as he rose. His reddened cheeks passing close to hers, too close perhaps, close enough to smell her perfume.

'It's a pleasure and thank you for the entertainment. We were just visiting the Cathedral and saw your predicament. Do you often stop here to fly kites? Or were you trying to read it?'

"No! I'm actually looking for a job, I was in the middle of making notes and the wind caught it." He couldn't help but smile despite the embarrassment.

'Really? What is it you do?'

"Well…I.." Jim didn't tell the whole truth. He didn't think a wire works salesman sounded too good and besides he had only met the lady twice before now and even then only for a short while. "…sales. I'm in umm." He made an attempt to fold the paper back into some sort of order. It wouldn't have mattered any way as they were interrupted by the sister.

'Are you joining us for coffee? Kym and I are just going to Pizza Two and Pancakes or whatever it is.'

It seemed to be an order rather than a question as having picked up the remainder of Jim's paper and talking over her shoulder, she walked towards the Cathedral gates with Mrs thirty something following on behind; her head doing a double take between Jim and her sister as if she wasn't sure where she should be.

Half an hour later refreshed with a good cup of real fresh brewed coffee, Jim remembered he had promised to return to the agency and the plump faced lad who had prepared his CV.

"Ladies, I love your company and I thoroughly enjoyed the coffee but I have to go I'm afraid. I'll get the bill though."

'No you won't!' it's our treat, in payment of the sand castles. You can get the next ones. '

With a cheerful "Thanks" a smile and a wave he was off; He uttered a sigh of relief. "That was a close call. I've just about got enough to get me home." Through the cobbled lanes, past the buskers and round by Jarolds. Up the slope by Shire Hall with its soap stall and Crystal shop. And he was back at the employment agency. The plump faced lad was nowhere to be seen.

'Can I help you?'

"Yes I was in earlier and saw Umm.."Jim fumbled in his pocket for the card he had been given

'Was it Gary or Malcolm?'

"Here it is. It was Malcolm. He said to come back after lunch."

'Oh! I am sorry. He's had to go out to see a client. What's your name and what do you do? I'll see if I can help.'

"Daily, Jim Daily and I'm in sales. I sell wire wares or rather I did, and thin gauge metal extrusions."

'yes…thin gauge metal extrusions..' she drew the words out as if trying to take in exactly what Jim had just said and what it meant.

'A bit out of our league there I think. We have plenty of office jobs and catering but I can't think of anywhere

40

round here that does wire work. Rather specialist you see.'
Her head was bent forward as she spoke more into the grey
four drawer metal filing cabinet than at Jim. Searching
through the files, not wanting to make eye contact until
"Ah! I've got your CV'. 'Hm, Yes, Hm, well, Yes!'
Looking up and sounding happier. 'Yes , well. I'm sure we
can do something for you.' The noises were approving
even if she did still avoid eye contact.

'OK take a seat.'

Officious now and in control, pointing to the chair. As
he sat he realized why she had a difficulty with eye contact
and he felt guilty. She had what his Dad called Road
Safety eyes, they looked both ways before crossing.

Jim felt embarrassed for her and wished he hadn't
stared. For the next ten minutes he tried to avoid her gaze
but with her eyes going in different directions it seemed
wherever he looked one eye or other was looking back at
him. Like a rabbit trapped in the headlights he found it
difficult, not knowing which way to duck or dive.
Nevertheless he couldn't help smile at the nice young girl
with the quirky face and prominent squint. He spent the
next hour in her company and was impressed by her
diligence in trying to get him an interview. She managed
to secure three. Two in sales and one with the County
Council in emergency planning. Relieved with the
prospect of three interviews and confident he would get
one if not two jobs he set off for the Castle where he
would get the bus back to Hornham.

On the bus sitting confidently and pleased with his days
efforts he started to open the paper, then remembering the
disasters that followed his earlier attempts thought better
of it. "May be I'll just watch the day go by". In no time at
all the bus was entering Hornham. Staying on the bus until
it turned into Main St, past the Church, and shops stopping
by the road to the school. He hopped off and crossed to the
phone box. Shook a few coins from his pocket and phoned
home, or what had been home.

"Hello! It's only me,"

"What do you want?" snarled Betty on the other end of the line.

'I just rang to let you know I'm going to pick the boys up.

"How can you? You haven't got a car!"

"I haven't got a bike either at the moment', he said, a smile in his voice, determined not to sink to Betty's level. 'So I'm going to walk."

'Good luck! But you get 'em back here on time that's all'

Jim did as asked first picking up Thomas from the school and then on to pick up Mathew from old Mrs. Nash who looked after him in the afternoons from 2 til 4.

The boys were so pleased to see him, he was able to chat to them and listen to their simple conversations 'Betty was so lucky, but she never saw it as such, What a waste.' He thought to himself as they walked slowly along the street. This was real quality time, almost as good as the weekends. A stop at the Mace for some sweets some washing powder and a couple of frozen chicken portions, served to act as a half way respite from the long walk. Then off again along Links Avenue and through to the park.

The only thing missing was Betty… His mind went into free wheel again around and around the events of the past few days. Should he have said this, should he have said that, what if he had done this, or not done that? A constant turmoil of questions but at the end of it all the outcome was always the same. They were separated! And that was what he had to face. His mind went back to the way she had snapped at him on the phone and the negative way she had spoken to him about the house. She was a very negative person. It's strange how when you are in love you concentrate on the things you like about a person and when that love starts to fade your concentration drifts towards the things you dislike. He realized this was happening with him and Betty.

42

'Dad the swings are broken and there is mud on the end of the slide.'

"Well let's see if we can fix it then and maybe give the slide a wipe."

All four swing seats had been wound around the cross bar several times leaving them 5 ft. in the air so that little children couldn't reach them. Jim fixed that easily swinging the seat and chains back over. He placed Matt in the rubber crate that served as a child seat. Picking it up from the grass where some fool had left it. Ten minutes was then spent pushing the boys to and fro. Jim was at peace. If only he could do this every day. He went quiet, his mind drifting into nowhere.

"Dad what are you thinking?

'I was just thinking that it's about time someone built a proper play area.'

"Please Dad Please, Please."

"Not this year boys we have too much to do to start building play areas.

Not this year, May be next."

Wednesday Evening 2ⁿᵈ May

'Where you bin boyee and how did you get on? Are we employed again?

"Not yet Peter but soon. I've got three interviews and a new CV: that should help."

'Well better than a bus but I don't go a lot on them foreign cars. Where is it?"

'No, a CV, not a 2CV. It's not a flipping dust bin on wheels. I mean a Curriculum Vita' Jim tried to stifle a chuckle but failed.

"Croyst! I thought Curriculum Veetie was one of them cumoonicative diseases. Ass whoy I bin avoidin the woman in the post office for three months. Well how'd you get on then?"

'I did alright. I have to ring in the morning to confirm actual times but I have two interviews tomorrow and one Thursday. I also got to see the boys. I picked them up from School. You know the worst thing? Saying good bye to them at five o clock and not being able to tuck them in at night. That hurts, really hurts."

"Well, as we int so flush I have something else that moyt hurt. I managed to swap a few veg for a couple of pheasant. They bin stewin a while and if is Lordship dunt mind peelin a few tates, we could ha ourselves a meal.'

"I bought some chicken but they'll keep. Pheasant sounds much better."

Jim did as asked and peeled the potatoes then made himself scarce for a few minutes. Peter heard the clatter of his bicycle and assumed Jim had gone off to cycle round to his home to tuck the boys in but no sooner was it gone than it returned.

Jim stepped into the Kitchen a broad smile on his face. Holding two plastic carry outs from the Wherry full of their finest Yare Ale. "Peter we are going to celebrate!" And they did. Pheasant stew, home grown vegetables and mashed potatoes all swimming in rich country gravy. Washed down with local ale. You can't beat it.

Chapter 4 A dog gone wet weekend

Thursday Morning 3rd May

Jim woke early the next day. He was up, washed in the icy cold water, and ready for the off. He made a pot of tea on the old stove and placed a pot of porridge on to cook for Peter. He hurried out of the door, across the rickety scaffold boards and along the driveway towards the bus stop.

'Oh! Hello! We are not open yet but you are welcome to come in for a coffee.' He was waiting on the doorstep of the agency as the staff had arrived. They looked curiously at him as they entered the building. Turning round to take a second glance as they did. Each locking the door behind them as they went in then came the lady who had arranged the interviews for Jim ' …You are the first on my list so if you are there while I phone it will speed things up for all of us'

He sat patiently and listened in while the young lady explained that she had the perfect candidate for the job to each customer she phoned.

Jim attended two interviews that day and felt both had gone well. As a salesman he was used to being interviewed and felt confident that he would get a job by the end of the day.

He returned to the agency a little out of breath having walked from one side of the City to the other and then back to the centre but was pleased to be told that he had in fact been offered both jobs. He didn't much fancy the one selling print space for Jarold's, a great company but it wasn't really his thing. " I'll go for the job with Lawrence and Scott. I think" '

'Good choice I think Mr. Daily, they're well known, good local employer and sound as a pound. I'll let them know and as soon as they have taken up references they will let me know. When are you available to start?'

"As soon as they want. I would prefer Monday though if that is OK?"

A chance to see a little more of the children and do some work on the house with Peter. A broad smile crossed his face. Employed again. Thank heavens.

'Mr Daily, or may I call you James,? We don't seem to have your telephone number.'

"no it hasn't been connected yet., Didn't I tell you? A new house you see and they haven't got round to putting in the line. Can I ring you tomorrow lunch time?"

Arrangements made and Jim was off bouncing with a confident air down the street. He bought a paper and reflected that he bought it to read the news and not the situations vacant. He headed towards the bus stop. Yes, Norwich is a Fine City.

The sun was casting shadows across the old Norman castle as he boarded the bus to Hornham.

Back in Hornham in time to pick up the boys again and share with them his news.

Desperate to tell his parents the news and also make sure they all still felt part of the family he persuaded the boys that the long walk via the chemists around the corner and past the dress shop was worth it. They could get to see the expensive sports cars in Hornham Motor Company and they could also speak to Grandma and Grandpa on the phone and tell them Daddy's special news.

'Daddy, Why are phone boxes always smelly ?'

'Yes Daddy, Why are they?'

"I don't know? May be it's because you have to spend a penny or two to use them."

'Can we do that, can we?'

"No you can't. Well maybe you can, when I say Whee!" picking Matthew up as he said it and pretending to drop him, "you say Whee too." They did, not sure where he was going with this. "Now you can tell mummy you went whee in the telephone box."

46

Nothing gets little boys more than toilet humour. Even at their young age it was not lost on them.

'Gamar,! Daddy's got a new job.'

"You are supposed to say hello first Matt"

"helloDaddy'sgotanewjob." All in one breath without a pause. Matthew had told Ganmar, somehow he never could pronounce Grandma, it was understood that Tom would tell Granddad. Man to man talk. Big boy's stuff. The conversations didn't last long. At five pence for 3 minutes twenty pence didn't go far." Look Mum, I just wanted you to know first; got to go the pips are going,

"well done son, we knew you'd get a job straight away, you are a born salesman.'

'Yea, thanks Mum, love to you both, see you tomorrow or may be Friday. Say Bye Bye Boys.'

'Bye Bye Boys! Ha Ha ha!' they yelled together. The innocence of children, they had done it so many times but they still enjoyed the joke. James got them home in time. He wasn't sure if Betty was pleased or sad. May be she had wanted an argument. Jim was in no mood for one. A new job, a new beginning as he saw it and he certainly wasn't going to spoil things wasting time arguing with Betty. Farewells said and with a promise to deliver them to school tomorrow Jim waved the boys goodbye and set off toward the Loke and to tell Peter the good news.

Hornham seemed to have a different look to it as Jim strode through the village.

The evening sun was still bright in the sky and although not hot it was clear and light, casting shadows and light which danced through the new spring leaves on the trees that lined the roads of this pretty little Broadland village. He took his Jacket off and carried it with one finger over his shoulder. A walk along the river would be good he thought, longer but so much more enjoyable on such a fine evening and anyway I've got plenty of time.

Past the Medical Centre, across the railway line and through the boat yards. He sat himself down for a moment on the key heading by the Hornham Yacht Club.. The tide was out and his feet dangled a foot or so above the water. Throwing pebbles in the river and watching the sun glisten on the ripples he felt pleased with himself. "I'll treat Peter to a meal at the Pub" he said aloud. Which really meant that he couldn't be bothered to cook and fancied the easy solution. I can afford it now. His mind drifted towards food, he could almost taste it.

"Don't darling, Don't!" A ladies screaming voice sounded in sheer panic. Looking up across the river towards where the sound had come from he strained his eyes to see a large dog had jumped from a boat. A big Broom's cruiser. The dog was making for a small group of ducks and a few Canada geese that the old lady had obviously been feeding. It looked like a Labrador or may be a retriever whatever it was it was enjoying the chase as were the gaggle of wild fowl which swam tantalizingly close , keeping just a few feet in front, just far enough away not to get caught by the powerful jaws but close enough for the dog to think it was catching up.

"Polly come back! Polly, come here." The lady bent forward and banged her thighs with open palms but to no avail. Poly was too intent on catching her prey. She made a lunge for a slower and fatter than average Canada goose but missed it by inches as it flapped its wings to provide that extra bit of lift, just sufficient to stay out of trouble.

The dog went under, came up a few seconds later coughing and shaking her head. Still came the screams from the old lady on the boat. "Polly, Polly! Come here!"

Polly turned towards the boat but the river was wide at this point where it turned and she had swam further than she had realized and was being taken by the current, while the boat had been going against it and had taken a few yards to slow. The dog was beginning to whimper as it eventually reached the boat encouraged by its owners frantic screaming. The old lady bent over to pick her up but couldn't quite reach. The captain of the craft had now appeared and tried to use the boat hook on Polly's collar. Unfortunately managing only to make matters worse, as he knocked her further under. Not once but twice. A small crowd was gathering behind Jim. Craning forward to see what was happening. The dog was visibly distressed and sinking further into the river as she clawed at the side of the boat trying to gain enough purchase to get on board.

"Oh she's drowning!"

'Save her!'

"Oh No! I can't look"

'Oh someone do something!'

Splash!!

At that moment Jim was in the water and swimming towards the drowning dog.

'Yes! Go On!'

"Go on mate,"

'Oh Please, Please'

Egged on by the crowd he swam the 20 or so yards to the dog. Sensing a life raft or shining knight come to her rescue Polly turned and started to swim towards Jim and although weary with her powerful front paws, scrambled up his chest. He went under taking a mouthful of pure river water surfacing only to be met by Polly looking for her life raft. He took a gulp of air and turned his back on the frightened beast and struck out for the shore. As he did so she placed two wet and hairy paws on his shoulders and scrambled with her hind legs to gain a grip on his lower back. Swimming breast stroke gulping air between strokes and going under from the weight on his shoulders he put all he could into his efforts, His legs stung as the dogs back claws continued to kick, scratching him as it did so. He reached the shore and the dog tried to scratch her way up the vertical key heading. Jim had visions of her not being able to make it. A man grabbed her collar but at full stretch was unable to pull her up. This was a big heavy and water soaked dog. There was nothing for it. Jim took a deep breath and using the wooden planking of the key pushed himself down into the murky water. His feet touched the mud some six or seven feet below and he pushed up wards with all his might he came up right below a mass of flailing legs and hair, he grabbed what he hoped was her rear end and propelled her upwards at a rate sufficient to allow the long arm of the other man assisted by a few others, to get her on to the boardwalk. Jim's face broke the water to the sound of cheers. He felt proud of his efforts, pleased to be appreciated but then realized they were cheering the bloody dog. Attractive women were petting it, men were congratulating the bloke who had dragged her out and no one was worried about poor Jim.

He swam to a nearby boat and used the blue nylon mooring rope as a ladder to assist him on to the shore. He sat there exhausted for a few minutes, wet, smelly, scratched all over and beginning to get cold. As he stood up someone patted him on the back saying 'well done mate' and he nearly fell back into the water. A lady from a nearby boat gave him a small towel as she handed him his jacket and asked if he was OK. "I'm fine, I think, I do this all the time you know, Hornham Pet Rescue. Thanks for the towel, I had better go home and change. I think I'm on call to rescue two swans and a wood pigeon later."

He wasn't sure if she believed him or not but as he padded and squelched his way along the river front and around the corner towards Peters place he looked back briefly to see Polly reunited with her owners. Soaked as he was and smelling like a dead pike in the heart of summer he felt satisfied with his days' work.

"Chroist Boyee, Wart yoo bin dooin this toime?"

'Nice Day; I thought I'd go for a swim. No not realy, Someone's dog fell in and I dragged it out.'

"Well you buggered up your suit boy. I hope they paid you well." Peter was looking down as he turned Jim around. "You're bleeding as well. Best I run you a bath."

'That'll take ages' why don't I have a quick wash to get the worst off and get changed and we can walk to the Wherry and I'll have a shower on the way at the boat yard.'

The pub was packed but they found a table in the corner and ordered their meals. Jim was paying as he had secured a job. 'Put it on the bill Peter' Peter was impressed, in all the years Peter had been looking he had never been able to get a steady job and here was Jim out of work only a few days and already back in full time employment.

Two meals, three pints later and both were ready for the short walk home.

'table 24, What do I owe you Barry?'

'You don't, table 24, 25 and 26 were together'

"Well, yes they were, but it was crowded and we couldn't find a seat so we separated them and stuck the spare ones on the end. No one said anything."

'You got a result then, because that Mr. Stone paid yours as well.'

"Today **is** my lucky day." That's twenty quid I've just saved. If you see him though, tell him I owe him, I don't want to do him down but it does help just now."

Friday Morning 4th May

Jim again woke early but had been beaten by Peter and rose to be greeted by the smell of bacon and eggs being cooked.

The bacon had been swapped for some vegetables, the eggs had no doubt been acquired by a similar barter, and the mushrooms looked fresh picked. A full fry up, porridge and a cup of tea. He was set up ready for the day.

'Any chance you can give me a hand with those timbers later today, after you have dropped your young uns off?'

"Happy to Peter"

They sweated from 9.30 until 1.00 with only a break for a glass of orange. He wondered where Peter got his energy from? A short break for a cup of tea a ploughman's lunch of fresh bread, cheese and some homemade pickles and they were off again. By 3pm the timbers were all in and trimmed with slate to bring them level. 'Thars a good job boyee, You int a bad worker when you gets a gooan. I'll put a stew on while you gets yourself washed and pick the lads up an we can get one in at the Wherry if you're up for it?' Jim didn't need telling twice, He collected the boys and spent a happy hour with them chatting as they walked home via the park. This was settling into a routine which he knew he would miss when he started work next week but the money was vital to keep the bills being paid. He delivered the boys home and hoped to have a few words with Betty but she was in no mood for a chat. 'look I'm busy. You might have all day to do nothing but I have a house to run so I am not going to stand here and make small talk with you. If you want to talk you can do it through my solicitor. Oh and he wants to know who your solicitor is?'

"Well I don't have one."

'Well you better get one then coz I'm not hanging around waiting for you. I'm getting a divorce so as me an Bill can live together proper.' With an obvious annoyance showing on her face she slammed the door.

Jim knocked quick and hard in a mixture of temper and frustration shaking the door with each thump of his fist.

'All right there is no need to knock the house down.'

"It's my bloody house!"

'No it's not it's mine and the kids. I told you. I got a solicitor and I know what's mine' As the tempers had risen so had the voices. Jim could hear crying in the back ground between Betty's words. Peering around and over her shoulder he could see his two boys standing by the stairs. They both noticed them and the moment of silence that followed was broken by a small voice pleading, "Please don't argue, please, we will be good but don't argue." Both boys were crying and seemed to be blaming themselves for the argument.

"I'm sorry boys it's my fault. I shouldn't have shouted at Mummy."

'Too bloody right now look what you've done.'
Gesturing towards the stairs where the boys stood.

'Mummy , please! Please Mummy, please don't shout.'

"Boys, I'm going to go then Mummy will stop shouting"

'Daddy, please don't go! Please stay,'

"I can't Matthew, I wish I could but I promise I will see you tomorrow".

The atmosphere changed you could almost feel it. Matthew and Thomas were still crying but it lacked the intensity and there were more sniffles than tears. Betty was still scowling, her head bowed forward and her eyes and nose squashed up like a dog protecting a bone.

"I'll get a solicitor and we will talk in the morning when we are alone. This is hard enough on the boys without us arguing in front of them."

'Don't start again just go.'

He did just that. Not wanting to cause the boys any more upset. Looking back as he walked up the path he could see them, still crying but waving. Thomas put one hand on the window pain and the other around his brothers shoulder. Jim waved and blew them a kiss. He forced a smile onto his face and hoped the little lads could not see the tears that were in his eyes.

'Comes round here again and I'll punch his lights out. You tell him next time. Tel him I'll punch his lights out.' Billy Salter's repertoire hadn't changed. Betty wondered if she should have told him, but then again he had to know why she was so upset and why the boys were not in bed by the time Billy got in as they were usually. 'I'm going to go down the pub now and see Smithy he'll sort him.'

'Oh Don't Billy, stay with me and the boys. I'll get you your tea.'

'No! I'm off down the pub. I'll be back when you have got your kids to bed. I'll bring a few bottles back.'

Oh flipping heck! Work, I forgot to phone about Monday."

Looking at his watch, not too late it's nearly 5 and they don't close till 5.30.

He ran across the top field by the memorial Hall, along the lane by Mrs Callum's house and around the corner to the phone box.

'Oh Mr. Daily thanks for ringing in. Are you connected yet?'

"No they still haven't put us on. You know what these telephone people are like."

'Well oi'm glad youv'e rung because I have a bit of a problem. That job at Lawrence's has been delayed. Can you come in on Monday? I think we may need to re evaluate.'

"Re evaluate? How do you mean re evaluate? When **do** they want me to start?

Well I'm not sure they do that's why we need to revisit our options and asses our situation you see?'

"No I don't see. Either I've...."Beep Beep Beep "Oh bloody hell the pips have gone and I don't have any more change."

'Come in and see me Monday then an...'.the one continuous tone told him there was nothing more he could do. It was Friday evening. He'd had a row with Betty, upset the boys and now he wasn't even sure if he had a job to go to. What a week.

'You alright boyee? You look like you have just lost a fiver and found a shilling.'

"No I had a row with Betty. It upset the boys. We all ended up crying our eyes out. She says I need a solicitor. So she can get on with the divorce. I mean, It's only been a week and it seems she has it all worked out and I'm going to lose everything."

'Oi carnt elp yer there. I know nothing about solicitors and that. You'll hat er arsk down the pub. Bound to be someone there that knows.'

"Don't ask me. I am still married and I can't afford that, let alone affording a divorce. Ask Sam, he was married 3 times."

'Thanks Barry.' Unusual for a publican not to have an opinion thought Jim as he approached Sam who was clattering money into the slot machine. Without taking his eye of the flashing lights and between pressing the various buttons each time they flashed, he listened intently to what Jim had to say. "If I was you I'd stick with your Mrs. Lamb. You'll probably have to go private or whatever they call it but she must be as good as any."

'What,? you mean not go through the citizen's advice?'

"No! You find out where she works normally and book up to see her. She'll sort out all the legal aid and stuff and all you have to do is what your told an pay the bill at the end but if you have any assets they take it out of that."

'You don't reckon your solicitor then?'

"You're Joking. I went to Pratt, Pratt and Allsop, Allsop was out and I ended up with a Pratt. It cost me a fortune." With that the machine jumped into life and began spewing out 10 pence pieces.

'Cheers Sam.' the words were lost in the incessant noise of the jackpot of coins hitting the metal tray. Sam mouthed something in return, which Jim didn't catch but the gesture of the thumbs up said it all.

"Feelun better now then Boyee?"

Peter shoved a pint of Yare across the table towards Jim as he sat down next to him.

"Yea much. I'm going into Norwich again Monday and I'll sort out my solicitor and get things going with the employment agency. Tomorrow I'm going to have to go over to Wroxham and Salhouse I need to get my laundry done and I'll take the boys too if Betty will let me. I should be back by lunchtime so I'll do some more on the house if you wish."

'That house has waited years; a few more days won't make much difference boyee. . You spend the time wi your young uns. They need a father and the less they see of that gob on a stick Salter, the better. You want another one?'

"Yea, go on then. But then I'm going to go especially if I'm up early tomorrow."

He sat playing with the beer mat and supping his pint feeling as though the whole world had fallen in on him while Peter got the refills.

'Barry says that Mr Stone's lookun for you boyee. Apparently he says there is a score to settle."

"Oh flipping Heck, I'd forgotten. We sat at his table and he paid our bill. I think I owe him 20 quid. I haven't got that much on me. It's gonna have to wait till next week and I'll have to apologize."

'You can't. He int in tonight he's at Reedham'.

'Heloo boyees, har ya getting on then?'

"Jessie! You want a drink?"

'I'd love one Jim. A large red'd be nice.'

"I can't afford to pay Mr Stone but I can afford to get you a drink."

'I knew you boys would get on.' Jessie's eyes lit up and that wide smile cracked across her weathered face but it disappeared almost as fast as it had arisen the appearance changing with her thoughts. 'How's things with Betty and that?'

'I've heard it I'll get the drinks.'

'Cheers Peter.'

Jim again poured his heart out to Jessie just as he had nearly a week ago. She said nothing, just nodded at the appropriate moments and made the occasional hum or har. But the fact that she listened meant a lot to Jim.

'He's from the east end you know.' Peter interrupted placing Jessie's large glass of red wine down and changing the subject.

'Who is?'

'Mr Stone. Jim owes him twenty quid. He's bin avoidin im. Oi'm surprised you don't know him coming from London an all?'

"Well it's a fairly big place actually and he's a few years older than I am. May be he went to a different school"

'Well I hear he's well connected with the east end mobs and used to knock around with the Grays.'

"I think you mean Crays Jess."

'So you do know him? Well whatever, I know he loves his Mum and would do anything for her. He used to box a bit apparently.'

"That's all I need being chased by a queer boxer who thinks I'm avoiding paying my debts. What with that, a divorce looming, losing my house and family to a tosser like Salter and having no job. It's been a hell of a week."

Chapter 5 Bowler

Saturday Morning 5th May

Jim had risen early again; A thing he was getting used to. The dew was still on the grass an early spring frost was just clearing from the ground leaving a line of mist across the fields about six feet high, which made everything below it appear out of focus while the eastern sky was awakening to a larger than usual orangey sun with a tinge of silver brightening everything above the mist and sending rays of rainbows through the droplets on the trees.

"Life is shit at the moment, but thank heaven I still have this. Norfolk is beautiful and un-spoilt. Thank you God. And this is free."

'You all right boyee?' Peter stepped over the deal plank entrance, a carrier bag of mushrooms in his hand just as James was musing over the benefits of living in Norfolk. 'Breakfast?' He said holding them aloft as if they were a prize?

Jim declined although hungry, and made his way on Peter's bike to his other house.

He expected to have to wake Betty but found her already awake and even more surprisingly she was up and had by the smell of things when she opened the door, been cooking breakfast. 'I don't know what you want but if it's another argument you can forget it. I have said all I need to so that's that'

"No, I have come round to see if I can take the boys out. I'm going over to mum and Dad's and I thought they may like to come over with me."

'You haven't got a car and besides they are coming shopping with me to Norwich. Bills treating us all to dinner out and a trip round the Castle. So there!'

"So Bill's taking <u>my</u> children out is he? and I can't?"

'Bills *not* actually. I'm taking them, he's paying. He has a job and works for a living. Unlike some. If you want

58

to take 'em out you can do it tomorrow. They are all yours from 10 till 6. Not before mind as me an Bill are having a lie in."

'Dad?'

'Get in!' She snapped.

'Is Daddy coming with us?'

'See what you've caused? Clear off and stop upsetting the kids. Come back tomorrow. Get up them stairs and get changed. We're going out!'

The door slammed. He could feel the tension but did not want to upset the children any further. It was obviously difficult enough for them already and they were feeling the strain as much as he was. He resolved to get as much done today as he could so that he could have some time with them tomorrow.

Two busses and an hour later he was in Wroxham. "Crazy, a ten minute car journey takes an hour by bus but then, this is Norfolk"

He struggled off the bus with his two carrier bags of laundry and vowed that if he ever had the opportunity he would open a laundry and dry cleaners in Hornham. It was the one thing the village lacked. He also vowed that he would call it anything but Roy's. Roy's of Wroxham had been a good customer of his and were a good successful company but as he sat in the launderette just a little too far away from the river to watch the boats, he had nothing better to do than watch his washing go around in the two big silver machines and as he did so his mind wandered. He couldn't help but think that every other shop in a village being called Roy's was overkill. There was even a Miss Roy's for the ladies. All you ever needed under one name. His machines seemed to take forever and then as one finished he had to rush and get the load into the tumble dryer. I can't be doing with this every week. I'll have to think of another way around it.

Two hours, he thought as he waited in line for the bus back to Salhouse, two hours just watching washing go around. Betty may have her faults but she did enjoy washing and ironing and Jim always had a clean shirt to wear. And what's worse I've still got to iron this lot. The bags seemed heavier on the way back. Smaller, but heavier. He struggled on to the bus the two bags balanced between his knee and the driver's shelf while he fumbled for change and noticed the only vacant seat was next to a lady who looked as if she had been eating for England and won. Wearing a summer print dress and sweating like a bull dog on heat she took up two thirds of the double seat. "is this seat taken?"

Her face swiveled around as if it were not part of her and she gave a one eyed stare towards him. He could see a row of fake pearls and looked for a chin but noticed there wasn't one. Her neck and head seemed to rise up from her large bosom as one with a pug faced expression slapped on to it.

Jim couldn't help thinking he had seen her before.

'For you or your bags?'

Well, I was going to put the bags on my lap.

With that the large print dress and its rolls of fat started to shuffle towards the window. As it did the rolls started to wobble and seemed to gain a momentum of their own eventually stopping as they hit the inside edge of the bus. Jim sat down quickly dragging the bags on to his lap, worried in case there was a rebound and he would end up with less seat than he'd started with.

"It's my washing you see," half apologizing and half explaining, "I'm only going to Salhouse so it won't be long."

'It's OooKay Spin a long toym since oi ad a young man share moy seat.' She smiled just enough so he could notice a large gap in what had once been a row of front teeth and now was obviously stifling a laugh. Jim could tell from the little chuckle and the fact that the ample bosoms were jiggling up and down but nothing else was yet. Then the beads joined in and then the layers of fat below. Jim thought it would stop but no. It kept going as if really pleased and happy. 'You wait til Oi tell moi Dad. He'll larf!'

'Scuse me mate,' *'Sorry!'*, "Excuse me,"

People pushed past as the bus came to a stop at the other end of Wroxham. Jim was forced to lean over and squeeze ever closer to the large lady to allow them through. 'OooH', she purred 'Oi'm Jane, und you are?'

"Moving!   There's a seat," pointing as he lunged towards an empty double bench seat "I'll allow you some room" He didn't mean to be rude and realized his flippant remark may have been taken as such so decided to say good bye when he left the bus in case she felt upset.

And Jim didn't really want to upset any one.

Six minutes later the bus rounded the corner into Salhouse. Holding on desperately his bags in hand with one out stretched finger holding on to the rail at the back of the seats he worked his way towards the door, "Bye Jane,"

"Boyee Mervyn." A smile appeared on the slapped face making it look more like a bulldog on heat trying to swallow a sticky toffee than anything human. Jim smiling back at her he realized she'd missed his quick remark and thought his name was Mervyn.

'I'll put the kettle on, What you got there then son? Do you want something to eat? How long you stopping? How are the boys? What's happening with Betty?

Have you started the new Job yet? Do you want something to eat.? How is Peter?

Ham all right or would you prefer cheese?' The questions came quick and fast so fast in fact that as usual he didn't have a chance to answer one before she'd moved to the next.

'Will you shut up woman and let him answer!'

'Well I haven't seen him for a week I have a lot I need to know'

'Haven't we all I'd lov,'

"Yes! Mum I'd love a cup of tea." He interrupted, "I've been to Wroxham and I've got my washing with me so can I borrow your ironing board and iron?"

'It'll be much quicker if I do it for you, give us it here, Father you make the sandwiches and tea'.

The words he'd been hoping to hear but hadn't dared to ask. Ironing never was his strong point.

The next hour was spent filling his parents in on the events of the past week while his Mother ironed and tut tutted while his father sucked on his unlit pipe. It wasn't lit as he wasn't allowed to smoke in doors any longer except on special occasions and even then the windows had to be open or the fire roaring so it didn't notice. That more or less restricted it to Christmas and the Queen's birthday so in between times he filled it with tobacco and just sucked it. Poking the tobacco down every now and then with his index finger.

"So that's it basically, I'm up the Barking Creek without a paddle."

'Well I'll do your washing and ironing for you for starters. That way you'll be able to concentrate on getting a job.'

"Mum, that would be great but I can't ask you to do that. I do Peters as well and it wouldn't be fair."

'Well He's taken you in and that's hardly fair either so if it's all right with Father it looks like I'm doing the washing and ironing for all of us. Besides it will make me feel better because at times like this we have to pull together."

'I'm trying to think what I can do.' John looked totally dejected and struggled to his feet using the edge of the lounge chair and one of his walking sticks to prize himself free. 'I'm goanna See Keith next door'

"Dad, just you and Mum listening is good enough don't underestimate that. I really do appreciate all that you do."

'I know son but I feel useless. If I were more mobile I'd be helping you a lot more I'm going to see Keith.' Jim's Mum raised her eyebrows skywards and gave a look as if to say she'd heard it all before. Jim was about to speak but she raised her index finger towards her lips as if to say shush. As the old man hobbled out of the house Elizabeth explained that her husband felt less and less valued as he was no longer able to get about. He could just about get next door and He and Keith had various projects they were working on in Keith's shed and garage. Home brewed wine and beer being one of them. Keith was a kindly old chap of about the same age as John and had run a pet food franchise until his sight had given out a few years ago. Two more cups of tea and several shirt folding sessions later and Jim was about ready to return to Hornham.

'Jim! Jim! I've got you something, Or rather Keith has, He say's you can borrow his car.'

"I didn't know he had a car? I thought he was blind"

'Not totally, It's what we've been working on. It's a right little goer, He was going to give it to Christine but she's happy with her little allegro. Come and have a look,'

They all traipsed next door as Christine turned the handle of the metal rollover door and lifted it to reveal there in the garage, the front end of an old Fiat 126.

'Isn't it a lovely finish. Keith ran his hand over the ultra-smooth paint finish like a master craftsman admiring his work. 'Your Dad's done the engine and I did the spraying and polishing. You should have seen it before we started. You wouldn't have believed it'.

"Oh Keith, I'm not sure I believe it now." It was beautifully painted in red. Unfortunately none of the red panels actually matched, Each panel was beautifully finished and as smooth as any showroom model would be and they were red all right; but each was a different shade of red from the next.

"Keith, what can I say? It *is* er, um,,,unbelievable."

'Keith's worked really hard, the shine on the paint work is just amazing. ..'

"Yes, Yes it is"

'...And the engine, you hear the engine. Keith! Get in and start it up. Let him hear it'

With that Keith felt his way around the car and opening the driver's door climbed in. There was a little wait while he found the ignition lock. A little shuffling of the gear stick while he located neutral and a further few minutes when turning the key the engine failed to fire. Then suddenly a loud bang! followed in quick succession by a few coughs as the engine fired up. Keith gunned the engine with a heavy right foot on the accelerator and the garage was filled with a heavy blue smoke.

'I put that SLP in the tank and carburetor and it'll take a few minutes to clear.'

Smoke billowed out of the garage as the entourage retreated to the garden. Keith seemed oblivious to the blue fog he was creating and continued to rev the engine hard.

"Flipping heck Dad how much did you put in?"

'Only a bottle.'

"What in the tank?"

'Yea, and one in the carb and one in the pistons'

"That's enough to do 30 gallons. This car only holds 5"

'Well it was all in litres I don't understand litres.'

They all turned silent and stared as an apparition came towards them through the blue smoke like Moses descending from Mount Sinai hand out stretched, it spoke.

'cough! cough! Well what do you think? cough! I seem to have got a tickle in my throat Cough! Will she do you a turn until you get a company car? She's all insured and still has an MOT. I was doing her up for Christine but she prefers the little blue allegro'

"Um, well I don't know what to say, I am lost for words, it really is good of you but I couldn't. I mean,," How do you say no politely? He tried but he couldn't and just gave a sigh.

'I knew you'd love it son and I know you feel humbled but when your principles affect your pocket it's time to pocket your principles.'

Jim could see that his Father wanted him to have the car. It was his way of doing his bit for a son in trouble.

"Ok Dad you win, but I'm not insured."

'You are with owner's permission, and you got permission. It's only a loan though but you can keep it as long as you need it.'

"Thanks Keith, Thanks Dad. I really do appreciate it."

Twenty minutes later Keith, Christine, Elizabeth and John were waving good bye to the little soft top car that had been so lovingly worked upon.

As it neared the corner Jim changer down a gear and as he rounded the bend and accelerated a large bang and huge cloud of blue smoke signified that may be a little too much engine cleaner had been used.

"When your principles affect your pocket you should pocket your principles? Where did you dig that one up from?" Asked Elizabeth with a wry smile.

'I used to know a bloke who lied and cheated on his business partners. That was how he justified it. It worked though didn't it? He's got a car and we will see more of him and the grand kids now he's mobile.'

The little Fiat 126 was a small car with an air cooled 900cc engine positioned at the rear. The front was the luggage compartment with a space for the spare wheel and tire Jack. It was a two door, four seater although with two people in the front there was only room for a small child or two in the back. It was however a vehicle and as far as Jim was concerned it would take him from A to B without having to wait for busses. "I'll have to lower the seat though; my head keeps rubbing against the canvas roof." This roof folded right back from front to rear and was obviously designed for the sunshine of Italy and the Mediterranean. It may not be exactly what was required for the British summer but it would be fun on a sunny day. Happy that he had a pair of wheels he wasn't going fast but was keeping up a steady pace on the narrow country road daydreaming as he passed the farm with the little pond in the front garden and on down the narrow country lane.

Barp! Barp! An impatient boy racer was behind, right up his tail. He looked once and then again as he recognized Bill Salter, the centre of his wife's attentions, eager to pass this slow little fiat in his flashy Ford Capri. Changing down as he approached the Salhouse and Norwich Road junctions Jim allowed the fiat to coast for a few yards, slowing the vehicle almost to a stop. He looked both ways and accelerated hard across the main intersection. As he did so a loud bang and a few flames from the secondary ignition were followed by a huge cloud of blue smoke out of the exhaust completely engulfing the Ford Capri in a thick fog. Although unable to see, its driver decided to follow the fiat and promptly drove one wheel into the ditch on the opposite side of the road. The junction was only off set by about 3 feet but it was enough for the nearside wheel of the Capri to dig into the soft mud and the rear wheel drive did the rest as it spun 180 degrees to end up facing the wrong way on the wrong side of the road. Slammed so tightly into the verge that the driver and female passenger both had to get out of the passenger door.

Jim didn't wait to find out what happened next. Thinking it best to make a hasty retreat he followed the road through to Hornham, satisfied that he had been able to see off a brand new Capri with his little "toy" car.

'Christ Boyee, What you got there? it looks like a bowl of cherries on four wheels.

"Don't laugh, it just got me from Salhouse to Hornham in less than 2 hours twenty minutes."

'You could walk it in less than that'.

"Not with two bags of freshly ironed clothes you couldn't. And I have negotiated that my mum will do our washing and ironing in future in lieu of rent."

'What rent? You int payin rent remember?'

"No but if I was it would be in lieu."

'I int worried about the loo. I needs to get a proper roof over our heads fust.'

"Well, now I've got a set of wheels how about I go and get some cement and we start on them gables? We got four hours before it gets too dark to work."

"Last bucket of muck. Can you make it do?"

'It'll do fine boyee You clair up, n' I'll finish hair.'

They had got the loose bricks of the gable end finished and partly completed the work around the chimney stack. The beams and roof trusses were next but that would have to wait. They'd shored up the ends of the house and as long as there was not a major gale in the next few days all would be well.

'Good Job today boyee, You can ha tomorrow off.'

"Cheers Peter, I'm going to take the boys out to the Beach in the morning. Do you want to come?"

'Ass noice boyee but I'm too old fur the beach. I'll just potter about round hair. You want Gamon, mushrooms and tomatoes or you dining out tonight?'

"Where'd you get gammon from?"

'Snot wot you know it's who. I swapped s'mornins mushrooms an' some tomato plants with Old boy Long. You won't find a better butcher.'

He was right; Long's had been the village butchers for years and much of the meat they sold was from their own farm so you knew it was good. They served not only the village but most of the restaurants and local pubs as well.

"As there is nothing on our telly why don't you go and get washed, I'll cook the supper and we'll have a pint in the Wherry/".

It was just after eight o clock as they walked in to the crowded public bar.

'you just missed him' Barry exclaimed as he drew off two pints of Yare and passed them over without even being asked.

"missed who?"

'Mr Stone of course. He was in for a meal again. He says you and him have still got to settle up. He's taking his mum and the dog back to the boat and reckons he'll be back in at ten to see you.'

67

"Oh Christ! That is all I need. What do you reckon I should do Peter? I certainly haven't got enough money to pay him and I don't fancy my chances in a fight with an ex-boxer."

'Well, Ten o clock did he say? That's enough toime for two pints and I should suddenly feel unwell, You'll ha t take me humm. We'll ha an early noight an you can figure something out in the marnin. Hows that suit?'

"Sounds good to me." A game of cribbage, a chat with some of the locals and it was time for another pint.

Ann was laughing as she pulled the foaming beers taking her time to let it settle before drawing some more. 'D'you hear that?' Speaking and laughing at the same time, while topping up each glass, 'Bill Salter was run off the road earlier today. Nobody was hurt so it serves him right. Him and that flash car. He reckons he's going to swing for him if he catches him.'

'Talk about *me* feigning sickness you look white as a sheet. You all roight?'

"Day by day it gets worse Peter, I am now being chased by Bill Salter as well as Mr stone. I'll just have this one and go. Before anything else happens."

Jim lay there that night not able to sleep. It was all going around in his head. He felt useless, and an abject failure. His marriage was over, he couldn't see his children, he couldn't get a job, he owed money he couldn't repay and at least two people were after him. He tried to think of positive things and a way out of his predicament but couldn't. The more he lay there thinking the bigger the problems seemed to get.

"Why me? Oh God why me? Someone help me please. Show me what to do."

Chapter 6 Cribbage in the Wherry

SUNDAY 6th May

It was morning, the sun streaming in through the blue tarpaulin bathing everything in the building in a pale blue hue. "I must have dropped off." He looked at his watch. Eight thirty. There was a mug of tea at his side. Still hot and steaming.

"Thanks Peter!" he called out as he wrapped his hands around the warm china mug before sipping it gently. He was soon up, washed and dressed.

'thought about your problem then ha ya boyee?'

"Yep! Sure have, I'm going to take the boys out today. We will call in at my parents, I'll see if I can borrow some money off Dad. I'll pay Stone with that and tomorrow I'll get a job. Don't care what I do but I'll get something.

"What about Salter? How we gonna sort him out? If he reckons you wrecked his car we could be in serious trouble."

"I've thought about that one Peter and I reckon I'll just have to get him on his own and,, is that porridge?" changing the subject quickly. Peter gave him a sideways glance. He'd never taken Jim for a fighter, well not one that would be willing to stand toe to toe. May be he was wrong?

Jim parked the car around the corner from his former home and walked the last few yards. No need to pour salt in the wounds. He would have to pick his moment to confront Salter and the place, today and here wasn't it. He collected the boys and walked with them towards the car.

'Where are we going today Daddy? Can we go to the beach? Can we go swimming? Can we go to the pictures?'

"First boys we have to get a car. Lets' take this one." He opened the door wide for them to enter.

Their faces were a picture of shock and amazement.

Daddy this isn't your car we can't take it, it's not ours.

"You are right it's not ours and normally we wouldn't take it but I have borrowed it and we have permission to use it as long as we are careful with it."

With exclamations of Oh Daddy it's great, what fun, press this, press that, can I pull this, and what does this do? The trio set off.

The boys were safely strapped in the back and from his view through the rearview mirror he could see they were enjoying the ride. They didn't care that it wasn't new or that the colours were all shades of red. All they knew was it was new to them and therefore an adventure. When they found out the roof folded back they were amazed.

'Daddy does it have a name?' "I think we are going to call it 'Bowler'"

'Bowler? Bowler, I like Bowler.' 'Yes so do I'

Thomas and Matthew discussed it and it was agreed it was Bowler. After a short pause while he had obviously been thinking about it Thomas leaned his head to one side then the other and questioned slowly and deliberately 'Dad, why is it Bowler?'

'Yes, that is what I wanted to know why is it Bowler? Is it a dog you once had?'

'No! Silly, that was Ben. Bowler is a man. Like a butler or something.'

'What is a butler?'

"A Butler is a servant Matthew." James interjecting quickly to keep the peace. "and no it's none of those things. It's because Peter said it looked like a 'bowl a Cherries' so it's Bowler."

They arrived at Jim's parents' home where the boys were treated to glasses of fruit juice and cake. Jim knew how much it meant to his parents to see the boys and taking them to visit was the least he could do after his Father and Keith had gone to so much trouble to loan him the car.

"Don't feed 'em too much Mum, were off to the beach soon." '

'I'll make you a packed lunch. I've got some lovely chicken and some Peanut butter and those cheese triangles you like so much boys eh?'

'Yes please Gamar and can we have some more apple juice?'

"Matthew, what have I told you about being rude and asking?"

'Don't ask don't get that's what Bill says' It was as if Tom had driven a nail through Jims heart. Here were his children copying the words of a fool and he could do little to stop it.

"Well young man that's bad manners and just because some people don't have any it doesn't mean you should copy them." The atmosphere had sunk like a lead balloon. The phrase "young Man" meant; Don't argue or try to be smart. Dad's not happy.

'Right you Boys, come and help me in the kitchen and we'll get a packed lunch for you to take to the beach I might even find you an ice cream for you to eat now if you're good.' Jim's Mum knew the way to a young man's heart. 'Your Dad and Keith are down the shed, why not go and join them for ten minutes while me and the boys get the lunch.?'

He quietly pushed the shed door open and the two old men nearly had heart attacks as they tried to hide the bottles of illicit home brew.

'Crikey son! Don't you know to knock on a man's shed before entering? It's sacrilege. Its like entering a teenager's bedroom, you never know what they might be up to and there are certain things you shouldn't see'

"Such as Dad? You don't mean you have mucky magazines under the cushions do you?"

'At our age the only mucky magazines we get to read are Gardener's world aint that right Keith?'

'I don't even get to read them. He has to read 'em for me and I have got to be honest if it was your dad reading porn I don't think it would do a lot for me.'

"Yes, Point taken, what's the big secret then?"

71

'Keith's pea pod!'

"Pardon?"

'Home brew son. Strong enough to rot your socks. Sweet enough to charm the birds from the trees. Try some?'

A glass of cloudy pale green liquid was waved towards him by Keith's out stretched hand. Not wanting to seem ungrateful he went to take a sip. The first thing he noticed was the smell, like rotting cabbages. That hit the back of the throat even before the drink did. He drank a small amount. It was sweet, like peas and sweet corn cooked in butter but as it went down he could feel it burning. It hit his stomach and seemed to burst into flames making him breath out from way down within himself.

"Whoar!!" his breath was taken away."Whoar,,," still unable to speak his father broke in with 'See Keith, I said he'd like it. We've saved you a few bottles. I was going to give it to you yesterday but Mother was about and she doesn't know about it.'

Jim recovered sufficient breath to utter a few words. "Whats in it? it's like fire water."

'That's Keith's secret recipe.'

Keith smiled and looked proud. 'Well it's a mixture of pea pods and corn kernels fermented with yeast and honey. The secret is in slowly adding the honey. That's what gives it the kick you see. You know it's ready to drink when it goes clear.'

Jim lifted the glass and peered through the cloudy green liquid. His quizzical look was spotted by John who gave a wink and a smile as if to say don't tell him. The poor old bugger's blind and what he doesn't know won't harm him.

Jim joined the old pals and declining another drink on the pretext that he was driving, sat himself down on an old wooden beer crate and explained what he was doing, as he did so a bell rung out. 'That's Elizabeth, Your Lunch must be ready Jim, I'll come and see the boys. And I'll bring a couple of bottles but mind Mother doesn't see 'em.'

Jim didn't like to refuse he hid the contraband away in the car and went in to get the lads.

'Look Dad Gamar's given us some money for an ice-cream'

"Crikey, I almost forgot, is there any chance you could lend me some money? It's only until I get myself sorted. I'll have a job and be earning soon but Betty has frozen the bank accounts and I'm living on some spare cash I had and the money you lent me last week."

'I've got my Christmas money upstairs and a little put by in case something happens, let me go and get it.' "I don't want to take your Christmas money Mum" 'Let her Son, she wants to help. You and the boys are all we've got so you take it. You can pay it back when you get straight.' This time Jim did feel humbled. There he was borrowing off two pensioners who hardly had a spare penny to their name and yet little did he know that in giving it they felt more pleasure than they would in spending it on themselves.

The car park at Happisburgh was crowded and Jim had to park Bowler on the far side by the single track road, nearer to the lighthouse than he would've liked. Only because the boys always wanted to walk to it and stare, marveling at its red and white candy stripes and huge great light on top which seemed to dwarf them as it held them in its own magical spell. Eventually after what seemed an age, they descended the concrete slope past the lifeboat station to the beach. They turned left and walked a few hundred yards in the direction of Wallcot. Behind them were the cliffs and on top was the caravan park from where music was playing and children's laughter could be heard.

'Can we go up Dad? Can we go and see what it is?'

'Please Dad! Please!'

"OK come on but It may only be for the people on the camp site."

As they clambered up the steep path cut into the crumbling sand and mud cliff, the music and laughter

73

seemed to die but on reaching the summit it burst out at them as if welcoming them into a cacophony of sound and light. They were on the edge of a neatly mown playing field. Its perimeter surrounded by mobile homes all pointing towards the sea and between our trio and the caravans was a small old fashioned style fair. There were about twenty small stalls with hoopla, roll a penny, darts, cork guns, candy floss and more. A grand old maroon painted generator was providing power for the music and lights, as well as enough horse power to run a merry go round. The boys were in their element. Thomas was so excited he was jumping up and down and Mathew didn't know where to look next. It wasn't the first fair he had been to but it would probably the first he would remember. They wanted to go on everything. But first was the merry go round. Mathew in a plane as it was safer, and Thomas on a motorbike. Jim stood back and watched as the ride took off, remembering his own childhood and the simple pleasures of his first fair and days spent at the seaside.

"thought it was you. How are you? Did you get that job?"

Jim turned as he recognized the lady's voice. "Hi Kym, Yes I'm fine. I'm here with the boys, they are on the roundabout."

'So are mine, we were round the other side and I spotted you so I thought I'd say hello." Jim waved as the boys came round and then waved again as Chris, Emma and cousin Mickey came round after them. There was a bit of a pregnant pause as they looked at each other and looked away again and then back, both wanting to talk but neither really knowing what to say or how to start the conversation. And when they did speak it was both at once. "Well did you" .."How did your sh.."

"Sorry you were going to speak" 'No no, I interrupted. You say what you were saying'

"No I insist, ladies first"

'Well I was only going to ask how you got on? Your job interview? The last we saw of you, you were rushing back to the agency to get a job.'

"Yes, well I got one in fact I got two but there was some mix up and I'm not sure what happened but I have to go and see them again tomorrow."

'I hope it goes all right. We are supposed to be off back down to Essex next week but I'm not sure we will go we may stay here for another week or so. The kids love it.'

"Can you do that? Just take them out of school?"

'Yea, I can at the moment, I'll explain in a minute.' They both assisted the children to dismount from the ride and as the children played on the role a penny they chatted. From the rola penny to the darts from the darts to the hoops and the hoops back to the darts. Not a goldfish or cuddly toy was won between them. As consolation they each got a candy floss and watched it being made. The young lady who hardly looked old enough to go to school let alone serve on a fair ground stall, twisted the stick around the drum turning it as she did so in order to capture the hot sticky stands of pink sugar. From there it was a quick stroll to the beach and as the children played they talked some more. As Jim drove back that evening he couldn't remember what they had actually talked about. Everything and nothing. He felt good, he had enjoyed the company of Kym and her children, there was no pressure and there was nothing to prove. He was able to be himself and they had discussed all sorts of topics from the merits of living on the Norfolk Broads and local villages to the quality of day light for artists painting. He hadn't realized that Kym was an artist; she looked too normal to be one. He also didn't realize that her brother in law was a plumber. It's strange the things you learn when you have an hour or two with someone interesting. The time seemed to fly by. "Hold on boys! Acle bridge. Are you ready?" As if with one voice all three let rip a loud "WHEEEE!" as their stomachs churned from the motion caused by the hump back bridge. Jim's head nearly went through the

75

canvas roof which delighted both Mathew and Thomas but only served to remind Jim he must lower the seat somehow. They parked the car around the corner as he had done on collecting the lads. It wasn't time yet to show it to Betty and the boyfriend. He would have to at some time but not yet.

Saying goodnight to his boys since leaving home was never easy and it was getting ever more difficult for Jim. He had always loved reading them bedtime stories and had not been able to do so since he left. Betty didn't want Jim to hang around and certainly seemed reluctant to talk about anything. Tonight was no exception. She quickly ushered the boys in and slammed the door in Jims face. He walked up the drive and looked back to see the boys waving from the front bedroom. He waved back, smiled and stifled a tear as he headed to the little car for the short journey home.

'Yer quiet boyee' Peter paused only to hand over a plate of sausages in batter with mashed potatoes. 'And I int really had a family m'self but I spose they gi you lots to think about.'

"You can say that. The trouble is I love them so I find it hard to be without them". I can't help but think that they should have a family around them, me and Betty, but I know she's finished with me and has been for some time, only I couldn't see it. And she loves 'em too but I'm their dad and I want to be there to tuck 'em in, to read them a good night story, to teach them to laugh, at themselves and at life; And to be good human beings, And Oh! Bollocks! Why did I have to go and screw it all up?""

'Dunt think ya did boyee. Und you shouldn't neither. You bin a good dad to them boys and your still being. Some people always think the grass is greener on the other side. She'll see. It won't be long and she will try to tie him down and he will up and leave but by then you'll have moved on. She's gone for the flash money and the fancy sports car but as soon as he smells nappies and is expected to show commitment he'll be off. You mark moi words."

Jim felt better and after a plate of toad in the hole and a strong mug of tea he settled on the porch to watch the night sky as it slowly darkened casting glorious hues of red and crimson across the few wispy clouds as they streaked overhead; The broads and the trees framing a classic Norfolk sunset.

'Life might be squit boyee but with a sky like that would you want to be anywhere else?'

"No, it's beautiful. I think it's so good that we should break out the home brew my Dad gave me."

'I int sure it's that good, but it will help to keep the chill out I suppose.'

Monday Morning 7th May

It was 10:00am as Jim walked into the employment agency. He spotted Malcolm who he had seen on his first visit but he was busily engaged in a phone conversation as the girl with the road safety eyes smiled and waved so he made his way towards the desk and sat down opposite her.

'I was hoping you would be in earlier.'

"I'm sorry I took my boys to school and came in immediately after. One minute I had a job and the next I didn't. Is there a problem?"

'I'm sorry about this but it seems there is a difficulty with your references. Your last employer insists in saying you were sacked but refuses to say why and Laurence's won't take the chance you see. If it's not a rude question why were you sacked?'

"I think I was sacked because I was a foot taller than the boss and I come from London; but you can't really put that on a form or as part of my CV so I'm not sure what to say"

'Oh' she said nodding her head with a knowing smile. 'I think we'll put it down as you left on a mutual understanding that you would seek a more challenging role elsewhere. However it may make things more difficult if our customer wants to check references. Where else have you worked?'

Jim gave the name and address of his former directors in London and his previous employers of some ten years ago and hoped that would be ok.

The cross-eyed lady who Jim found out was called Louise, agreed to find some more positions for Jim and make sure his references were good. He made his way back to the car park and home to Peters place in Hornham.

For the next few days he phoned in to the agency each morning. The message was always the same. 'Sorry nothing for you at the moment. Please ring in tomorrow'

He busied himself with helping Peter to work on renovating the property. The highlight of his day was dropping the boys off at school and collecting them at the end of their day. It seemed to him that it was their highlight too as he listened to all the things they had learned at school and play school and at how clever their teachers were.

It was Thursday evening, the 10th May. The boys had just been delivered home, and as he walked slowly back to Peter's Jim was worrying about how he was going to pay for the next meal and where he was going to get a job. He'd got the Eastern Daily Press again. There were lots of jobs but few that would suit a wire working salesman. And even fewer that he really wanted to do. But he would have to take something and soon, or he would have no money at all.

'What you need is a pint'

"Peter that's your answer to everything."

'Listen Boyee, I int got this old and this ugly by not knowin when someone needs a pint. 'n I can se you needs one. You've worked hard this week so Oi'm buying. Dun argue.'

The Wherry was unusually full for a Thursday Peter and Jim had to almost push their way through to the bar.

'Two pints of yare please and how come it's so busy?'

'Oh it's the football. World cup qualifiers or something. Barrys got a telly set up in the next bar so all the sensible ones are this side and the football lovers are next door.' Pointing to the public bar. They looked across, the bar was packed with familiar faces. Jims eyes met those of Mr Stone looking back towards the restaurant bar. There was an instant recognition, Jim looked away immediately but it was too late and he knew it. "Shit! Where am I going to find the money I owe him?" He looked like a boxer although too old to fight, but still muscular and fit enough to handle himself. Certainly fit enough to sort Jim out. Jim looked again. Mr. Stone was still looking. Although this time he was staring. Staring right at Jim. He raised a finger and gave a nod of the head as if to say I want to speak to you.

As his knees went weak Jim smiled back.

May be he could give him an IOU? May be arrange credit with Barry and Ann? May be just say sorry and throw himself at the mercy of Mr. Stone and accept a good hiding may be.., It was too late Mr. stone was there next to them holding a pint in one hand his other by his side, fist clenched. Jim saw the glint of a silver knuckle duster and tried to look away and not stare.

'I've been trying to get you for the Last week or so. You are a hard man to track down.'

"Yes, sorry, I've been busy", Jim mumbled, "Job hunting". It was all he could think of to say at the time. He hoped his nerves didn't show. His mouth dried and he could taste the fear at the back of his throat.

'We've got a debt to settle,' his hand raised slightly as he uttered the words, Jim instinctively took a step back and again saw the silvery glint of a knuckle duster as Mr. Stone's hand reached out towards Jim's stomach and stopped!

'Sorry I can't shake your hand properly I've got the bloody dogs lead. It's in the car at the moment fast asleep. You saved it didn't you? In the river the other day. I really owe you. My Mum's devoted to that bloody Dog and if you hadn't dived in I don't know what would've appened. As I say I've got a score to settle. Let me buy you a beer and you tell me what I owe you.'

As Peter laughed Jim's sigh of relief could be heard in both bars above all the noise and chatter, Mr. Stone didn't quite get the joke but politely carried on as if nothing had been said. 'Do us a favour, Hold the dogs lead while I get the beers in.' Jim found himself happily holding a silver choke chain and leather handle that only minutes before had looked so menacing.

'You here on holiday or what?'

Mr. Stone placed the drinks on the shelf above the two old ships wheels where Peter and Jim had found space to stand.

"I've lived here for a few years but grew up in Higham's Park in London".

'You never lose the accent see.' I'm up here quite a bit and Muver loves it but some of 'em talk funny though don't they?

'Well oi i'nt sayin Nuffin' Peter quipped with a smile in his voice which showed a mischievous irony that wasn't lost on his companions.

The evening continued with Mr. Stone insisting on buying the beer and as Jim explained their situation with the house renovation, his job or lack of one, and his relationship with his estranged wife, their cockney dialects became more and more prevalent. "There I go again" he thought. "Telling the world and his wife my troubles and I hardly know him."

"We gota go I think, Barrys calling last orders and I have to get up in the morning to take the kids to school. Fanks ever so much for the Beer you really didn't need to. Next time s'my round an also I owe you for a meal that we had; apparently you didn't know it but we took a table next to yours and you ended up paying for our meal. Can I pay you next time?"

'No! No problem, Just say you owe me' Jim Noticed the sideways glance and wondered what it meant. First Jessie and now Mr Stone. He was building up debts of gratitude but it was better than owing money.

'Thanks for that boyee', Peter interjected as if to move the conversation on 'and we only know you as Mr. Stoon. We can't call you that all noytt. Blast me boyee whars your fust name.?

'don't use it much but any man who risks his life for a dog and can keep my muver appy can call me by me first name. It's Leyton.. It's usually saved for me muver and close friends only. Me parents met in the blitz in the east end of London. So they christened me Leyton.'

With that the three men shook hands, Leyton climbed into his car. The old fashioned Jaguar roared into life and as the engine started he pressed the button winding the automatic windows down. 'If you still need a job at the weekend try the Larkswood 'otel I understand they're looking for people. Fanks for the chat an' f saving the dog, see you arand.'

The twin carburetors gave a throaty roar and the dark blue jaguar glided smoothly up the hill and away into the night. As they stared at it disappearing into the distance Peter slowly reflected.

'Could a bin wuse I spose. His parents could a met in Scunthorpe.'

Friday 11th May

The next morning Jim settled into his by now familiar routine; collect the boys deliver them to their schools and phone the agency. The reply was the same. 'Sorry Mr Daily we have nothing for you at the moment. Would you like to ring back in an hour and we will see what we have for you'

He sat on the bench seat at the corner of the Street and Highview Avenue and read yesterday's situations vacant. He ringed several sales jobs and vowed to send cv's. He read an article about last year's grain harvest, the price of houses and a foolish notion of closing the Brewery. Heaven forbid!!! How could anyone think of closing a brewery?

55 minutes gone, that's good enough! He was back on the phone this time however the story was different. 'We have a job you may be interested in. It's sort of sales but it needs a bit of decorum and a sense of dignity. Which I think you have got. They won't just have any one. You can drive can't you?'

"Yes! Of course I can. Is there a company car with it?"

'Oh Yes! there are several but,,'

"Great it's not all office based though is it?" Shouldn't have said that. Whatever it is I'll take it he said to himself hoping the inference in his words would not be seen as a reluctance to work.

'Well you are out and about some of the time collecting and delivering, I'm sure they will explain.' "Good," 'Well they'd like to see you, Do you know St Stephens round about? Well you go over there and take the first left and left again past the church and they are on the left as you drive round. It's the Co-op you can't miss it. Ask for Mrs Watson. If you are free this afternoon at two I'll let them know.'

"Yes I'll be there. I'm not sure about van driv.."Beep beep beep. "Bloody pips, I've got no more money . tell 'em I'll be there".

Jim had never done van sales before but he was willing to give it a go if it meant he was back on the sales ladder. He could always use it as a spring board. May be he'd be the team manager in charge of several van salesmen, after all he had been in sales for ten years. His spirits lifted with the prospect of a job he headed back to Peter's to get washed and changed.

Jim heard the door as he was drying himself. Peter was just back from Acle Market. He'd cycled there with a full basket and a back pack of early spring veg plants he had been cultivating in the green house and under tunnels of plastic. A new idea that jim was sure wouldn't catch on but it had enabled Peter to expand his growing season for now.

"I'm going in the City Peter if there is anything you need?"

'Well funny you should say. Mate o moin Erik , he's got sum old double length pallets saved for me. He's on the hairport. I'll gi ya his address. You take the croo barr boyee an ya cun brake 'em up soos they'll fit in your little jalopy. You'll ha ta separate the long uns coz thars wot we needs fur flooring joists.'

"I wish I'd never asked."

'Dunt be darft boyee, you know we int got the money to buy new so this is next bess thing.'

In his heart of hearts Jim knew Peter was telling the truth but he couldn't quite bring himself to admit it. He'd always sold new and was not a fan of recycling old junk.

"Up St Stephens around the back of the co-op? Stupid woman! She's got her left and rights mixed up. Typical! can't read a map and doesn't know left from right."

He left the little fiat in the parking space under the old city wall. If it weren't for the colouring of the little car it would have made a great picture. A shining cherry red car framed by a red brick arch against a back drop of the old black and grey flints.

The colours as they were, it would look more like a Picasso than a Lawrence or even a Newby and certainly not worthy of being displayed where people would see it.

Walking into the small entrance at the back of the Co-op on the left he spied a small glass window hiding behind it an obviously busy office. He pressed the bell and was embarrassed as it stayed down and ringing long after he had lifted his finger. The glass suddenly parted and a fist hit the bell stopping the sound instantly and with a look of "Why didn't you do that" a squeaky little voice enquired. 'Yes?'

"Hello, I'm here for an interview with Mrs. Watson."

'I think you are in the wrong place wait there' squeaked the voice as the glass closed like a guillotine falling on its victim.

Three minutes later the squeaky voice slid back the glass to reveal a sneering face with the words "I told you so" written all over it. 'I was right you should be over the road. At the back of the night club or theatre or whatever it is now. Opposite the church. There is a Co-op sign you can't miss it. It's in there. Mrs. Watson is waiting'

The glass doors slid shut almost as fast as they had opened, the words "Good Luck" emanating from the squeaky voice being lost cut in mid-sentence as the glass doors slammed. A five minute walk through the underpass round the furniture store and Jim was there. He could see it clearly. The Co-op sign he was surprised he had missed it first time. "Maybe she did know her right from her left. Well," he sighed, "it is not van sales, and they obviously do have company cars. Two are parked outside I'm not sure they would let me take them home though." He couldn't help but chuckle and smile as he pushed the heavy plate glass door open and stepped into the Co-op Undertakers.

'Mr. Daily? You're late!' It was the voice like an old school teacher telling off the naughty pupil, spoken so fast and crisply that you dare not interrupt. He turned to see her grinning like a Cheshire Cat with a Norfolk accent that had a mouse trapped in it's claws.

"The one thing we look for here is promptness; funerals wait for no man. If we are late for a funeral the wrong mourners weep over the wrong coffin and we end up without a tip. My Husband and I , He's a Director . A real Funeral Director you know; He can't abide lateness.'

"Sorry Mrs. Watson, I went to the wrong Co-op" Jim offered his hand but Mrs. Watson was unmoved and

84

turned raising her nose but still talking and ignoring the gesture of friendliness and respect.

'We expect you to be on time, you will look smart and be available to sell and advise the mourners when they need it. You will have to dress in black of course. With white shirt and black tie. And after a short period if you are acceptable to me and my Husband he is the Funeral Director you know, we will issue you a uniform.

Well you can start on Monday our first funeral is at 10.00 but we have some laying out to do. We always do after the weekend, so be here at eight. You know the wages I assume.?'

"Well actually No! I know very little other than I am expected to drive and that my experience as a sales man will be useful"

'I despair with these agencies. I have told them time and time again of the caliber of the person we need and they always send me people who will not stay any longer than a few days. I sometimes wonder what is up with them.'

Still looking up towards the ceiling rather than at the person she was talking to

'The Salary is three thousand pounds per annum plus a share of the tips.

We work Monday to Friday with occasional overtime at weekends and evenings. Collecting customers laying out, that sort of thing. The overtime is greater in the winter than the summer…..' She wittered on but Jim had already decided that this elderly looking lady with bleach blond hair and a funny accent was not going to tempt him to be a pall bearer.

"Thanks ever so much for the opportunity but I think this job is not for me."

'What!!?' came the rapid reply. She seemed amazed and oblivious to her own lack of charm or warmth.

'You are not pissing off as well? You are the third one today.'

Jim was stunned to hear such swear words from someone dressed as a lady. His first reaction was to reply "No, I'm not pissing off, I'm fucking off!" but he thought better of it.

"I am ever so sorry but I don't think this job is for me" with that he turned and made his way through the engraved glass door and back towards his car with a cry of

'My Husband won't like this. He is a Director you know' ringing in his ears.

"Yes" thought Jim. "A director all right, a flipping funeral director,; And heaven help him if he had to live with her. It's enough to turn your hair white."

It was 4.30 by the time that Jim returned in the little fiat loaded with dismantled pallets collected from Eric's engineering works at the airport. Some of them having been too long for the little car Jim had reluctantly poked them through the roof.

He had received some strange looks from passing cars.

'Did you get the sales job then boyee?'

"Yes I did but I didn't want it. It was an undertakers and I couldn't have worked with the old lady who ran the place. I know I can't afford to be fussy but I won't sell my soul. I have to have some self respect."

'I agree Boyee, There's more important things in life than money. You have to be able to hold your head high when you walk the street. Some can do that and some can't. Let me gi you a hand with them timbers.'

That evening Jim took the laundry to his mothers. She fed him as usual and gave him one of her special frozen meat pies to take back for him and Peter. At least he had some food and clean clothes to wear. But he still didn't have any prospect of money coming in or a job. He resolved to follow Mr. Stone's suggestion and try the Larkswood. As he left armed with the pie and two bottles of his dad's home brew, his mother tucked two five pound notes in his hand saying 'just in case you need a proper drink and take them boys out tomorrow on me.'

"I will Mum. Thanks, and if I do can I bring 'em over for tea?"

'If you don't we'll be upset. Stop at a phone box in the morning and let me know so I can prepare. Is Saturday feast OK?''

I'll ring Betty and let you know Mum. It should be good but you know what she's like."

A few moments later and it was all agreed. There was a sting in the tail though. Betty and the boyfriend Bill were going out to a special black tie dinner that started early at 6pm and didn't finish until well into the early hours. Jim would have to have the boys overnight or get them back before four..

"all right them, I'll pick them up tomorrow at 10.00"

Chapter 7 Larkswood

Saturday, 12th May

The Larkswood was a top quality establishment in its day and hosted dinner dances, weddings, banquets and large private functions. But these were on the decline and it had been let go by the previous owners as they moved towards their retirement. New owners had recently taken over and they appeared to be ploughing money in to bring it back to its former glory.

The outdoor swimming pool had been overhauled and brought inside with the clever use of a double glazed conservatory. A gym had been set up in the former garages and the restaurant, toilets and bars fully refurbished. Two stable blocks were in the process of being converted into a suite of holiday accommodation units and the key Heading was being replaced in time for the main holiday season.

It was nine in the morning when Jim arrived, and other than Mr. Franks and his sons from Thorpe doing the key heading there were little signs of life.

The sounds of sawing and banging ceased as one of the carpenters called over 'If you are looking for the manager he's gone into Hornham, He'll be back in five minutes if you want to wait.' Jim did just that but it was 35 minutes later that the manager turned up. His muscular frame, short cropped hair and arrogant swagger made him look more like a night club bouncer than a Hotel Manager.

'Can I help you?'

"Yes I was told by a friend that you were looking for staff."

'We might be. Who told you? What can you do? What qualifications do you have? And is it live in or live out?'

"I've got no qualifications but I've been looking for a job and my friend Leyton suggested I pop in and see you because he understood you were hiring people. I live locally and I am just looking for a job until I can get myself sorted. I'll even do part time work if necessary"

'Physically fit?' Hard working?' The bouncer spoke quickly as if he had asked the questions a thousand times and just wanted to get to the end of the process.

"Yes of cour…"

'can you drive? Will you do split shifts? You're not an alchy or anything are you?

All this time Jim was nodding. "I enjoy a drink but I'm certainly not an alcky"

'Right, Start Monday. Kitchen Porter. You'll be fetching and carrying, washing pots n, pans peeling the veg and 'elping the Chefs. You all right with that?

"Yes I think so but what's the pay and the hours?"

'Split shift 9.00 till 2 then 6 till 10 that's 8 hours 'coz somewhere in that you will get an hour's break. Wages are seventy pence per hour paid weekly in arrears. You work Monday to Thursday split shift with Friday 9 till 6 straight through. I don't usually need you weekends 'coz that's the students and they are cheaper than you. If you are all right with that Mr. Daily you can start Monday.'

"That's brilliant," the obvious relief showing in both his voice and face he offered his hand which the bouncer took and squeezed hard. "Sorry I don't know your name."

'It's Paul, Paul Berry actually but my staff call me Mr. Paul. Makes it easier and that way no one gets too familiar'.

It was ten fifteen by the time Jim got to pick the boys up. He was just about to ring the bell when the door suddenly flew open and Betty pushed past him. Not stopping but half turning her head as she hurried up the driveway and yelled behind her.

'The boys are upstairs getting washed. Lock up after you. I've got to get my hair done for tonight's Ball.'

Jim thought for a moment as he passed into the small house he had once called home, Ball? What Ball? It then struck him. It was the Norwich Metal Workers May Ball which he had always taken Betty to. This year he hadn't received an invitation and what with the relationship break up between him and Betty coupled with losing his job, he had forgotten all about it. How come Betty and Bill Salter were invited? Who would have invited them and why? His thought pattern was interrupted by yells of delight and hugs from both the boys.

"You are all wet! Come on, Go get yourselves dried. Thomas what is that around your chin?"

'I was playing Father Christmas like you showed us with your shaving foam'

"well get upstairs and wash it off or we can't go out."

As Jim began to follow them up the stairs his hand touched the banister and he noticed the black dinner jacket on the stair post.

His jacket.! The one he bought last year in the sales to avoid the cost of hiring one.

Pausing one foot on the stair and one off, he looked around for the trousers. There they were in the kitchen. Betty had obviously been taking them up ready for Bill Salter to wear to the Ball. Jim's Ball. The one he always took Betty to. He began to boil inside. Jim was furious but not just furious he was hurt. First he had stolen his wife, then he had moved into his house and now Bill Salter had stolen his dinner jacket. The phrase don't get mad get even kept racing through his brain. If he took the jacket they would just hire another one and they would know that they had got to him. If he left it and did nothing they had won another victory.

Jim continued up the stairs and organized the boys with washing and drying themselves. At a point where they were nearly dressed he left them to it and went into his old bedroom. He soon saw what he wanted. Taking the can of hair lacquer from the dressing table he proceeded back down the stairs, lifted the jacket and sprayed a considerable amount of the lacquer into the lining between the shoulders. He replaced the jacket on the stair post and spent the rest of the can spraying the back where the post formed a bulge. Not content with this Jim went into the kitchen, opened the drawer where they always kept odd bits of string, half used batteries and other "just in case and useful one day" items. He rummaged for a few moments and found what he was looking for; an old tube of superglue.

With a pin from the same drawer he carefully pierced a few holes in the tube, not too small not too big. Just sufficient to allow the glue to form a skin if undisturbed. He placed this carefully at the bottom of the inside breast pocket. 'Daddy, can you help me get my shoes on?' The interruption made him jump. He left the sabotage and went to help the boys.

"Right boys! Your choice, beach, broads or Petits?"

'Beach! There was no question. It was their favorite place when it was fine and at the moment it was a lovely spring day. "Happisburgh it is then. Last one to see the light house buys the ice lollies."

Half an hour later they were settled down on the edge of the concrete slipway eating ice lollies and gazing down on to the soft golden sand below. The tide was going out and leaving little rivers in the sand which exposed the bright shiny stones and broken shells making noises as they raced and tumbled to join the receding tide.

Shoes off they walked along the virgin sand where the sea had been some little time before. As they walked the boys busied themselves looking for the tiniest small shell they could find while a light westerly breeze calmed the sea and made it look almost inviting. Underneath the sandy cliffs beneath the red and white lighthouse they sat and ate some sandwiches, cake and biscuits, which they had purchased from the market on their way through Hornham, washed down with a can of drink each.

A lady came by with her dog quickly followed by a group of ramblers looking strangely overdressed for such a lovely day on the beach, wearing boots, shorts and tee shirts some carrying ruck sacks and some with jumpers tied around their waists.

"Come on Boys, shoes on and lets go and find some fossils!" they raced back along the beach passed the slipway and beyond where they had climbed the cliff to see the fair a not two weeks before. It was here that the best fossils could be found.

They chose a spot where the cliff was formed into a dense clay like rock and using a stick, and some shells they set about prizing stones out of the clay.

'Wow! I've got one! Look Look! Matthew had indeed got one. It was a circular shell forming a spiral; Fossilized some 10,000 years before and then covered in sand stone.

"It's an ammonite."

'What will Nana do?'

"No Matt it's not a Nana-might. It's an ammo-nite" Jim punctuated the words pronouncing the syllables so the boys could understand."

'You know? like in the A team when Mr T gets angry' Thomas had it all worked out. He was so pleased with himself smiling as he looked up to his Dad who was laughing.

"It sounds the same Tom and if that helps you remember it that's great but this one is a fossil and about 10,000 years old."

'Are we rich? Are we Daddy?' 'yes can we afford another ice cream?'

"No boys, we are not rich and yes, we can probably afford another ice cream Then we had better be going back to Grandma's for the rest of the afternoon and Saturday night feast."

Sitting on the sloping Jetty enjoying the sounds of the sea lapping against the sand and shingle beach as they themselves lapped at their ice cream cones, they were setting their minds to leaving when they were joined by Emma and Chris together with Pauline, Simon and Mickey. My sister will be so sorry to have missed you, she was only saying yesterday that she hadn't had a chance to say goodbye. "Spring holidays over? You going back to Essex then?"

'Well yeas and no. We have decided to move up here permanently. It's so nice. It's quiet. There's the beautiful beaches, the broads and it's so much nicer to bring children up. Basildon's alright but we can sell our place and buy a palace up her for the same money.'

"That's why we moved up." We, the phrase ran off Jim's tongue without thinking. The fact that he was no longer a "We" and was now only a "He" flashed through his brain. He dismissed it. That's twice this morning you've been brought back to reality Jim boy. Get a grip, he thought she was wittering on in reply but he was only half listening. "Yeah! Yeah! That's right" he mumbled.

'As I say it would be nice and she will be sorry to have missed you. Where should we go from, Wroxham or Horning?'

"Sorry I was miles away, looking at the children."

'A day boat! From Wroxham or Horning.?

"Well either is good. From Wroxham it's a lovely trip to Coltishall or from Horning to Salhouse and Ranworth. The views of the broads and the wildlife this time of year is absolutely magical. If the weather is good you can't beat it."

'That's what we thought, so its agreed then. We haven't been to Salhouse yet so Horning it is. What time should we pick the boat up? Oh they are alright, Simon's playing with them. He's not as good at sand castles as you but he trying.'

"Ten till four will give you six hours and that's plenty of time to take a lazy trip to Salhouse and back. Especially if you take yourselves a picnic. The kids will love it they can even paddle."

'OK. If we get ours you get yours and then we can pool it all together.' Jim's puzzlement was interrupted by Simon returning.

93

'I just said to Jim about coming with us tomorrow and he is well up for it. He says from Horning to Salhouse with a picnic would be good.'

'Well done Jim' slapping him on the shoulder as he approached. 'it will be good to have a bit of male company. I've been out maneuvered by two women for the past three weeks and I don't stand a chance.'

"I think I know how you feel." His mind filled with all the things he should be doing. Helping Peter fix the plumbing at the cottage, fixing the entrance plank which spanned the bog, running in the roof timbers etc. etc. But there again the boys would love a boat trip, Horning wasn't far from his mothers they could get back for a later lunch and he did have a job which gave him time off to help Peter during the week. Argument settled! A boat trip it was. With people he hardly knew but the kids all seemed to get on fine so for their sake he should give it a go. The rest of the afternoon was spent getting to know Pauline and Simon a little better. He found the more he was with them the more relaxed he felt and began to enjoy their company; which was good considering he was going to be on a six hour boat trip with them tomorrow.

Saturday feast a mixture of sandwiches, crisps, hoola hoops, cheese biscuits and sausage rolls always went down well, especially as it could be consumed without the formality of knives and forks in front of the television while watching Saturday night TV programmes. It was concluded with the boys being washed dried and put into their favorite pyjamas ready for bed. 'Read us a story Dad, please.'

How could he resist, this was special time for both him and them, something they shared together that no one else did. Their own special time. Tonight was Rupert. Jim always put extra rhymes in and included names of people the boys knew. It was ten past eight when he went into the lounge. He was as tired as they were but felt he should spend some time with his parents before leaving to go back to Hornham. He'd thought about staying, crashing out on the sofa but Peter may wonder where he'd got to; So home it was in bowler the little red shaded fiat. The drive from his parents seemed to disappear in Jim's mind. He was engrossed in thoughts of wishing to be a fly on the wall at the ball Betty and the boyfriend were attending. It would have started by now. They'd actually be on the dessert and coffee. Or maybe the speeches? That'll serve Bill Salter right, there's nothing worse than boring speeches. His mind wandered back to last year when his boss got drunk on port wine and fell asleep after the toast to the Queen. As the next speaker finished there was a short round of applause. Dickson's head had been bowed in slumber but jerked up, awakened by the clapping and like that huge fat seal at Pleasurewood Hills he joined in with the clapping. The moment it stopped he resumed his comatosed position only to repeat the performance several times over. As the speeches waned on more and more people noticed which made things worse. They started clapping and laughing at the most in appropriate places and the guest speaker couldn't understand why his speech had gone down so well but encouraged by such a receptive audience added four extra minutes to his speech. "shit" I should be there now not him!! Especially as he's got my bloody suit.

Sunday 13th May

Jim turned bowler onto the car park of the Broads Day Hire centre at Horning. The little red fiat was filled with Matthew, Thomas a picnic in three carrier bags, their swimming things and most importantly excitement. The boys were on fire with anticipation. This was a real treat for them. Betty hated boats. The boys and Jim loved them. 'There they are, there they are', Tom was first to spot the others and could hardly contain himself jumping up and down but still strapped in by bowlers safety straps.

Matt joined in making the whole car bounce up and down on its rear springs. It took Jim all his patience to stop himself from shouting at them to pack it in. They seemed to burst out of the car as soon as it came to a standstill, the passenger seat being flung forward and the door opening almost in one movement. 'The boys are excited and they are not the only ones eh Kym?' 'Thanks Pauline' throwing a sideways glance towards her sister, Kym's gaze returned to Jim,

'No our lot are excited too we had trouble getting the trio sleep last night.'

"I know. I have had similar and to keep them quiet this morning my mum made them help with the picnic. What we have got heaven only knows but I'm sure it will be good."

'I do like your little car. Its quaint and quirky. It suits you.' Kym ran a hand over the front panel where it joins the bonnet as she stroked it she realized what she had said and blushingly tried to back pedal. 'No I didn't mean you were quaint and quirky, it's just its unusual. The colour is so different and well, it's just different. But nice.'

Jim noticed how easily she blushed and how she would lean her head slightly from one side to the other when she felt awkward. "You are right. It suits us just fine at the moment. It goes from A to B and cost us nothing so I can't complain." She obviously felt embarrassed and he didn't want to deepen that embarrassment but he did wonder what she really meant.

'Come on you two, boat to load up.' Simon interjected picking up two of the bags and placing them into Kym's hands as a sure gesture of you carry these and get a move on. With the cars locked, food on board and all the children wearing life jackets they set off out of the small cut and into the main stream turning left towards Salhouse and Ranworth. The boat was nothing special. The seats were very basic as were the controls. 'Forward to go forward, back to go back. 'Remember it steers from the rear so it is slower to respond than a car. Simple as that.

Have a good trip and any problems find a phone and let us know.' 'Is there a speed limit?' Simon didn't want to break the law or worse, upset the locals. His future customers. 'Four miles an hour' came the reply from the smiling boat mechanic, 'but with a full load I doubt you'll need to worry.' The instructions were simple but sufficient. Jim had handled one before so was given the task of steering out of the little marina and into open water. The front cock pit held four, two in front and two behind. There was bench seating at the rear for another four or five. Plenty of room for the children and an adult so everyone took it in turns to supervise. Simon was desperate to steer so Jim handed over the controls in the first wide stretch of the river. "Now don't all move at once" Jim directed proceedings to ensure the little craft didn't topple over. "Simon you move to there. Pauline you move to where Simon was. Kym you and the crew of pirates stay there and I'll move to your seat Pauline. Ok? Go". 'Do I go here?' They all followed the carefully choreographed moves, the boat rocked but it certainly didn't tip and Simon was safely where he wanted to be, behind the wheel of his own craft. "You need to pull back a bit Simon you are tending to over steer." Simon moved his chair slightly towards the stern. "No I meant don't give it so much throttle and remember she is slow to respond. Give her some time to follows your instruction and wait for her to respond." 'More like a woman you mean.' 'Hey! I heard that' Pauline interjected, giving him a sharp prod on the arm. 'Sorry dear, only joking.' As Simon settled in to his role of captain Jim turned his attention to the crew. "Right you lot, you are the pirates and we are your captives so you must tell us what you want us to do. If we need to go slower tell us that too. Don't be silly mind as we have only captured this vessel for a few hours and have to return her shipshape and Bristol fashion. Isn't that right first mate?" Kym was stirred into life having been thoroughly absorbed with Jim's talk to the crew. 'Aye, aye captain if you say so.'

"Right then, first one to spot a kingfisher wins a prize."

'What's a kingfisher? What's it look like, how big is it?' Jim dived in his bag and brought out a map of the broads turning it over showed them the various birds to look out for. They ambled their way along the river spotting swans, coots, moorhens and plenty of Canada geese. They stopped to let the boys answer the call of nature and were discussing why it was always boys that had to stop for a pee, when the floating ice cream man came past. He was hailed by the pirates and crew leaving them a few minutes later, each with a 99. The boat became silent as they licked away at their ice cream cones so silent that they hardly noticed a kingfisher swoop overhead and glide effortlessly onto a dead tree stump some ten feet away from them. He sat, looked up river and down and then peered into the dark water about seven foot below. Kym was the first to spot him at about the same time as Jim. They gestured to the children to be quiet and pointed to the spot where the kingfisher was sitting. His blue and green plumage catching the dappled sunlight as it shone through the early spring leaves of the beech and oaks that lined the bank of the river. Suddenly there was a flick of the head, the plumage seemed to rise at the crown of his head and he was gone. Straight down, into the murky water below only to emerge moments later with a fish. The bird itself was only about four inches tall and the little fish was about half that size. With a shake of the kingfishers head the fish seemed to turn from horizontal to vertical and disappear down the throat of the beautiful bird.. They were not sure if it was the noise of the children's excitement or the approaching motor cruiser that frightened it but a look both ways up and down the river and it was gone. Not beautiful in flight, just another bird. But to see it doing what it has done and perfected over hundreds of years was a real experience for them all. They sailed on towards Ranworth where they stopped for a while and bought a coffee for the crew and lemonades and cokes for the pirates. Simon and Jim were tempted to try a beer from the Maltsers but a look from Pauline put paid to that. Back on board and a slow trip back towards Salhouse Broad lay ahead where lunch was planned. As it was Jim's turn to be coxswain he first steered the boat around the broad giving them all a view of where they had just been. Ranworth was a sleepy little place. Typically Norfolk with its little thatched cottages, a pub and a few essential shops gathered into a rural farming community based around the land and the broads; Looking almost if time had stood still, single track roads leading down to the staithe which was the centre of village life in summer and always lit by the afternoon sun opening onto a wide broad; Home to thousands of ducks, swans and other waterfowl that used this area as a stop off to and from distant shores. "You seem miles away, you ok?" He asked as Kym sitting next to him in the canvas director's style folding chair, as she gazed across the water. 'Sorry,' she replied, 'I am. I am just amazed at the tranquility of it all. It's so peaceful. You wouldn't believe there was a care in the world when you are out here. It's just so lovely.' Simon leant forward, 'Beats Basildon any day. Now you can see why we are moving up here.' Simon and Kym chatted on about the merits of Norfolk above the urbanization of south east Essex. Kym had half turned in her seat, legs resting on Jims. Almost stroking his ankle with her own. He was slightly taken aback but didn't move his legs. He was strangely comfortable. His personal space was invaded, as was hers, yet neither said nor did anything, an intimate moment shared by only them. Steering the boat into Salhouse Broad broke their momentary closeness as the pirates shouted 'land ahoy!' The little craft soon approached the shallow sandy shore which rose up to become a sloping grassy hillside with areas of short grass cut by the geese, intermingled with gorse and old oak trees.

'Wow! This is beautiful, is this where we are stopping?'

"Sure is Kym, the children can have a paddle while we get the picnic ready."

'I can't believe this place, it seems to be in the middle of nowhere. No shops, no cars, no nothing, only a few boats and millions of ducks and geese,. Can you only get here by boat?' "No there is a path but it's about a mile long so most people don't bother. My parents live about a mile and half up there but hardly ever come down here."

The sun shone, the children paddled, the grownups talked and joked and they all enjoyed the picnic. Especially the swans and Canada geese who polished off all the crusts and crisps the group couldn't finish. Simon was sitting on the trunk of a fallen oak tree looking down out towards the broad, with a wide grin on his face as Jim approached. He had been watching Jim teach the kids to skim stones.

'I fhink ish bruddy marverous Jim, marverous. I um reerie pleashed we came here. Do you want shum of your mums lemming aid?' He stumbled forward with hand out stretched offering Jim a three quarter empty bottle of his Dad's home brew.

"Oh my god! Who else has had any?"

'No one, they didn't like the taste but I fort it wash ok. I drank theirs so you wouldn't feel hurt. Hic!!'

"We had better get you back to the boat."

I don't fink hive quite got my shea legs Jim. Hyum having trouble staying upright on this log. Hit keeps moving.'

"It's not the log moving it's my dad's home brew"

As Simon started to fall backwards Jim made a grab for his arm but only managed to catch hold of his shirt. He heaved it towards him. A few buttons flew off but it did the trick and prevented him falling back. If only it had been that simple, the momentum was now forward towards Jim. Simon's reflexes although dulled by the drink, were still intact and he grabbed hold of Jim's upper arm with one hand and his shoulder with the other as he moved from the log towards Jm. At the same time Jim's mind seemed to go into slow motion as Simon came towards then over the top of him. It was just then Jim realized he had his finger stuck in the bottle of homemade wine. Flat on his back and still moving with Simon rolling over him he had no choice other than to follow him and like a snowball rolling downhill they quickly gathered momentum. One second Jim was on top, then Simon, then Jim, then Simon again as they cart wheeled down the slope until with a splash! they hit the water.

Everyone was laughing at them. Two grown men playing rollovers. They sat side by side in about one foot of water, looked at each other and laughed. There was a great pop! as Jim pulled his finger from the miraculously unbroken bottle, took a swig and offered it to Simon. 'Fanks, ish good thish lemming aid.' The only one not amused was Pauline. She was even less amused when she found out Simon was drunk. As penance Jim was put in charge of steering the boat back to Horning marina, the two girls looked after the children and Simon slept it off in the co-pilots seat. Jim couldn't work out why it was his fault but Pauline was convinced it was, so it was. She was a lovely lady with a great sense of humour and fun. A fairly well covered lady of comfortable proportions but not one to be crossed with thought Jim.

Forty five minutes later and they were tying up at the marina. The boys were saying their farewells as Pauline and Kym got Simon into their car and Jim bent forward to load the rubbish, towels and remnants of their day out, into the bonnet of his little red fiat. There was a tap of a warm hand on his back just on his belt in line with his hip. 'Thanks for today, I really did enjoy it and I know the children did; yours and mine. You are very good with them you know. I've never known Mickey so attentive. And Emma thinks you are great' "Yes I'm good with old people and young kids. It's just the middle range where I miss out." Her head tipped slightly towards the floor and to the left, she gazed at him coyly looking upwards, 'I wouldn't say that.' She reached up on tiptoes and kissed his cheek. Without waiting for a reaction she turned towards the car and stepping in said. 'You have Simon's number, please keep in touch. I know the kids would love. It.' With a wave of her hand she was gone. He watched as they set off with her in the back seat of Simon's car where they had squeezed three children and one adult in a space for three.

'Dad what are we doing now? Going back to Grandmas or going home?'

"Home I'm afraid guys. Sunday roast at Grandmas will have to wait."

'Can we do it again though dad.? Please.' 'Yes please Dad! and can you teach us how to do that rolling down the hill trick. It was great.'

"No I can't and it bloody hurts. Come on bowler! Home please and no messing about"

They pulled up outside of 33 Edward Gardens parking behind the Ford Capri. Before they could step out of the car Betty was there; hands on hips, looking like thunder. 'Where you bin with them boys, they're filthy.!?'

"You said you and what's his name were going out and they could be with me for the weekend. So that's what we did. You were going to the Ball Cinders, don't you remember?"

'The less said about that the better.' With that she turned to go inside ushering the boys in front of her. 'Bye Dad.' 'Yeah, bye Dad. Are you picking us up tomorrow?'

"Yes of course, 8.15 as usual." He waited by the car until they were in doors. He loved them so much and so enjoyed their company it broke his heart every time he had to say goodbye. He opened the car door but didn't get in. Waiting for just another glimpse of them. It wasn't to be, the curtains of the front bedroom were already closed and he knew that Betty would have marched them straight up stairs for a bath. He resigned himself to knowing he would see them tomorrow. He gave a large sniff and hoped no one saw the tears he wiped away as the car rounded the corner.

"Peter, If you haven't done tea I'm buying you a roast dinner at the Wherry."

'O'y been putting them trusses in n I could murder a beer. Roast'd go down well . Ha you got the money?'

"I start work tomorrow so who cares."

Sunday roast at the Wherry was always good but never special. It was value for money and with a choice of turkey, beef or lamb with Yorkshire pudding, roast potatoes, vegetables and all the trimmings, it beat cooking at home. Washed down with a few pints of real ale it was great end to a great day. Jim was reflecting on the good bits of the weekend when he noticed a shape of a lady he knew well, but these were in unfamiliar surroundings for her. Jim looked again to make sure. He was right, it was Millsy from Wilkinsons Wire works. She was with her husband and another couple but he felt he ought to at least say hello. "Millsy, sorry to interrupt but I felt I should say hello as this is my local and it would be rude not to." A broad smile crossed her face as she recognized Jim. Turning away slightly from her party as they looked for a table to sit at, she looked slowly up and down.

'Oh! Its soo good to see you. You're looking really well. How's things gooin? You're job, I mean and well.,,' There was an awkward pause, 'you know, everything?' Her speech suddenly speeded up, 'place ain't the same without you, you know, I refused to type that letter. I said he'd have to type it hiself.' She seemed embarrassed, awkward as it she had done something of which to be ashamed. 'In the end he got Gloria to do it on Satdee.'

"Yes, I understand he often does." She thought for a moment then the double meaning sank in. 'Ooh no! you don't think they do, do you? Oooh the dirty pair. No wonder he didn't want me to work Satdees, Well!'

"Mills, I haven't received any letter so I'm not sure what you are on about."

'It's not to you, it's a reference. I said I thought it was lying, so I said I wouldn't do it, so there! Well he wern't none too pleased but I got me principals. You know me. He didn't hardly speak to me at the ball last night, but I didn't mind, we had a good old laugh on our table. He had too many ports and fell asleep during the speeches. He only woke up when we all started clapping He'd jump up like one of those battery powered kids toys with and the tambourine and start clapping like mad. He'd look around all pleased, smile and fall asleep again. Well His missus weren't none too pleased neither, but he was at the other end of the table an...'

"Mills!" Jim had to interrupt, he couldn't stand the tension of not knowing, he had to know if it had worked or not. His sabotage. "was Betty there with Salter? What happened?"

'Ooh yeah, they were there, on his table, I wasn't going to say but it was Salter we was laughing at mostly. For some reason his jacket was all bulged out at the back and he kept shifting his shoulders left and right but whatever he did he couldn't get it to flatten. He looked like the hunch back of Notre Dame. Well, when he realized we was laughing he tried to take it off but it was stuck to his shirt. An to make matters worse he couldn't get his wallet out of his pocket coz that was stuck too. Betty had to lend him some money to get a drink. Martin from the warehouse said he wanted a scotch and when Salter said which one we all said 'The Bells! The Bells!' Well we laughed and we laughed but they didn't. They went home just after that. Oh, I'm bein called, I'll see you before oy goo.' Jim was aching to know more, What the reference said, or didn't say, what Betty did or didn't say. What's happened at Wilkinsons and much more, but he contented himself in the knowledge that just occasionally dirty tricks do pay off. If only he had been there to see it. He returned to the table to find it had been cleared of everything except a box of dominoes which Peter was proceeding to empty with a clatter onto the polished surface, turning them face down with one hand whilst making circular movements with the other in order to shuffle them. In the middle of selecting their pack of seven, Jim's attention went back to the bar as he noticed Mr. Stone accompanied by his mother and their dog entered the bar. Jim rose to greet them. 'What you having son?' "No it's ok Leyton, I've just got one in and I wanted to buy you one. I got that job you mentioned at the Larkswood. I start tomorrow, what would you like Mrs. Stone.?" 'Fanks Son, I'll av a barley wine if they got one.'

'Listen Son you won't be on much money so let me get them, we're only stopping for one.   Muver wants to get home'

"No I insist.   You bought them last time, remember? Peters over there, we were just about to play dominoes if you want to join us."

'Dominoes?' the old lady's wrinkled face lit up and widened with a thin narrow smile. 'I ain't played dominoes since father died. You'll have to remind me ow to play; come on Leyton.' Two and half hours later they were the last to leave the pub.   Mother had known very well how to play dominoes and won almost every game. Peter was full of beer and had not been playing at his best but didn't care.   Jim was still on a high after a good weekend and the prospect of starting work the next day and Leyton? Well he was complaining but only in a light hearted way that he'd brought the car and been on shandy all night.   Looking directly at Jim he waggled a finger menacingly.   'I blame you, you know, we was only stopping for one. Now she knows you boys play dominoes I'll have to bring her every bloody time, and next time we will get a taxi.   You want a lift?'   Peter turned from helping mother into the car.   'No its alright boyee by the time you ghet to the top of the hill we will be hoom.' They watched as the car glided up the hill complete with a full size nodding dog sitting proudly in the middle of the rear seats as if he were the owner being chauffeur driven. Millsy and her husband were just leaving too, they stopped the car to say goodbye. Jim told them of the new job starting tomorrow and how he hoped his luck was turning round. He thanked Millsy and via her passed on his best wishes to most of those that worked at Wilkinsons.

Monday May 14th

It was cold and overcast. There was no doubt it was going to rain but it didn't matter Jim had taken the boys to school and play school. He was picking them up from Mrs. Nash and school later. Today was the first day of the rest of his life. He had a job, he could see the boys morning and afternoon. He had a roof (well almost) over his head and he had a car when he needed one. He had friends, a little money, he had love and support of his parents and above all he had his dignity. He parked the little car in the shingled car park and went through to the reception area of the Larkswood Hotel. There was no doubt about it, the new owners were certainly spending some money on the place. The entrance was a set of wide stone steps with ornate planters at the foot and at the top. Above this was a canopy in kingfisher blue with the name Larkswood written in gold. To enter the building you went through two large full length tinted glass doors, each with a picture of a Lark engraved in the centre. The red and gold patterned carpet felt soft and deep underfoot. The colours were picked up and enhanced in the flock wallpaper. The lighting was from small spot lights inset into the ceiling. The reception desk set in the corner was small curved affair in mahogany with a brass foot rail and fittings. Pink tinted mirrors set in ornate gold frames behind gave an air of opulence and space. Opposite the reception stood a four foot polished marble column on which rested the bust of what looked like a Roman God. Two closed doors matching those at the front entrance led to what looked like a bar area and staircase. This was so much nicer than the entrance Jim had used previously.

'Yes. Can I help you?' Jim turned around. He hadn't noticed her before and wondered where she had come from. Looking about eighteen she had wavy shoulder length jet black hair with deep brown eyes and skin the colour of milky coffee. 'Can I help you?' She repeated. "Yes, I hope so, I'm here to work in the kitchen. My name is Daily, James Daily. I saw Mr. Paul on Saturday and he said report here."

'Yes, I'm sorry, Mr. Daily I'll have to get Mr. Paul the Manager. I think he wants a word with you before you start. I won't be a moment, if you'd just like to wait.' The slim pretty young thing pushed the mirror behind her which opened as a door into a back office. As quickly as she had appeared, she was gone. Jim was left standing there in awe of the splendor of the place. He could see why footballers, stars and celebrities were attracted to it. As he looked around the glass door to the bar area opened and Mr. Paul stepped through. He gave a quick smile as he held out his hand.

'I'm sorry Mr. Daily there' s been a bit of a problem, I need to speak with the owners before I can employ you.' Jim was puzzled, "You didn't say that on Saturday. You said turn up on Monday ready for work. What's the problem?"

'Yes I know, that was Saturday.. I received a phone call this morning and I have to check with the owners. I'm sorry, but at the moment I can't employ you. I can only suggest you come back and see me after lunch. The owners don't live here, they are based in London and I can't get hold of them until noon today at the earliest.'

"What am I supposed to do? Either you've got a job or you haven't." He was worried. He couldn't be too forceful and risk antagonizing his future boss but he wanted to know what had changed. Jim looked him straight in the eye saying

"What is the problem with the job/".

'There's no problem with the job. The problem is with you. I'm not sure you are the right man for us. I need to check with my boss. There is a lot of money being invested in this project and I am not prepared to risk it by employing someone of dubious character.'

"Who says I'm a dubious character?"

'I can't say. These things are confidential. On the one hand you have said and I understand, you are of good character. On the other hand I am told the opposite. I will speak with the investment company at noon. I can only reiterate that I can't give you an answer until then. I can say though that if we do not employ you we will pay you for one day so that you are not out of pocket'

"I'm not interested in the money. It's the job I need." It wasn't worth arguing. Jim knew he wouldn't get anywhere. He turned cress fallen, and walked to his car.

Chapter 8 Priorities

'You are back early',

Jim Looked up and saw Peter leaning out of the window.

"Yes I don't know what's going on but one minute I have a job and the next I haven't. I have to ring at 2.00 to find out."

James went to change into some work clothes and joined Peter They said nothing at first; Peter sawing a piece of timber while Jim held the other end, a look of sheer misery on his face. Some ten minutes and four pieces of sawn to length timber, Peter could bear it no longer.

'What happened then boy?'

"I don't know, I don't really understand it. I get there on time as arranged and then he says He's not sure he can employ me and has to check with his directors or owners or something in London. They're out so I have to phone back after lunch. It beats me Peter. He reckons I'm a dubious character or something. I don't know what to do. I still have no job and I'm fast running out of money. If it wasn't for you I'd have nowhere to live either."

'Well best you get working then boyee, Stop feeling sorry for yourself. We got a house to build and we'll get it done three times as fast if there is two on us worken on it' said as he picked up another length of timber and marked it off ready for cutting.

Peter was right and come lunchtime they had half the roof trusses in and supported. A job that takes two rather than one.

As they stopped to admire their handiwork James reflected on the fact that he liked hard work and was gaining a lot of satisfaction from helping Peter to convert a fallen down ruin into a home. He realised too that he had worked off his frustration and felt ready to return to the task of seeking a job.

Turning the little red car into the driveway of the Larkswood Country Club and having decided on the direct approach rather than a phone call, he felt ready for a show down. The tall 6'3" man squeezed himself out of the little red Fiat and tried to look composed. It didn't work. The equally large frame of Mr. Paul eclipsed him as he stood up.

'James, Sorry about this morning.' A wide smile broke across Mr Paul's suntanned face as he offered his hand. Griping Jim's firmly and pumping rather than shaking he looked him in the eye. 'I am told to ignore what I heard and go on my gut instinct; So welcome to the Larkswood, come through to the office.'

Jim was speechless. It seemed one minute he was the Devil incarnate and the next he was God's gift. He wasn't about to argue. He needed the job. And this one although not paying a great deal it was a job. It would allow him to see the children and it gave him some time off when he needed it.

'I'll show you round then.' His train of thought was interrupted as Mr Paul stretched out his hand inviting Jim to go ahead of him.

They went through the restaurant which opened out onto a large patio it's crazy paving adorned with shiny new aluminium cocktail tables and chairs leading to a large swimming pool bordered with wrought iron railings painted as was the rest of the rear of the building in Kingfisher blue. Around the pool were placed Romanic busts on marble columns in keeping with the main entrance. At the far end of the pool there was a small fountain and what appeared to be a Childs pool. The sun sparkled off the clear pool water reflecting the shine of the mosaic tiles beneath. They went down a few steps to the left.

'This is the outside pool bar, or rather it will be when it is finished We have the builders in as you can see and they are putting the finishing touches to the whole area. Whereever you turn there's either wet paint or someone

110

sanding down the area to receive it I'll be glad when it's all over. Should be ready in June.'

'We are still trading but won't be fully complete until about two weeks before the school holidays'

They turned around and ascended a wrought iron staircase onto the roof of the restaurant, where more ironwork gave way to a terrace matching the pool surround and patio. Here you could see the full extent of the pool and the lawns which were being laid with turf to form a back drop from the hard pool side, running out some 50 yards towards a laurel hedge and woods behind.

'Not bad eh?'

"No, it's absolutely beautiful."

'This is where we will do the wedding receptions. The small function room's behind us and we already have bookings for next year. We missed out this year but as soon as people see this they want it. My office is through here.'

Mr Paul took a little time to go through the paperwork and fill out all the forms. Everything was done in duplicate or triplicate with carbon paper between each sheet. 'A messy business but I keep a copy, you keep a copy and head office keeps a copy. I'll take you down and introduce you to the Chef before he goes. He's off now till tomorrow. Dave the second chef is on tonight but won't be here till 6, which is when I need you back here. Is that Ok?'

"Yes that'll be fine. "

They walked through the office towards the centre of the building and down a wide staircase that opened onto a large corridor leading on one side to the main bar, the other way led towards the reception and main restaurant while a set of double swing doors led to the kitchen.

'Hello mate, I'm Andy.' Jim took one look at him and immediately felt relaxed and comfortable, A jolly chap with a big beer belly a ruddy complexion and a welcoming smile. He was a little older than Jim and slightly smaller standing 6' but looking considerably taller in his starched chef's hat.

'You'll have to excuse me. I have to go and get changed. I have got to get home, the wife's lost her voice and I don't want to miss it. Nice meeting you. I'll see you tomorrow. Dave's in tonight. Nice bloke, you'll be alright but watch him he's an arse bandit. You'll see, he'll have your arse if you let him. know what I mean?'

He gave a nod of the head and a wink, took off his hat to reveal a bald patch like that of a monk in days gone by, then turning to look back briefly flashing another warm and genuine smile he was gone.

A further tour of the downstairs bar, function rooms, staff changing area and reception and his induction was complete.

'If you could return here tonight at six Dave will get you kited out with the wash up aprons and all the gear. I think you'll do alright with us Jim and I'm sorry about this morning.'

"Yes, what was all that about?"

'I can't say mate but you are on the books now so don't let me down.'

He squeezed himself back into the multi coloured red Fiat and returned to Peter's feeling more positive than he had for ages. Stopping off briefly to let Peter know how things went he hurried to share his good fortune with his boys. As ever they were full of their day and not really interested in his, Matthew had a new friend at play school named Nick, and Thomas was full of football and how he was going to play for Norwich City when he was older. They walked through the park chatting about their day and how Miss Humphrey's was so clever as she knew everything and how naughty Johnny Reid was in class. Matthew said Mrs Nash had a smelly cat that made him sneeze but she made sandwiches with the crusts cut off. That was posh! and just like Grandma did. Today had been a good day overall. He had started the new job and been able to collect the boys and walk them home. He had helped Peter prepare the timbers for the roof and he was going to meet the other members of the Larkswood Restaurant team. Maybe things had turned around... the thoughts still drifting through his mind they turned into the driveway of the family home. Betty opened the door and welcomed Jim with a scowl. 'Where you bin with them this time?'

"Nowhere! we just stopped off in the park for a go on the swings and the boys were telling me all about what they have been up to?"

'What have they been up to?' Her words were fast and accusing. Always looking on the black side.

"Nothing there's no need to worry, they were just saying what happened at school that's all" 'Well they can tell me later their teas ready.' Ushering them in she closed the door leaving him once again staring at the frosted glass of the small porch. He knelt down and shouted through the letter box. "See you tomorrow Boys! I'll pick you up at eight fifteen.. Goodnight"

The door flew open 'I suppose you think that was funny do you?' Betty was in the door way arms folded, chest out and scowling as usual.

He was half way up the drive; looking back over his shoulder without stopping he smiled delivering a cheery "Good night Dear"

'Humph!' The door slammed with enough force to rattle the pane and make the knocker fly up and down with a crash.

He was determined not to let her get to him. Not today. He was in a positive mood and he intended to stay there.

Ten minutes to six. He checked his watch again for the fourth or maybe fifth, time. He didn't want to be late.

Entering through the front door of the Larkswood he approached the reception. 'Hello Mr Daily' the cheerful voice of the young lady had a friendly ring to it as she

113

welcomed someone she knew. 'You are all right tonight but in future if you can come in round the side you'll find it easier. We sometimes have guests and Mr Paul says it looks better.'

Point taken he thought, after all I am only the washer upper. He was ushered through to the restaurant kitchen.

'ello Mate,' another cockney accent but this one was different. It had a strange ring to it

'I'm Dave. I take it you're the new Plonge?

"Sorry? I'm the washer upper. Jim Daily."

'Yea, that's wot I said. This is a Fwench style westawant. Me and Andy were twained in London see, and the KP is called the plonge' seeing the puzzled look appear on Jims face he continued 'KP is Kitchen Porta. That's you. I'm Sou. Sou Chef, and Andy is Head Chef. But you just call us chef. You'll soon get used to it. Main fing is do what you're told and if you don't know ask. Let's get you sawted out with uniform.

Jim noted the obvious speech impediment but said nothing, not wanting to embarrass either of them. Dressed in his chef's whites Toni's sallow complexion was extenuated.. With a large nose, deep brown eyes he walked with a swagger as if he was the top dog and knew it but Jim took an instant liking to him he was about the same age as Andy or may be a little younger as his complexion did not look as lived in as the Head chef but he too had a warm smile that showed his rosy cheeks off to full effect.

Jim was introduced to the sink, a large commercial unit with 2 extra deep bowls and a swivel tap that could fill either. There wasn't a plug in either sink which he found strange. Just a pipe sticking up so the water could flow continually without over filling. Jim started upon the mountain of washing up that was already in the sink.

'The first bowl is for washing the second for winsing and the dwainers for stacking and dwaining. Not woket science is it? It's a quiet night tonight that's why Andy has it off. I'm off tomowo and Satday Mawnin. He's also off Tuesday or Wednesday depending on bookings.'

"Does it get very busy then?. "

'I'll say. We're good at what we do and the twade is building up nicely. We have got another woman who helps out,. She is called Effel.'

"Ethell's an old fashioned name is she very old?"

'It's cockney. It's not her name, it's what she does, F All.' Dave smiled and chuckled to himself. Jim wasn't sure if the joke was on him or Ethel or on both of them but laughed any way and continued cleaning pans.

The doors to the restaurant flew open and a big buxom lady dressed in a waitress uniform that hugged her well proportioned but ample figure breezed in.

'Table six is in, four of them, what's the soup?'

'Cweam of potato with caw-wianda and wed onion. Special is wump steak on a wokket salad. Oh that bloody Andy, He does it to me evewy time. And the sweet is wum baba with wazbwies and stawbwies Oh Bollocks!'

Jim couldn't help but laugh he was pleased to see the ample waitress was laughing too. It was then that he realised the meaning of Andy's parting comment about Dave and watching his R's.

Luckily Dave was laughing along with them ' I'll get that bugga, You see if I don't'

The night seemed to fly by and at 10pm the last orders having been served Jim took to sweeping up and moping the floor.

'You've done weally well Jim. Back in tomowo?

'Yes I'm supposed to be in at Nine. I have to drop one boy off at school and then play school for the other first.'

'My Nick's just started play school. Loves it!

"I think he was with Matthew today; My youngest"

The next twenty minutes were taken up by as much chat about children as it was work.

Later that night climbing into bed, tired from a long and exhausting day. His body said sleep and as he began to drift off he realized how satisfying it felt to have a job and be tired from working for a living again.

Tuesday 15th May

Having risen at seven and deposited the boys at school Jim drove to the Larkswood. 'I want you to peel 2 bags of potatoes today' Andy saw the look on Jims face 'Not by 'and, We gota machine downstairs. Ave you met Effel? .Effel!

The shout went up and a mature lady of sixty or more years came around the corner. She was slightly hunched over but neither that nor her weathered expression and wide smile could hide the fact that in her youth she had been an attractive lady. As the days wore on Jim was to discover she was a lovely old lady with a dry sense of humour and although she appeared never to get into a sweat always working at a steady pace, she managed to peel a lot of vegetables, prepare a lot of Salad and do a large amount of food preparation for the chefs.

'This is Jim the new KP. Show 'im where the spuds are will you? But don't you go lifting them. That's what he's ere for'

Out of the kitchen and down a short flight of steps was the cellar, It doubled as a wine cellar and as a veg room. The floor walls and ceiling were all of concrete it turned out it was the old air raid shelter put in during the second world war. ' It floods at times when we have lots of rain but they have a pump for the water and the drain so we can still use it as long as we keep things on the duck boards.' There were plenty of things on the boards, large bags of potatoes, nets of carrots and wooden crates filled with cabbages and cauliflowers. " What's behind there then?" he pointed to a low wooden door securely fastened with a padlock.

'That's the wine cellar. We have to keep a clear path so the waiters and barman can get to their stock in a hurry. It's the expensive stuff in there.'

Jim was introduced to the automatic potato peeler which took half a bag at a time. 'Water on, electric on and spuds in. '

"It makes a hell of a racket!"

'Pardon?'

"I said it makes a hell of a racket"

'Yes! It will make your ears ring if you are down here too long. When they come out you have to eye em up.'

How do you eye up a potato? Surely one spud looks as good as the next and if you did fancy one over another would that be right and would it be something you would admit to? As these thoughts went through Jim's head Effel lifted the loose fitting rubber lid, reached in and extracted a potato from amongst those spinning and rumbling around. She reached down still clutching the potato and almost as if from nowhere produced a pointed knife and proceeded to cut the black bits out of the not quite peeled potato. With a speed of a well practiced hand she proceeded to demonstrate what eying up a potato meant. With that she opened the door to the peeler allowing half a bag of potatoes to rumble noisily into the sink.

For the next two hours Jim was rumbling and eying up 2 bags of potatoes. The finished articles ending up in plastic dust binsand topped with cold water.. He was glad to get out of there and his ears were singing exactly as Effel had predicted. Sitting down for a cup of tea with the chefs and Effel gave a welcome relief. They were joined by Nikalos the bar manager from Crete and Berryl the waitress from Hornham.

Both of them were friendly and greeted Jim with a warm hearted smile and pleasant handshake. He felt he knew them from somewhere but couldn't quite place it. As he sat at the table his ears only ringing when he thought about it, he mused on the range of cultures there were

117

employed at the Larkswood and the cosmopolitan feel it gave to the onlooker however; he was to find out over the next few weeks that all in the world garden that was the Larkswood was not as rosy as at first it seems.

'How you doing Boyee? 'Glad you're hume. I need you to muck up while I brick the middle wall. You want some lunch?'

"No thanks Peter, I'd love a cuppa though. I'll just go and change."

For the next two hours Jim laboured for Peter making cement and passing up bricks and mortar from ground to first floor.

'Nairly done Boyee, you still alright fur time?' "Yep! I got to be at Mrs Nash's by four thirty." He was. A little dirty having had no time to wash but he was there to pick up his little monsters.

The usual walk through the park and up the slight incline leading to Edward Gardens. As usual they chatted about their day but as they approached their home Thomas stopped looked up at his father and said 'Dad why can't you still live with us? I promise I will be good. We will do all the things we should we promise we won't fight. Or be naughty.'

"Oh come here you two", sinking to his knees and reaching out his arms to embrace them both. "It's not you that's the problem. I love you both to bits even when you are not being good. No matter how bad you are I will still love you. Me and Mummy love you. The problem is Mummy no longer loves Daddy. When you get older this sometimes happens. Now I have this new job I will be able to see more of you than I did before. I can pick you up from school and drop you off".

'But you can't read us a story any more or tell us not to be frightened at night'

"Not during the week Matt, but maybe we can arrange for you to stay with me and Peter at the weekends. I'll talk to Mummy and see what she says. Come on let's have a big cuddle and then I'll race you home." They did just that and ended up out of breath and laughing as Dad was last again having started out in the lead.

Betty as usual was not amused. She opened the door and turned her back on the three of them. 'Come on in you two your teas ready. You can close the door.' Jim knew the signs, she was in no mood to discuss issues like staying over. He decided to leave it for now.

He ran home to Peters house at The Loke, picked up the car and drove the few miles to the Larkswood. Evenings were different from days. During the day the restaurant was only partly filled with a few business men, the odd elderly couple enjoying the cut price special of the day, the twitchers, most of whom seemed to go for the vegetarian option and a few boat owners. There were a few tourists but the newly refurbished (well almost) Larkswood was not on the tourist maps or in the brochures yet. In the evenings the restaurant went up market. Norwich City footballers with wives and girlfriends rubbed shoulders with the local rich and nearly famous. Couples celebrated special events and occasions. Hair dressers dressed to impress dined with boyfriends and girlfriends. This was becoming the place to be seen in.

The staff too were different. Beryl was still there as waitress but she was faster and moved with a more determined and hurried pace. She was also joined by Lucas, a Turkish waiter who wore a blue jacket and showed gold fillings when he smiled. They shared the tables although Jim never did quite work out how they knew who had what table.

Jim was put to work straight away washing up the pots and pans that had been used during the afternoon to prepare the evening meals. The evening started slowly with each of the waiting staff bringing in orders for their tables. Andy the Head Chef calling out across the small kitchen for the orders to be prepared. Andy was in charge of vegetables, fish, soups and roasts. Whereas Dave was in charge of grills, steaks, and starters.

Jim was in charge of a double bowl sink full of hot water. As the evening wore on the restaurant became busier and more frantic. Mr Paul made an appearance from time to time occasionally helping out the waiting staff and making sure the food was served quickly.

'Hot!' the cry would go up and a once silver tray, used to grill the steaks and fish would come flying into the sink narrowly missing Jim and making a bubbling and hissing sound as it boiled the water whilst it sank. From the other side would come glass coupes and small starter plates, followed shortly after by fish or soup plates and then dinner plates. 'Hot!' the cry would go up again as another silver flat would be slung into the sink. 'Two medium away Chef! 'Yes Chef' 'Table four two minutes' Table six slow it up'. 'Bring nine on' 'A well done and a blue' 'Yes chef' 'Away Chef'

It was a world away from anything Jim had been used to before. It seemed to the uninitiated that this was a frantic mish mash of garbled phrases that had no connection with anything or each other almost like another language. For an hour and 45 minutes this crazy to-in and fro-ing of sounds continued unabated and as it reached its peak the whole atmosphere became hotter both metaphorically and physically. And then without a sign or apparent spoken word the atmosphere changed. It was as though everyone had breathed a sigh of relief.

The pace slowed down Andy took off his hat and stepped out of the back door to cool off. Dave started clearing down his grill area while Beryl and Lucas kept bringing crockery and cutlery in for Jim to wash.

It was ten thirty, the chefs were dressed in civvies ready to go home, Beryl and Lucas were serving the coffees and liqueurs and Jim still had a mountain of washing up to do.

It was almost midnight when Mr Paul put his head around the kitchen doors and told Jim to leave it until the morning.

He climbed into bed tired out aching and satisfied. What a weird world a restaurant kitchen is he thought. He started to offer a silent prayer for someone to protect his boys, his family and.... as his eyes closed he drifted into a well-deserved sleep.

He returned the next morning not looking forward to the mountain of washing up. As he walked in he was amazed to see it had already been done. "I'm sorry about the mess I left you Ethel."

A knowing smile passed briefly across her face and with eyes opening wide she gave a puppy dog grin.

'Thas alroight boyee, you'll soon get used to it and you'll be amazed at how fast you become. '

The next few days were taken up with more or less the same routine except that Jim noticed how each day at the Larkswood he had learnt something new and that Ethel was right. He did quickly get the hang of it speeding up considerably in the process. On hearing the words 'hot Plonge! He instinctively stepped to the left allowing room for a sizilingly hot pan to hit the water. When Dave called for a few more silvers, he had quickly learned to reply 'Yes Sous!' The response to Andy was always 'Yes Chef!' As the next few weeks wore on he and they discovered he was much more than a kitchen porter. He became a part of a well-oiled machine turning out top quality meals, on time and to satisfied customers. What's more he was enjoying it. He had a sense of purpose and self-satisfaction. It wasn't a lot of money but his life had started to turn around. He was able to see the boys off to school, in the morning, work at the Larkswood until after lunch then help Peter with the cottage in the afternoon before collecting the boys and returning to work in the afternoon. The money although not great was enough. He was able to pay Peter for food, building materials and a few beers. It even left a few pounds over for him to take his boys out at the weekends. There wasn't much left over for clothes and luxuries but at the moment he had sufficient. He was surviving. So much so he even stopped looking for a better paid sales job.

'You look pleased wi yourself Boyee; whistling away there?'

"Not so much pleased Peter, More contented I'd say. This is the first time since me and Betty split that I can actually say I am pleased we did. I see more of the boys now, I have a roof over my head and I actually feel I am alive.

It's the Whitsun Holiday next week and I'm hoping to have a day or two off if Andy can get the students to cover for me."

'If the weather is good I was hoping to get the roofing felt on and the battens in place but it will keep.'

Jim didn't need to look at Peter's face he could hear the disappointment in his voice.

"Good idea, What about if my parents have the boys Saturday and overnight and we do it then?"

'Could do, depends on the weather though, and can't do it in the rain. Not while we are living under it. And it's more than a one day job but,,,'

An awkward silence followed, the mood had changed. It was hard being full time kitchen porter, part time builder and full time parent, especially without help. Sometimes something had to give.

"Mum, it's me. I was wondering, Is there any chance the boys could stay over at yours this week end? Peter and I need to get the roof on and it looks like being good weather"

'Oh! Jim you know we would love to but your Dad and I are meeting Dora and Dennis at Hunstanton. We are doing Sandringham and the Coast. The rhododendrons will be out and you know what a spectacle that is,'

He had forgotten that each year with age old friends from Bristol his parents would holiday for a few days around the North Norfolk coast. The Queens estate at Sandringham was particularly beautiful as the vibrant mix of colours set the whole area alive contrasting so well with the natural woodland setting of the Queen's own woodland all of which was open for the public to enjoy.

The spectacle never failed to amaze anyone who saw it. He remembered a time a few years ago when he and Betty together with the baby's as they were then, went to view it stopping at the wooden tea rooms to buy a cup of tea, a freshly made sandwich and a plant from the plant stall outside. He jolted himself back into focusing on the job in hand.

"Ok Mum no worries, I'll sort it somehow"

'I have got your washing though dear and your dad has some more of that wine you seemed to enjoy so if you can pop over at some time it's here.'

The wine! Yes that's it! It's worth a try "Ok Cheers Mum, Speak to you later"

His mind was racing; there may be a way after all. He fished in his wallet and found the number for Simon.

"Simon? Yes Hello Simon, It's me, James, Jim, Jim Daily"

'Sorry?'

"Yes you remember the boat on the broads, rolling down the hill at Salhouse and ,,,"

Jim was beginning to worry, there were silences and pauses in the conversation where there shouldn't be.

'Of course I remember Jim, How could I forget? I was just trying to get you going. How are you?'

Sighing with relief Jim replied he was OK and went on to explain that he needed some help and wondered if Simon was available? 'You are in Luck, Kym's coming up so her and Pauline can take the kids off somewhere and I'll help you. One condition though, No more of your Dad's Lemonade.'

The next call was to his old work colleague Mick Mates, he too readily agreed and even suggested that he could bring along his father in law who used to be roofer. Too old now to climb ladders but full of enthusiasm and happy to give advice.

"Peter we are on for Saturday and possibly Sunday! I have called in a few favours and organised a couple of friends to lend a hand. I reckon if we crack on we could have the roof trusses battened out and the felt in place in time for Sunday lunch at the Wherry. What do you think?"

Peter was proud man, a man of principle and not used to taking help from strangers. That is why the place had been left for so long. His wrinkled nose and furrowed brow told Jim he needed to sell the idea to him.

"Peter all they want is to feel useful. They have offered their help and if we let them I'm sure we will have the opportunity to replay the favour at some time in the future! That's how it works. You took me in when I had nowhere because my Dad had done you a favour or two in the past. These lads are the same. We don't have to pay them, they are not after what they can get out of it, they just want to help, have a bit of a laugh and share a beer at the end of it!"

'That's sorted then but what about your kids?' Peter didn't sound totally convinced.

"That's sorted too. I'm sure Betty will have them for the day. I can have them Sunday afternoon and the rest of the week if necessary."

'Go on then boyee, let's give it a goo. As long as the weather holds good, let's have a crack at it.'

Time off work was agreed with the exception of one night during the week which the students couldn't cover. Now it was just a case of agreeing things with Betty. Dropping the boys off on Tuesday evening Jim chanced his luck and asked the question which somehow he knew would not be greeted with great enthusiasm. He had been wondering all day how to say it. All combinations of what to say had gone through his mind. He rehearsed them all several times. Can I?, Will you? You need to... I want ... none seemed to fit the bill. In the end he decided on the honest and straight forward approach. The door opened and the boys were ushered in.

"Betty, I was wondering what are your plans for next week. Half term?"

'Why?' snapped like a terrier chasing a ball.

"Well if you can look after the boys on Saturday I will gladly have them for the week. so you can have some time off with what's his name."

'You know very well what his name is and I am not sure. We were going to go out Saturday to well, wherever. You'll just have to leave it to me. I'll let you know.' The door closed with its customary slam and Jim was left feeling he was not being shown the whole picture. It took until Friday to resolve the matter. Betty was having the boys on Saturday and Jim would collect them on Sunday morning at nine, returning them that evening, collecting them each morning at the same time for the rest of the week. As long as the weather held it was a good plan. It did and it was

Saturday 26ᵗʰ May

Saturday arrived early with a call of 'Teas ready boyee, are you?' It was 6 o'clock and Peter had been up picking mushrooms at God knows what time. He had even found the time to prepare a breakfast for them complete with eggs and fried bread.

'We will stop at ten for bacon rolls and tea, what do you think? First thing get that tarpaulin off.' Peters hidden message was right. There was a lot to do and if they didn't have a schedule they wouldn't make it. The weather was just right. Bright, just a few small clouds scuttling across a pale blue sky, with just a gentle breeze. A typical Norfolk Broads morning. The sounds of the birds could be heard above the old rattle of a boat engine with the smell of bacon cooking as Hornham started to wake up. The sewing ropes on the windward side of the bright blue tarpaulin were loosened. Peter furled the sheet and shook it like someone putting a duvet on a bed. It billowed and just seemed to float over the house and then dropped in a crumpled heap at the other side, half in the muddy dyke and half out.

'Come on Boyee, dun't just stand there. Gis a hand to fold her.' Jim jumped into action grabbing one end while Peter unhitched the other. As they folded and wrapped the sheet a car drew up. As Simon got out and opened the boot to reveal his tool box, Pauline wound down the window smiling towards Peter and Jim. 'I'm dropping his majesty off, then Kym and I are taking the kids to the animal adventure place. We will be back about four. Want us to bring you anything?'

'No we are fine.' The boot slammed shut,

'Bye love, and don't have any of his dad's home brew remember.' With a wave and a smile she was off and just as she turned the corner a black marina estate turned in The Loke with Mick Mates and his father Patrick. Quick introductions followed and it was agreed that Mick and Jim would do the high level work balancing themselves between ladder and roof while Peter and Simon passed the roofing felt, nails and battens up. Patrick suggested they rig up a small pulley at the gable end so things could be sent up easily. This took a little while to rig up but proved

126

invaluable. Mick at one end of the roof, Simon at the other each being supplied by a loader below, the work commenced. After three hours of "to me, to you", Hammer! Watch out below and 'Walsham' which was Peters term of chastisement when anyone did anything stupid, the roof started to take shape.

"How's it looking Peter?"

'Alright but don't step back to admire your work. Finish this next line of felt and stop for a break.' Sitting on milk crates and orange boxes and the chairs Peter and Jim had already, they enjoyed a laugh and a brew accompanied by bacon sandwiches. Patrick and Peter got on well talking of the old days when Norfolk was cut off in the blizzards, when you could leave your door open and everyone knew everybody else. Mick and Simon found they shared a common interest in fishing and Jim? Well he was just happy that all was going to plan. Tea break over they continued well past lunch and into the early afternoon. Their fevered work rate only being disturbed by Pauline and Kym complete with children turning up with cakes and buns from the local bakers.

"Another couple of hours and we can do this. What do you reckon?"

'We can give you till six then we have to go. You ok with that Dad?' Patrick nodded agreement reluctantly. He had enjoyed the day and would have liked to have seen it through to the end. As they beavered on, the two ladies took the children for a walk returning just as Mick and Patrick were leaving with only one section to complete.

'Well, That's it then, call it a day.'

'You still have one bit to fit Peter.'

'I know Kym but we need two up top and two down below.' Kym looked puzzled and studying the faces of the three men asked 'Why can't I go up the ladder. Pauline can you look after the kids?' 'No that's too dangerous. I'll go up top, you pass the bits up'. Within an hour the job was complete. The tarpaulin lifted back over and everyone feeling satisfied they had done a job to be proud of with even the children joining in passing nails and catching bits of cast off tarpaulin. Peter was especially pleased. He'd never thought they would do it.

'Pub then, dinner on me.'

'But we've got the children.'

'They don't eat a lot do they?' Pauline smiled at Peter's response. It was obvious they were all invited. 'OK but only for a short while.' The Wherry was crowded with the usual regulars jostling for space amongst the holiday makers and boat owners.

'Come and join us mate.' Leyton pulled over one of the felt covered barrels which served as stools. A bit of pushing and shoving enabled them to create just enough space for Kym and Pauline to sit down next to Leyton and his mother.

'This is Kym and Pauline and Simon, don't know if you've met but this is Mr. Stone and Mrs Stone his mother.'

'Ay no need to be so formal. It's Leyton and Doris.'

'As you're friends of Jims you can call me Mother. Ee's lovely ee is, You know he saved my dog Poly? Jumped in, no fort for imself and saved er. Gaud bless im. Ow'd you know im or is it Peter? Ee plays a mean game of dominos.'

"I'll help you guys get the beer in. Whose avin what?" Simon took the children to the playroom while Leyton Peter and Jim ordered the food and drink. Leyton waved his finger at the barmaid. 'On my bill.'

'Noo, Noo its not, oime payin. They deserve it we got the roof on in one day which is better than I ever thought'

'Then I'll get the next lot, and no arguing.'

'We're havin dinner too. You gonna join us boyee?'

'We were going on somewhere else but I'll see what mother wants.'

A table for 10 was laid up in the restaurant section of the pub and a meal enjoyed by all. Jim found himself sitting opposite Kym and not for the first time noticed her smile. Not just her smile but her face, her eyes, her hair and her ears as she laughed and threw her head back. She was wearing jeans and a check shirt with a pleat in the back and short suede cowgirl boots. Nothing special but he realised he liked the whole package. 'Shit! Got to stop thinking like this, I'm married.''

'Was this the then Jim? You day dreaming?' Jim took a breath about to reply

'That's right' Peter interrupted 'See that terrible bruise there?' Pointing to a small red spot on his right forehead,. 'You cockneys can't talk the Queen's English. He's up the top and shouts "Look out!", so I did and got hit by a bloody great piece of wood. He should'a shouted Look in! It would've missed me then.' The laughter and conversation flowed, Pauline took the children back to the playroom leaving Jim and Kym to chat.

'You enjoying the job?'

'That's wot I wanna know'

'Yea, go on Jim is it any good?'

"It is actually. It doesn't pay very well but the people are nice. I get to see the boys and I get weekends off."

'Wot the customers like then? All snobbish I suppose.'

"Well I don't see them really but we have our regulars and quite a bit of passing trade from the boats. It's an upper class restaurant with French cuisine and last week there was a family in from Birmingham. The waiter was serving the lady her food and she said in a very strong Birmingham black country accent. "What's these?'

The waiter looked puzzled and shrugs his shoulders saying 'It is what you ordered Madam'

'Now! theese int wot I ordid. Oye ordid cootlet dan yow, petty poir un French froies! Yo'em brung moye chops, chips n peas. I could'a ad that at ome.. Sow take diss awoi and bring me wot I ordid.'

The crowd laughed and wanted to know more but just as Jim was about to recant another tale Pauline returned with three very tired children. As the party started to break up with everyone thanking everyone else for a good days work, Jim suggested to Simon that if they were at a loose end tomorrow they were welcome to join him at Waxham Sands. "There's miles of golden sand and usually a seal or two. There's also a shop, loos and a barbecue place but see what the weathers like. If you fancy it we'll be there. Turn right at the thatched cottage."

Chapter 9 Waxham Sands

Sunday 27th May

James picked the boys up as agreed. They were excited as ever and Betty seemed pleased to pass the responsibility of them to Jim. 'You bringing them back tonight or what?'

"Yes if that's ok. If I can arrange for them to stay over at mine during the week is that ok too?" 'What in that ruin down the Loke? You're mad aren't you?'

"It'll be like camping for them. Up to you, just let me know then." Boys ushered out, door slammed. "Come on kids lets go to the beach. An ice cream for the first one to spot a sea."

'Will we really see seals?

"Yes we should do if we are lucky and if there are not too many people in the sea."

Waxham Sands caravan park lies a quarter of mile from the main road toward the sea and is bordered by a large ever stretching sand dune that forms the tidal defences of the Norfolk coast. On one side the Northsea and the other the Norfolk Broads. Stretching from Gorleston in the south to Hunstanton in the North interspersed by the occasional coastal cliff, a bank of sand and shingle was all there was to stop the sea from crashing in. It has been breached a few times in the past 100 years but the people and the land recovered so the various governments of the day were never going to spend much money on proper defences. There is not a lot of economic value in protecting windmills and wildlife even it is a unique part of Britain and Europe. In a way it is the uniqueness of this environment that attracted Jim and many like him, to leave the hard city life for a tranquillity and beauty that cannot be held in the hand or owned by anyone. The early morning skies give the marshes a colour all of their own while the clear clean evenings allow sunsets that artists flock to paint. Each county of Britain has individual qualities and prides itself on them but Jim couldn't think of a better place to be as he drove down the long track between the fields and short cut grassed area leading to the campsite.

'Daddy where is the sea?' "Over the hill there, help me with the things and I'll show you."

A wind break, 2 buckets and three spades as well as a bag of food and drink was a lot to carry. They made it over the sand dune and turned right walking along the sandy beach. 100 yards and they were virtually on their own. He hadn't mentioned to Thomas and Matthew that they may be joined by Mickey and .... 'Hey look, wow!' Tom and Matt had spotted their friends and rushed along the beach to greet them.

'Christ, when you said get to the thatched cottage and turn right I didn't realise you meant a cottage on the beach. What happens when the tide comes in?' Simon held out his hand dropping his bags into the soft sand. "Good to see you Simon and thanks for yesterday,"

'Pleasure mate.' As Jim bent down to pick up one of the bags two hands touched his shoulders and a kiss was placed on his cheek. It was that perfume again, he could smell it, a freshness yet alluring fragrance,. It was........ who cares, he thought. Its female and very pleasant. Another kiss, this time from Pauline. 'Are we building sand castles again today or what?' 'What a lovely spot, glad you brought the wind break.' 'We have a picnic. What about you? I'm sure there is enough to share.''

'Pauline give it a rest.' Simon's interjection was right on cue as the children came charging up. 'Make us a boat', 'make us a castle', 'make us a car'. It was as if all the children wanted something different except Matthew. He was quieter than usual, not his normal happy self.

"What do you fancy Matt?"

'Make a house with mummy and daddy in it and a big garden by the seaside.' Like a knife through butter his simple request sliced right through Jim's heart. That's why he's quiet. He is being torn between me and Betty.

Oh God, I wish there was something I could do. May be, I could..... 'Jim you ok?' Kym's voice showed real concern.

'Come on kids lets collect sea shells to decorate whatever it is the dads are going to make for you.' Pauline's motherly instincts had kicked in and relieved a tense and awkward moment and like a mother hen, swept her brood along in front of her their minds focussed on the prettiest, largest, smallest or knobbliest sea shells.

"Am I ok? No, No not really. I think we are all feeling the strain of the break up, The kids may be more than me." 'It's no real consolation, I know, but kids are very resilient. I went through similar last year and I sort of know how you are feeling.'

"It's slightly different for you. Your husband was a fireman and fell from a ladder in the call of duty". 'Ha ha; I wish he had,' her ironic laughter caught Jim by surprise. 'He died painting someone's house. He was moonlighting as a painter and decorator. All the fire crews do it. He had been doing that job for about four weeks when he fell. I'm sure she was his bit on the side. There was definitely more going on than just decorating. Anyway, that's history, we are talking about you. If you want to talk sometime over a coffee or something I'd be happy to listen. In a way I'm still going through it so maybe we could share out thoughts'. "Thanks Kym, I'm sorry about your husband, I didn't realise." 'Not many people do particularly the kids and that's how I want to keep it. Their memories are precious and it doesn't matter if they are not 100% accurate as long as they are happy memories.'

"I like that. And that's what I want for my lot."

He turned to see Simon digging and piling sand. "Simon, how about we make Bowler? We could even do it life size and fit all the kids in." 'Not sure we can match the colour.' Two hours later and the children were adding the finishing touches. Helped of course by a few additional children and what seemed like a stray dog. Lunch came and went with everything being served with a few grains of sand but no one went hungry. By three o'clock the warmth of the sun had started to wane and the party began packing up. Bribed by the promise of an ice cream the children helped carry the beach towels, buckets and spades back over the sand dune past the beautiful thatched cottage which positioned anywhere else would be worth a fortune. As Pauline and Jim packed their respective cars, Simon and the gang as they were now called, played football. Kym helped Jim load the windbreak into the front of Bowler. As they bent forward she spoke quietly. 'I meant what I said you know. If you do want to talk I'm a good listener.' "Kym that's really sweet of you but I can't burden you with my problems. You have enough of your own." She smiled at his embarrassed awkwardness. 'I know' she said 'but may be I'd like to share mine!' She turned her head slightly towards him as he turned his. They were inches apart. As she took a little inward breath her lips opened slightly, he closed his eyes. Whack! They were each startled to receive a slap on the back. 'Come on you two, I need you I'm losing.' Kym laughed again with that familiar touch of irony as Jim wondered if he had read the signal right or was he mistaking her friendliness for something more than it was. "Women! Why are they so bloody complicated? Anyway I don't need a relationship. I've already got one, not a good one, but I've got one."

Heading towards Great Yarmouth, about a mile from Waxham the two cars turned off into the car park of a beautiful windmill that served as a tearoom; its bare and red bricked walls adorned with paintings by local artists. James Allen, Elizabeth Hyam and Jim Lawrence stood alongside others, each with their own style of brushwork and use of colour. A few bits of sea fishing memorabilia added to the ambiance serving as an ideal backdrop to the display of homemade cakes and pastries. Tea and cakes were ordered with orange juice for the gang. '

'Lovely spot that today Jim, shame we didn't see a seal.'

"Yes it's a great place to go. I'm off this week and thinking of taking the boys camping there for a night or two. I was thinking of having them at the house but it's a bit unfair on Peter."

' Well if you are going let us know we might join you, if that's ok?'

'Pauline, he might want to be on his own.'

"No, that would be great. The more the merrier as far as I'm concerned. It's good for the boys to have someone to play with and it takes the pressure off me. I'll see what the weather is doing and let you know." Pauline took charge as usual and went to pay.

'The owner just showed me his Newby.' 'I beg your Pardon?' They all looked stunned. 'Richard Newby the painter. I've always wanted one, but could never afford it.'

'How much is it then?' 'Oh Simon you are a love but we couldn't afford it. Besides his one is sold. He's exhibiting at Holt though. How far is that Jim?'

"About 35 minutes from here but you'd do better to have a day there. It's a lovely place full of arts and crafts shops and antiques. There's a couple of lovely tea rooms as well."

'Come on, time to go.' Jim and Kym chuckled as Simon tried to change the subject.

'Oh Simon we could have our own Newby in our new house. Wouldn't that be .....'

'Now look what you have done.' Smirked Kym, 'You know she won't shut up now. Well not until he gives in.' Jim smiled at Kym's pretend annoyance. "Don't blame me he laughed, I only said Holt was a nice place to visit."

'You're back earlier than I thought'. The scowl on the face and tone of voice hadn't changed. "Sorry Betty, the boys are knackered. They both fell asleep in the car. I had to wake them up to bring them in."

'Oh so you bring them back here for me to feed and put to bed after you've wound 'em up.'

"They don't need feeding. Just a glass of milk or something and I'll put them to bed if you wish?" 'No you won't, not in this house.' Jim took a deep breath "Betty I think we need to talk. This attitude is not doing the boys any favours."

'Not today. Tuesday! And not here.' Her voice was softer and as she spoke her gaze went quickly left and right as if checking she was not being overheard.

'Assembly rooms tea shop 10 o'clock ok?' It wasn't a question or request it was an instruction. One Jim was pleased to agree to as he really felt they should try to resolve things amicably.

"Ok, Tuesday morning. The Assembly Rooms."

'Yes!' The customary slam of the door. "Why the Assembly Rooms that's normally the reserve of the over 50s. Oh well, at least its progress."

"Peter!" , there was no reply. "Peter are you in?" There was still no reply. Jim felt the kettle and noticed it was warm. He used the water to wash and shave. He changed into some clean clothes and set off for Peter's other home. The Wherry. Peter was sitting at the bar with a pint and a basket of chips. 'Hello boyee, you want one?' The basket was pushed towards him and Peter's weather beaten hand raised a half empty glass. "No I'm fine. I just called in to let you know I'm popping in to work to see if they know what days they want me to work. I'm thinking of taking the boys up to Waxham camping. They loved it up there today. I shouldn't be too long."

'Ok boyee, I'll see you at hoom.'

Jim squeezed Bowler into a space between a Rolls Royce silver shadow and a pale yellow Mercedes Benz. He walked through the back entrance to the kitchen past the bins and the old iron stove where they burnt the excess cardboard.

"Hi Andy, sorry to trouble you on a Saturday night but I thought I'd catch you before things really got going."

'They already have, that wedding's running late, and we have a 21st birthday in the Wetland suite who have all come in early. What with that and a full restaurant we are well up against it.' Jim hadn't seen Andy stressed before but the pressure was certainly showing now. Dave and Leo the casual chef, were busy with restaurant orders while Andy was in and out of the walk in fridge with trays of sandwiches, quiche, canapés, sausage rolls, chicken and plaice goujons. Jim didn't ask to be involved he just followed Andy into the fridge and collected the trays of food and started to decant them onto silver ovals ready for service. Slices of lemon and sprigs of parsley were added before they were placed on the trolley for the waiters.

'Black Forest Jim, it's on the bottom shelf and the pineapple'.

"Yes Chef" replied Jim as he picked up the two gateau's. 'Hot plonge! A silver flat taken straight from the grill whizzed past him narrowly missing the gateau's and sizzled through the grease laden water as it disappeared into the sink.

"Whose on wash up?"

'One of the students, he's over the other side clearing the function'. 'Hot plonge!' More sizzle but this time the oval flat dish bounced into and then out, of the nearly full sink. Jim grabbed a cloth, retrieved it from under the hot cupboard where it had skidded to a halt returned it to the sink and started to wash up. The restaurant orders gathered pace to shouts of 'table 4 away' 'Table six, two sole, one duck, 2 prawn cocktails, 1 melon.' 'Jim get them will you? in the fridge.'

"Yes Chef, No chef,! not here!

'Bottom shelf,'

"No chef.!"

'Hold the sole hold the duck. Those bloody students, I told em to make the starters and they've buggered off.'

"I'll make 'em chef. Give me a few minutes."

Jim hadn't made prawn cocktail before or cut an ogen melon but he'd seen it done and it didn't look hard.

'I'll stick the garnish on, you just do the bloody things and make it quick, it's for the governor.'

Jim pictured them, lettuce finely chopped, hand full of prawns, a dollop of sea food sauce; a pinch of paprika, lemon and 5 slices of brown bread buttered and no crusts.

'Looks good, 3 prawns on top.'

"Yes Chef."

'Tails facing same way you twit, Mr. Paul's table away.' Andy was still talking twice as fast as normal the urgency was still there in his voice but the desperation had diminished.

'Good, like the melon. Do them all like that in future.' Jim turned to Dave "What did I do with the melon?"

'You thwaited it.' Dave responded to the puzzled look on Jim's face. 'Kwinkle cut it in half. We only normally do that with lemons.'. The frantic pace continued as the two students returned to assist with the washing up. It was nearing ten thirty and there was a lull. 'Dave, Jim, have a break alright Leo?' 'Yes chef. But they need a knife to cut the cake chef.' 'Jim run this over the function will you.?' Andy passed him what looked more like a ceremonial sword than a knife.

As he walked from the kitchen towards the function suite he saw the familiar faces of Mr. Stone and his mother. 'ello Son, thought you said you weren't working tonight.?'

"Hi, I only came in to find out what shifts I'm on next week but they were busy so I stayed and gave them a hand. I have to go, they need this in the function room."

'All white son, catch you later.' Returning from the function room he met with Dave.

'Mr. Paul's looking for you'

"Me, why?"

"I don't know. He didn't say. Mind you he don't much he tends to keep things to himself, plays his cards close to his chest that one.' It was only the second time Jim had been in Mr. Paul's office, once at his interview and now.

'Don't bother taking a seat we are busy and I've got to be front of house. Just wanted to say a few things so we know where we stand. You are a kitchen porter. Don't talk to my customers. It may be good for you to be seen with them but it might not be good for them to be seen with you. Ok?' Not giving Jim a chance to reply he continued 'Don't ever park that toy car on my forecourt again if you have to drive it park it round the back out of sight, not between the carriages of the high and mighty. Alright? And lastly,' there was a pause, Mr Paul's demeanour changed. 'Thanks! We were up against it tonight. Andy says it would have been a disaster if you hadn't pitched in. I appreciate that so have a drink on me.' Mr. Paul shook Jim's hand pressing a ten pound note into it as he did so. "Thanks Mr. Paul you didn't need to."

'I know that but I appreciate people that support me and my business. Just don't tell anyone else or they'll all expect it and don't spend it here.' Jim turned to leave feeling as if he had received a rollicking on one hand but praise on the other. A strange combination.

'Oh! While I think about it. Andy says you live at the Loke and you've got a field there doing nothing.' Wondering where this was going Jim hesitantly said yes. 'Well we've taken off so well here they want me to open up the lawns behind the new rooms. I need somewhere to store some building materials and a caravan until September. I'll pay you twenty five quid a week but I need to shift 'em early next week.

"Errrm,, Well,,," Jim wasn't sounding enthusiastic. "I think so but I need to check with Peter. It's actually his place but I think it will be ok, can I let you know tomorrow?"

'It will be cash mind. I don't need no receipts or anything'

Dave was still on his break sitting by the potato sacks in the cool night air as Jim joined him. 'What did you get then sack or pwomotion?'

"Neither really, he rollicked me for talking to the customers and then asked me to store some building materials on our field." 'You got a field?' "Yes but it's not mine, its Peter's and he was hoping to put a horse or two on it."

'Hawses? Well don't start me on hawses.'

"Don't you like them?"

'It's my speech impediment, No quite the opposite' I love 'em. We used to go widing quite a bit living in Epping Fawest. There was a Fwench woman down our wode who had a pony to sell. I explained it was a pwesent fwam me to the wife as we both love hawses. I'd seen it gallop and it stood beautiful too, so I said would it be ok to manage at twot? She thought I was speaking Fwench and had said ménage atois. Well she told everyone and after that we had to move.'

"Ha ha, was it too embarrassing?"

'No we kept being pestered, notes fwoo the daw, invites to parties and all sawts. So don't talk to me about bloody hawses. Mind you, it was pwitty though. But maybe a bit too big for the bedwoom!'

The afternoon of bank holiday Monday had been spent with the boys at Ranworth Village Fair. A rambling collection of old fashioned games. Roll a penny, skittles, catch the rat and more. There was the obligatory raffle and a brick-a-brack gift stall all run by locals to raise money for the Ranworth Church. With the scene set on the green overlooking the broad it was a beautiful picture of old England where the pace of life was unhurried and people had time for each other. Jim was glad of the opportunity to slow down as the morning had been a frantic rush to get the ground ready to receive the building materials and caravan. It hadn't helped that Betty wanted the boys picked up in the middle of it. Peter was very good about it and even set them small tasks so they felt involved and useful. In the tea tent between homemade chocolate cornflake cakes and orange juice Jim posed the

140

question of camping. It was received with great excitement. They spent the next hour talking of nothing else. What to do, what to bring, what to wear, could they do the cooking? Would mum be sharing their tent? Ouch? That one hurt. Jim danced around it with a "We can ask but she may be doing other things" Back to the car and during the short journey to Hornham the discussion was still on camping. ' What colour tent will it be dad?'

"Blue if it's still ok. It's in the garage at home. We can check it when we get back." The tent was indeed there. A small hole where the mice or moths had had a chew at it but it looked intact. A little camping stove and grill, a kettle and his dads old army billy cans completed the equipment list.

'You thinking of staying in that? You're bloody mad!' Betty was her usual supportive self.

"It'll be fine when I've re-proofed it. I'll take it now and then I can peg it out to air it. So it's agreed then you have the boys tomorrow and Wednesday. I'll have them Thursday till Sunday evening." 'Yea, if you like, whatever.' Betty seemed even less enthused than normal.

"I'll sort out food, beds and all that, can you sort out a bag for each of them with their clothes. We are going to Waxham Sands so best pack some swimming things." 'You ain't going in the sea?' A question and statement all in one. "No but we may paddle and if they have them it will be easier." He sighed and wondered why everything had to be a discussion point. Couldn't Betty just accept what he said and say ok. It never used to be like this. "Right, I'll see you tomorrow." 'Hmph!' Not a yes or a no just a 'hmph!' As if to say yes but I don't want to.

Tottering across the deal boards spanning the muddy dyke he could smell something wonderful coming from within the building he lovingly called home.

"Gosh Peter that smells lovely."

'Ass duck al a'range isn't it boyee. What you said about the posh menu got me thinking. So I used the 2 old

141

oranges and a tangerine we had. Mixed in a few stock cubes and veg and it'll be ready in about 20 minutes.'

"Where'd you get the duck?"

'It's Canada goose actually. There ain't enough on a duck to feed two.'

"What? Was it wild?"

'Wild? It were bloody furious, but only for a minute or two.'

"Oh! Peter I don't think I can."

'Listen boyee, thars as free range as you'll ever git. One minute he's as happy as larry, next he's bagged and gorne. No pain, no fear, no cruelty. Better and more hoomain than you'll ever git from a supermarket and besides, there's too many of them anyway.' He had a point and 20 minutes later when it was served up with fresh new potatoes Jim couldn't resist it.

"I must be honest Peter it does taste good and with the new potatoes, are they yours?

'Best you don't ask boyee . Mine will be ready in a week or two meanwhile these won't be missed'. Jim spent the evening sewing up the holes in the tent.

'Save the cotton reels you'll need 'em.' Jim couldn't think why but did as instructed. It was nearly dark when he finished pegging it out in the field. It looked ok in the dark but he was unsure how it would be in the morning.

Having risen early but still not before Peter, Jim checked the tent. It had stayed up at least that was something? There had been a little rain overnight and as he unzipped and stepped through the end his left foot met with a puddle. Not a great one, but it was still a puddle. Looking into the blue of the canvas he could clearly see pin holes he had failed to notice the night before. Pin pricks of white light shone out like stars in a moonless night. Maybe 2 cans of proofer rather than one he mused. He discussed it with Peter over a cup of tea and some porridge. 'Use the tarpaulin as a fly sheet. Its same colour and it will give you a covered entrance if you do it properly.' "I'll have to raise it though or it will rub and the rain will just pour in." 'What do you think them cotton reels are for boyee? Come on I'll gi you a hand.' The tent stood 6 foot tall at the centre ridge, 6ft wide and 8ft long. 11ft if you included the bell end. With the tarpaulin it was 15ft x 8ft. 'We'll leave it pegged out so you can proof it later when its aired a bit. Plenty big enough for you three I say.' It was and sufficient space to cook in the awning section if necessary. He shaved, put on a clean white shirt and a pair of trousers that actually had a crease. A few dabs of aftershave and he was off to meet Betty.

He approached the Assembly rooms via the rear entrance which led off the car park rather than from the front. Along what must have been a servants entrance at one time. He turned into the Georgian hallway that still displayed an opulence of another era. White plaster columns leading from the oak stained and polished floor to a ceiling some 15 feet above decorated with ornate plasterwork. A grand piano stood in the corner open and with sheet music in the rack from yesterday evening. A reception room lay off the hall used now as a tea room and restaurant. It had once served as a drawing room for the rich and famous. He spied Betty seated at a square table laid with a neatly pressed and starched linen table cloth. She saw him but as she did so her eyes darted around the room as if searching for a hidden object.

"You alone?"

"Yes of course, aren't you? What's with all the cloak and dagger stuff?"

'He's after you you know.'

"Who?"

'My Bill! He knows it was you who stuck his suit up. He reckons he's gonna punch your lights out. He's never bin so embarrassed.'

"Well could you just remind him it was my suit not his. It was my wife he was entertaining at my works do and if threatening to punch my lights out is the best he can do then he is not much of a man."

'He is, he's more of a man than you'll ever be.' Immediately defensive and snapping like a terrier.

"I seem to remember you said that once before." The approach of the waitress allowed them to change the subject. "Lets get down to why we're here shall we. I've noticed the boys are becoming upset and have started to comment about us not being together."

'Well we ain't are we, and as far as I'm concerned, can I smoke in here?' Betty always smoked when either nervous or stressed. Jim reckoned this time she was both.

"No I don't think you can it's an upper class tea room not a cafe. I was surprised you chose it." 'I chose it so he wouldn't see us. I told you he's gonna punch your lights out and mine too if he knows I'm talking to you.' "You're exaggerating Betty, but go on." 'Well as I was saying we are over. I'm not struggling to make ends meet anymore, I've got someone with money that wants to show me what life is about. It it wasn't for the kids we'd be off to Australia or New Zealand, he could still box over there.' Jim didn't quite understand the reference but made a mental note to check with Peter. "Ok, so we are over." As he said it he realised he meant it. There was no way he wanted to spend the rest of his life with such a mercenary and miserably grumpy woman. The sudden realisation of how he really felt deep down inside made him pause. 'An I'm glad you realise it. I'm putting the ouse on the market and I'll take all of it instead of maintenance.'

"Hang on, that house is mine as well as yours."

'Yea, but I'm taking the kids aren't I. You check with your solicitor. I checked with mine and I know my rights. Swas known as a clean break. You ain't got a pension and don't earn much so it's mine and the kids. You'll only have to pay basic maintenance till their 16 or go to university. I think you got a good deal.'

"Well funnily enough I don't." He was just about to tell Betty what he thought when the waitress brought the tea. That brief interruption was enough to allow him to collect his thoughts and focus on what he wanted to achieve rather than what he wanted to do. "Ok, I'll see my solicitor and I trust you won't contest the divorce. Let's get it done as quick as we can for the sake of the boys. I take it you'll agree to open access?"

'Course I will, I don't want to stop 'em seeing you and besides I needs my space!' The tea was fine but the conversation had left a bitter taste in the mouth as far as Jim was concerned. He paid up and even left a tip but still felt that he had been short changed as ever by Betty. Today's meeting had though, confirmed one thing, he and Betty were two different entities tied morally only by the fact that they had two beautiful boys and financially by the fact they had a house they jointly owned. He determined himself that he would get a divorce as soon as possible. So next stop, the solicitors.

He was lucky calling without an appointment Mrs Lamb had agreed to see him but he would have to wait 40 minutes. He decided it would be worth it.

She was very helpful and understanding although her view was that Betty's take on the likely outcome of a divorce settlement was correct. In normal circumstances the court would decide in her favour as guardian of the children. She would get the home in which to bring them up and Jim would be expected to pay to support that. At least until they left full time education.

The fact that he had no money was not the fault of the children it was his but any settlement would take his current earnings into account. It wasn't what Jim wanted to hear. "That means basically, I'm stuffed!"

'I wouldn't put it in those terms but , Yes! There are of course things we could plead and the fact you are countering the irrevocable breakup of the marriage with her infidelity goes in your favour. We could also if they agreed, go for a clean break. That generally means she gets the house and a large portion of any assets you may own. including any company pension.' Leaning forward feeling slightly trapped Jim looked her in the eye and almost pleaded as he said "Assets? I don't have any assets. I don't have a company pension or anything else."

'Well you might without realising it. You may have a case for unfair dismissal. I understand what they did but I'm more interested in why they dismissed you. I take it you still have not received an explanation?'

"No, not a word. All I know is what the agency said. And what Mr Paul at the Larkswood told me."

'OK, if it's alright with you we will explore that. I will put together some pleadings and will need to see you in a fortnight. There are some forms for you to fill out regards applying for legal aid but we can do that then.'

Jim felt better, relieved and even somewhat confident that all was not lost. He had someone who would fight his corner. Shaking hands as a gesture of thanks he left with a spring in his step.

Parp! Parp! As he turned into the Loke Jim could see Peter struggling with a deal board sounded the horn and waved as if to say don't struggle, I'm, here to help. Plop! The board squelched in to the muddy dyke sending a shower of black marsh mud skywards in little blobs some of which hit him as he clambered from bowler to assist. "Can I help?"

'I was thinking boyee, if they are delivering them building materials we need to get across hair without sinken. A couple of deal boards and two pallets should do us.'

Jim and Peter placed the second board in position followed by the pallets which Peter promptly jumped up and down on to prove they would hold. "They'll hold your weight Peter. What about a caravan?" Two more palettes and four more deal boards completed the bridge from the Loke to Peter's field. 'You could drive a tank across there now'. Peter and Jim were happy with their efforts. They were not sure how many building materials were turning up or even what they consisted of but they had worked out an area that was flat and dry and felt sure

they would be sufficiently out of the way so as not to
arouse the interests of any busybody who may be looking.
Jim checked the tent and started to apply the proofing
spray he'd bought that morning. It needed 24 hours to
cure properly and a second coating may need to be applied
read the instructions on the tin. It was decided that as it
was further into the field where the ground rose providing
a good dry area they would leave it up to help it air. Just
for good measure Jim also sprayed the seams of the
tarpaulin. It looked good, he was confident it would be ok
for him and the boys.

Eight o'clock, and Jim and Peter had been up for over
an hour anxiously waiting for the delivery which would
provide them with a little extra money that they so badly
needed if they were to finish the roofing and make the
cottage fit to live in over the winter. They were supping
tea as the sound of a lorry drifted in through the broken
single pane window.

"That's more of a mobile home than a caravan."

The low loader stopped and the driver got out
approaching them. 'Where is it going then. It is yours
isn't it.?'

'Yes, It's arrs boyee but I reckons we needs a crane.'

'I can get it on the field for you but I'll have to back it
up. Let's try that first'

An hour later after much swearing and some very
skilful driving the caravan was winched off the trailer onto
the field. Luckily the building materials had also turned
up and a dozen paving slabs were used to stop the legs of
the caravan sinking into the soft earth. The caravan was
actually a mobile home fully fitted out with kitchen, diner,
lounge, a double bedroom, a twin with bunk beds and
fitted seating in the lounge that obviously fitted together in
some fashion to form two more beds. There was also a
chemical toilet and shower unit. Proper little home from
home this. Peter was opening cupboards and inspecting it
all as if he had never seen a caravan before.

'When you said caravan I magined a small thing you tow behind a car. Oi didn't realise you meant a ready finished ouse.'

He was like a child with a new toy. 'Bugger me, s'even got gas on. An there's heating if we connect the lectric.' Peter was still musing over how good it was as he and Jim returned to help the lads who were delivering the building materials. There were bricks, blocks, tiles, timber and paving slabs, several tarpaulins, a cement mixer, scaffold poles and clips, together with about 50 deal boards that were also included. It was all tucked away behind the cottage where it could be seen from the river but not the road. The various piles of items covered from the elements with a few green tarpaulins, blended into the surrounds of what was after all now, a building site.

'You actually going camping then?'

"Yes Peter, I'm working tonight and going to go tomorrow Friday and Saturday. We'll probably be back on Sunday afternoon. Do you want to come with us?" Peter's face broke out into a smile as the sun catching his silver stubble emphasised the weathered lines around his eyes.

'Bless you boyee, I used to love camping but I also love my peace and quiet. I promised your dad I'd go over and see him so I'll probably do that.'

"We can pass there on our way to Waxham, do you want a lift?"

'Maybe boyee, we'll see, Oim off s'afternoon to see Richard Green about some sand and it depends when thas coming 'nd if I can do a deal.'

Jim arrived at the Larkswood early and immediately got to work on peeling the evenings veg. Andy had left a list of jobs which he expected done by 5.00 p.m. As far as Jim could see there was plenty of time. Service wasn't until 7.00 p.m. and wondered why the 5.00 p.m. deadline, but did as requested. Andy walked in at 5 dressed in his whites and threw a large full length apron at Jim. 'Here you go mate. Toni's off tonight so Leo's covering him and you are on sweets and starters. You'd better wash your hands and get prepped.'

"How about the washing up?" 'Paddy will cover that.' Patrick Flynn was one of the local students, a tall thin lad with fair almost gingeriest hair who everyone even his own family, called Paddy.

Wednesday evenings were generally quite but this was Whitsun week and the reputation of the Larkswood was growing. Orders soon started to pick up and Jim found himself working hard to keep up. It seemed that no sooner were the starters out than the sweets were needed, Shouts of "Yes Chef!" "No Chef!" "Oui chef!" Were followed by retorts of 'keep up!' 'Where is table 6 desserts?' 'Come on, those starters need to be away.' For 2 solid hours it was constant pressure eventually relieved with Andy asking, 'drinks?' Occasionally customers would ask to buy the chef a drink. Andy always had a pint of beer on hand and would open the swing doors to the restaurant, raise a glass towards the table that had sent the gratuity and nod visibly in their direction. He'd sometimes do it even though no one had offered a drink, this generally served as a timely reminder that it was acceptable to buy the chef a drink for all those wishing to flash their cash. A ploy which worked especially well with the local footballers and rich boat owners whose competitive streak extends way beyond business or sport.

'New waitress then, what do you reckon?' Leo was nodding in the direction of Donna. A nice young lady well spoken with a cultured accent. Her auburn shoulder length hair had a sheen that caught the light as she moved. At five foot four with a soft complexion and athletic body. Jim thought she looked to be in her late twenties. Or early thirties.

'Is she up for it do you think?' Mused Andy to the assembled kitchen team. 'The footballers will love her but she'll have to have a sense of humour. Only one way to find out, yours a larger or a bitter?' "Bitter please Andy, thanks. How do you mean one way to find out?"

'We will give her a scream test!'

"A screen test like in the movies?" Jim was curious. 'No! A scream test. I'll show you. If she screams she is young and innocent if she laughs, well, I'll give her a lift home.' With that Andy disappeared into the large walk in fridge pausing only to reach into the pot of flour and smear a large amount of flour on his nose. Standing in the fridge he selected a raw sausage from the tray prepared for breakfast, and placed this in the button flies of his chef's uniform. Dropping his long apron over this he walked towards the servery. Donna totally unaware of the interest the men were showing in her, smiled at Andy, saying 'Chef!" pointing to her own nose, 'You've got flour on your nose.' 'Thanks' said Andy lifting with two hands the large white apron to wipe it. Donna let out an embarrassed scream when she saw what she thought was the chef exposing himself. This quickly turned to laughter as he held the apron with his left hand and removed the sausage with his right. She blushed from head to foot but saw the funny side. All agreed she would fit in well. Andy decided not to driver her home.

As he drove the little car along the Loke Jim couldn't help but notice there were lights shining in the field. Not bright but soft orange and blue lights. About 4 in all that seemed to form a semi-circle. The cars head lamp caught some shapes and as he turned towards the cottage. Jim looked again his brain trying rapidly to work out what it was. Its tents, he thought, but who would put tents on Peter's field? Parking the little red car he went inside to find Peter sitting there cuddling a cup of something hot. 'Heloo boyee, are you booking in or just passing through? Welcome to the Hornham Camp site. Thar'll be two pounds per night per tent. Want a coco?'

"Brilliant Peter, who are they?"

'I thought they was with you. Turns out they saw the caravan, saw your tent and the other green tarpaulins and thought we was a camp site. Well, I didn't like to disappoint 'em, specially as they're paying; soo hair they are and here we be. Eight quid a night richer.' "That's great. Well done but what about services?". '

Oi didn't ask about their religion, any way I think they'll be gorn by Sunday.'

"No! I mean the toilets you fool, and running water."

'We got the stand pipe and the outside Privy. I have put a few of them slabs by that drain ditch thars needing filling so they can empty their chemical loos there. Taint perfect but it will do for a day or two till we can work out something better.' Viewing a look of concern on Jims face 'Blast me boyee we need the money. They need to camp so don't worry, It all works out. You camping in the morning still?

"Yes we are. How about you I feel guilty about leaving you to get on with things".

'Dunt Worry about me boyee. Oi'm takin it easy these next few days. Oi'm jus gunna clean out that old water tank wos gota goo inta the loft for the water, 'n maybe goo down the pub for a few bairs. After all I can't goo too far now as oi'm proprietor of a holiday camp'.

Thursday Morning 31ˢᵗ May

Jim was up early leaving Peter to sort out the campers. As he rounded the corner from the cottage towards the field he was surprised to see two people in what appeared to be camouflage jackets and trousers. Each of them had binoculars and a camera or two around their necks. 'Did you hear it?' Such an excited voice, Jim knew he had obviously missed something important. "Sorry hear what?" 'The bittern of course. The bittern!' Even more excited. "No I missed it." 'Don't worry Vivienne has it on tape you must listen.' The voice was getting faster and higher pitched with each sentence. 'This is so good. What a place to stay and the owls last night. Calling and replying, my gosh what a find.'

"Great!" Jim was not impressed and the sigh that followed his reply showed it. However the two twitchers were not deterred. Hearing sounds emanating from the other tents they raced off to share their experiences with their friends.

The car was loaded with tent, changes of clothes, cooking equipment an old lilo and a box of food. Some of which was donated by the Larkswood. A few stakes they wouldn't sell to their high quality customers but were fine if minced and formed into burgers. A task Andy had happily shared with Jim who it seemed he had taken to his heart and was happy to coach and mentor. Picking the boys up he proceeded to his parents home where he went in search of things they needed for the camping trip. Elizabeth made it into a treasure hunt for the boys while Jim's dad raided his cellar for homemade booze and a plastic container for water. Jim's mum also raided her pantry for extras, cakes, biscuits, flour, eggs, raspberry jam, brandy butter, cranberry sauce. "Brandy butter! What do we want with Brandy Butter?" 'You take it son, it's beautiful as a fat in the pan for cooking pancakes and besides, anything you don't use bring back.' Laden full to the brim with the food, 3 more lilos from the loft and enough homemade booze to launch the QE2, they set off. 'Dad are the others coming to join us?' "Yes I hope so Matt. I have invited them but I'm not sure if they can." He looked in the register as he signed in. "They are not listed as being here yet, so hopefully they will check in and find us." 'Can we go look for them?' 'Yes please Dad!'

"No! I need you to help me get the tent up first. Once we have done that, we can go anywhere we like." Jim and the boys continued to try and erect the tent followed by the fly sheet or blue tarpaulin as it was better known. "Pass me the peg by your foot, Hold this rope but don't pull till I say" Orders were given as much to keep the boys busy as to actually assist with erecting the tent. The finished article was not the most attractive tent on the site but it was theirs. It was large enough to sleep the three of them in comfort and had a porch where they could cook under cover. A couple of brightly coloured striped wind breaks marked their plot forming a barrier between them and a group of teenagers to their right. The plot to the left was vacant awaiting the possible arrival of the others. The manager of the site had promised to leave it vacant for 24 hours. It wasn't a problem as the site was only half full and there were plenty of spaces. "Right kids, let's go and see the seals." 'What about the others?' "Well done Tom, good thinking. We will leave them a message on the tent so they can find us." It was a warm Whitsun week with a full sun but a cooling westerly breeze and once over the dunes in the shelter of the tall grasses it was quite pleasant. The three of them settled down into a warm hollow and tucked into a picnic of sandwiches, cake and orange juice prepared by Grandma especially for them. She had even gone to the trouble of ensuring each had their own favourite flavour of crisps. Halfway through them they were interrupted first by a large Labrador dog named Barney and then by their friends.

'Got your selves a dog?'

"No I think He just smelt the crisps; do you want some?"

'We're fine we have our own. We saw your note. We are in the 2 plots next to you.'

Simon and Pauline settled down in the dunes while Kym took the children across the soft sandy beach to the water's edge.

'You didn't mind us coming did you?' Enquired Pauline with a genuine look of concern on her face.

"No I'm delighted you did. The kids love it and although they have their friends in Hornham it takes their mind totally away from the place if you lot are here."

'You must tell Kym that as she was worried that we may be intervening on a family holiday and inviting ourselves when perhaps we shouldn't be.'

"Oh it couldn't be further from the truth. I'll have a word with her." He got to get up but was prevented by Pauline tugging his shirt 'Not now you fool or she'll know I told you. Speak to her later' Jim did as Pauline had suggested and said nothing saving it until later on.

An exhausting day on the beach with sand castles, cricket and looking for seals preceded a sausage and chip feast bought from the site chip shop. Well it was a mobile chippy really with a sparse but adequate menu of chicken, fish or sausage all served with a generous portion of chips. but as far as the children were concerned it was the best fish and chips in the world.

'Can we all sleep together Dad?'

"No we can't but if you are good and promise to go straight to bed afterwards I'll read you a story"

'What all of us:?' 'Yes please all of us.' The five children settled down to listen to a Rupert story first one then as an encore another. By the time Jim had read half way through the second five little heads were nodding. Ten minutes later all were asleep in their beds the grownups having crept them out to their respective tents as the children fell fast asleep.

'Anyone want a tea?' whispered Kym as she pulled up a chair next to Pauline.

'Yes please, I'll give you a hand, Leave these two men to chat and look after the sleeping beauties.'

It was nine o clock and the sun had gone down a little while earlier It was a clear night and the brightest of the night stars could be seen glowing in the dimming sky. Simon was lying back in his canvas and metal chair admiring the view as Jim passed him a drink.

'Not your Dad's Lemonade again?'

"Yes so go easy. I remember how you were last time."

'What are you two up to?' The girls had returned with the tea.

154

'We are just admiring the stars'

'Yeah and drinking rocket fuel again I suppose? Jim Daily you are a bad influence on my Simon.' The wagging finger and words were overtaken by a warm and knowing smile from Pauline.

'Which stars are which then?' Kym asked as she too reclined in a small camping arm chair. "You can't see them too well from here because of the lights of the camp but if you go on the beach or lay in the dunes and look up you will see loads more. Look you can see the Plough from here" as he pointed skywards, "and the North star but if you want to see Casio pea or the Milky way you need to take a stroll away from the lights"

'Yes come on then let's do that.' Simon and Kym rose enthusiastically. 'We can't all go someone needs to babysit. Simon you and I will go later. Jim and Kym will go first.'

Pauline had said it in a Don't argue with me manner that they all knew so well. They both checked their children to make sure they were sound asleep and armed with a small torch set off over the dunes towards the beach.

"You are not afraid of creepy crawlies are you?"

'No why?'

"Well, lying down in the dunes is the best place to view from. It's warmer too and you are less likely to be taken for a seal by some well meaning soul walking their dog"

'Dunes it is then, lead the way.'

Settling down into a small hollow of sand and grass Jim began to point out the various constellations. The sky was black now except for a myriad of twinkling lights and half a moon at first Kym was making appreciative mummers as if understanding it all but as these lessened Jim looked across to see that she was no longer looking at the stars but was propped up on one elbow staring at him..

*Sorry, I'm boring you?"

'No you are not, it's quite the opposite. I could listen to you all day' with that she leaned over and kissed him, not

155

passionately but loosely and softly on the lips withdrawing just enough to see if there was a response. There was, as she rose away from him he responded by taking her in his arms returning the kiss with a passion running one hand gently through her hair the other snaked down her back. Their embrace was natural, a part of a courting dance which was choreographed through a mutual love and desire. Neither felt awkward or unsure they just kissed and embraced under the stars as if it were the most natural thing in the world. Jim could feel her body next to his. One leg between hers. Her legs wrapped around him as if keeping a prize locked in, never to escape. They rolled over as she fumbled with his shirt buttons releasing his chest to the open air so she could caress it, kiss it, bite it. They laughed as she sat astride him rubbing his chest pulling at the few hairs he did have. He was tall enough to be able to reach up inside her blouse and feel the small of her back. She leant back allowing better access as his hands tried to unclip her bra...

'You bin a long time. You all right?'

'Simon, shut up and put the kettle on. There's a lot of stars up there it takes a while to name them all.'

As they laughed at her remark Jim looked down and realised they were still holding hands. He broke away and looked first at Kym and then their hands as if to say let's keep it between us for now. Her smile spoke volumes. The eye contact said even more.

He lay in bed that night thinking how lucky he was, how good she was, how did it happen? She is gorgeous but I don't deserve her. Am I just a one night stand to her? Where will it go from here? what do we say in the morning? Do I just act natural or what? The next thing he knew it was light and Mathew needed the toilet but when you are camping for the first time it is exciting and any excuse to leave the tent and explore has to be taken. Thomas woke up and wanted to join them. Commencing a quick walk across to the toilet block through short grass dampened by the early morning dew was interrupted by a cry from Chris asking if he could come too.. It was light but the sun was hardly up. A quick glance at his watch told Jim that it was not yet six o clock. He vainly tried to quicten the boys. It was a waste of time. They were awake, it was light, they were camping and this was an adventure. Getting them to hold in their enthusiasm and excitement was like trying to hold back the tide. Thomas was jumping up and down, Mathew copying and Chris grinning from ear to ear.

There was nothing for it, If they were not to wake up the entire camp he would have to do something with them. "Come on you lot, get yourselves dressed quickly and we will go for a walk on the beach"

Joined by Emma and Mickey, Jim like the Pied Piper of Hamlet led his troop over the dunes to the beach. As they rose over the mix of sand and maron grass they were able to see the whole beauty of the Norfolk coastline. A beautiful soft golden sand stretching for miles either side of them giving way to a glass like sae gently lapping the shore with the rising sun in the back ground giving a silvery red glow to the azure blue sky. Gulls were dipping into the water skimming the crest of the small waves yet hardly breaking the surface. It was then that they saw it. At first they thought it was a dog; like a very wet chocolate Labrador or red setter it's head breaking the surface just long enough to afford it a good look around. Then it was gone. Leaving not even a ripple to show where it had been.

They raced towards the shore to cries of 'Did you see that ?' 'What was it?' 'It was a dog!' 'It was a seal!' 'It was a sea monster.!' 'It wasn't! What was it Dad?'

"A seal, Look there he is again. But be quiet or he will swim away"

No sooner up than he was gone. A few moments later rising again in a different spot.

'He's quick Dad. How fast can they go?'

"I'm not sure but... Hang on there's two, No Three."

He was right it looked as though there was a mother and two pups.

Just momentarily three heads were visible two smaller than the other that appeared to be holding back a little way behind as if checking the little ones were doing as they were told. The gang of five and Jim walked slowly along the beach keeping a look out for signs of life in the water. As they became less frequent they decided to return. The walk back seeming longer than the one there. They stopped every hundred yards or so to skim stones over the smooth rippling water and check each other's pretty stones or shells that if deemed suitable by all, were being taken back to camp as gifts for the grownups.

The camp had come to life by the time they returned, the enticing smell of sizzling bacon and sausages was in the air, people were going to and fro with pails of water, old ladies were carrying towels and make up bags into the toilets Men were filling up kettles and Simon was buttering bread.

Jim reached out to grab a slice and nearly lost his fingers to a swift blow of the buttering knife. ' Don't you dare. They're for the sandwiches. It's cornflakes or porridge first.'

'Dad we saw the Seals, We saw the seals. They were great!'

Breakfast was spent with the children talking between mouthfuls of porridge or sausage sandwich about nothing but their early morning walk.

Kym had been so busy cooking and serving the breakfast and Jim likewise getting plates and mugs of drink, that they hadn't had a moment to speak. He broke the silence. "Sleep well?"

'Beautifully thank you,' again it was that eye to eye contact, that soft smile and slight turn of the head to one side that although unspoken her reply meant so much more 'and did you?' The question between them was obvious Jim spoke volumes as he replied with just two words and a broad smile "Yes, Likewise"

Well that's it he thought, No regrets and a thank you. He was on a high. He didn't actually think, I'm on a high. But on reflection he knew he was. Simon too had noticed it. 'You love this don't you? Being out in the wilds, under canvas and with the children? You're beaming all over.'

"Yes I do Simon, You're right. I just wish I had enough money to do this more often. I get such a buzz from seeing the kids enjoy it too." He knew it was Kym that played a major part of his current euphoric mood but he thought it best not to say.

The day seemed to be a blur. He wasn't sure where the time went. It took until ten to get the breakfast things put away and the children washed, changed and ready for the beach. A game of rounder's, one of French cricket and a search for seals took up the rest of the morning; back to camp for a late lunch of sandwiches, crisps, cake, biscuits and milk followed by a return to the beach for a sand castle competition.

The evening meal was a classic Norfolk Fayre of Turkey Burgers served in a bun accompanied with pan fried oven chips and baked beans. All purchased from the site shop. The small jam tarts were provided by Jims Mum and the custard by Pauline. Maybe not the most nutritious meal but everyone was full and no one complained. Well, not about the meal but there were some groans about the obligatory homemade wine.

'Jim, can you and your lot wash up and Kym you and yours dry? Me and Simon will clear up here.' Pauline ever the organiser had it all worked out. The wash up area was a section on the outside of the toilet block covered by a small tiled roof. It was basic but it had 2 large stainless steel sinks inset into a long laminated worktop. There was hot and cold running water and a sign saying "NO BATHING" Jim wondered how anyone could actually "Bathe" in a two foot square sink but he mused to himself, I suppose anything is possible if you are desperate.

He began to fill the sink with hot water and a good squirt of fairy liquid. As the water rose the bubbles grew.

'Whoops! Too much washing up liquid. I thought you'd have been an expert.'

"I am but this stuffs twice as powerful as I'm used to; Have some!" scooping a large handful of soapy bubbles into Kym's face as he said it. The children loved it. Encouraged by their laughter Kym too scooped up a hand full of bubbles and lunged at Jim. He though, was too quick for her and too tall. Grabbing her wrist as it sprung forward he turned it around towards her. Again she ended up wearing the soapy suds. As he did so he pulled her towards him ending in a laughing embrace. The children laughed finding the moment of adult slapstick amusing being somewhat out of character for either parent.

The laughing of Jim and Kym was different. It was fun, but it was also an intimate moment. An invasion of each other's personal space they both welcomed and enjoyed. He helped her wipe the soap from her eyes and placed a gentle kiss on her closed eyelid as he did so.

On returning to the tents the children were full of the tale of soap fights and how Daddy covered Kym in soap but made it alright because he kissed her better.

"I don't think that's quite right Matthew. I just helped her clear the soap out of her eyes."

'Don't worry Jim your secrets safe with us isn't it Simon. Come on Kids time we got you ready for bed.' A knowing wink and a broad smile flashed across Pauline's face as Simon looked on, puzzled and little knowing what was or had occurred.

'Here you are 'ave a drink of Coco I've made a pan full. It'll help knock the kids out so they sleep like logs again. I think it must be the sea air. They really are enjoying it.'

The two men sat quietly outside the tent sipping sweet cocoa in the evening air listening as the ladies got the children out of their dirty clothes and into pyjamas ready for bed. A quick wipe with a warm damp face flannel was all that was required. A proper wash or shower in the morning would be needed and help to awaken the little ones while breakfast was prepared.

'They want a story!'

'Yes! We want a story, We want a story' the chant went up. And they all joined in. Even some teenagers from the next pitch joined in.

Jim rose from his seat "Come on Simon we are on."

'Me? I can't read stories to save my life.'

"Ok You can do the animal noises then. We'll tell them the one about the Zoo."

'Zoo? What one about the Zoo?'

"I don't know, we'll make it up. As I say an animal you make the noise."

All the children were huddled into Jim's tent on the blow up beds wrapped snugly in their sleeping bags with just their heads poking out as the two story tellers entered.

"Right you lot! We are going to tell you a story of the Norfolk Zoo.

Once upon a time there was a little girl who loved animals and wanted to travel the world to see all of them but she was too ill.." 'Ahh,'

'Oh is it a sad story? I don't want a sad story. Can't we have the one about Art, Bart, Smart and Fred?'

"No it's not sad; just you listen and tell me when we finish."

"This girl was saying her prayers when a fairy suddenly appeared."

'Ooh! Shut that Door' Simon was right on cue with his Larry Grayson impression.

"I'm your friendly fairy and can grant you a wish. What would you like?"

'I'd like all the animals in the world to visit me as I am too ill to visit them. She said"

"OK said the fairy" 'Ooh! Shut that door.' "waving her magic wand, I'll see what I can do. How about a Tiger?" 'Roar!!' went Simon. Not quite so much on cue this time but still good enough to impress the children. "and with that a big striped tiger with a long swishing tail appeared

161

Oh No! said the little girl he will eat my sandwiches Can you put him outside?

Ok said the fairy" 'Ooh Shut that Door!' "what about a monkey?" 'Hee, Hee Hee Hee,' Not content with the noises Simon was now doing the actions as well and in a tent with two adults and five children all balancing on blow up beds there was not a lot of room for error.

The story proceed to be told with Elephants, Seals, Cows, Horses and many more strange animals all being asked to wait outside in case they ate her sandwiches.

"...and then there was the Lama"

'Woo Woo, Woo Woo. Please leave by the nearest exit.'

"What's that?? It's supposed to be an animal."

'It was. It's the Fire A Lama' "I can't believe you said that" ' You wait till you get to the talking Donkey.

"The talking Donkey?" 'See Children? He called me a talking Donkey. Just because I have two big ears and a stutter he all, he all, he always calls me that.'

The children, Jim and Simon collapsed into laughter rolling and bouncing on the beds.

"Right that's it! Time for bed. We'll finish the story tomorrow."

As they left the tent a cry of 'We want a story! We want a Story! Could be heard echoing around the campsite.

Jim and Simon looked at each other then back at the tent from which they had emerged then back at each other. They couldn't understand it until as they rounded their other tents they realised that when living under canvas it is easy to forget how everyone else around you can hear every word spoken.

The request or rather demand, was coming from the teenagers tent next door and a caravan awning opposite.

"Sorry Guys," Jims loud voice boomed out to the unseen. " If you promise to be good we will read you another one tomorrow"

Hooray! Was the yell that went up accompanied by much clapping and from somewhere, a few sarcastic shouts of 'Thank you Daddy'

Kym and Pauline found it very amusing. While Jim and Simon were inwardly proud that their efforts were appreciated.

The children asked to sleep together and it was agreed they could for a while at least. The thought was that they would be moved to their own beds when the adults went to bed.

A pack of cards was produced from somewhere together with some cider and the remnants of the homemade wine. It was some three hours later while the late night snack of cheddar cheese and biscuits with pickle was being consumed that Simon asked if Jim could show him the stars from the dunes as he had Kym the night before. Jim nearly choked on a digestive biscuit as Kym burst into embarrassed laughter. Pauline as usual saved the day by quickly saying she'd like to go too if that was OK by Kym? 'I'm worried you might end up seeing Uranus earlier than you'd expected'

The innuendos passed quickly over Simon's head and the three of them set off across the dunes.

Returning some twenty minutes later alone Jim explained that Pauline and Simon were so taken by the view they were staying a little longer to take it all in.

'Thanks for that' she smiled,

"What? I haven't done anything"

'Yes 'she said softly still smiling 'you have you silly sod. And you know you have.'

With an innocent look and shrug of the shoulders he protested his innocence.

'Oh come here' she reached up and grabbed him in her arms pulling his face down to hers.

He gave no resistance and turned his head slightly to allow their lips to meet.

They kissed, as they had the night before. Their tongues entwining, his hands caressing her body as hers did similar around his back and shoulders. They fell, almost gracefully, into her empty tent, and continued to explore each other's bodies as they lay on the air beds kissing like young teenagers on a first date.

It was some time before they heard the over loud return of Pauline and Simon.

"We are just getting the beds ready for the kids" a red faced Jim said over his shoulder as he came out bottom first adjusting his attire as he did so.

'I'll put the kettle on. Do you want one Pauline my love?' Simon appeared happier and more attentive than usual. The night air obviously agreed with him.

'What do you think of the stars then Simon?'

'Unbelievable! I can't believe how different they look from here. Pauline was amazed too. We won't forget this night for a long while will we Pauline?'

'No! We are going to come back here again. It's something else. It sort of has a magical effect on you.'

It was Saturday. "change over day" and a lot of people were already leaving the site where Jim and the boys were rising from another well-deserved night's sleep under canvas. The boys had settled into it well thought Jim. They had not once complained and had looked at it as an adventure. The fact that they were sharing their time with Chris, Mickey and Emma had definitely helped. Jim unzipped the blue canvas and poked his head out to greet the morning. "Kettles on, want one"? Pauline as usual had beaten him to it. "Yes please we are just going to have a wash first and then I'd love one." 'You'll be lucky, place is full of people going home, queue is a mile long, specially the ladies.' "Right, that's settled then, we won't use the ladies. Come on boys, race you!" The challenge was immediately taken up by Mathew and Simon. All three raced to the toilet block and joined the throng of men and boys trying to shower, wash and wee as it had affectionately become known. They retired to their tents just in time to see the others clambering out of theirs.

Kym said nothing the warmth of the smile and the wide open eyes said it for her. Their relationship had moved on. No longer just friends, they had a shared bond, a deeper mutual understanding.

'Sounds good to me Jim'
   'What are you two cooking up?'
   'Nothing Pauline just saying it might be nice to go along the coast for a drive. There's a lovely steam museum and a war memorabilia centre to look at.'
   'I take it you're joking? Me, Emma and Kym ain't interested in any war memorabilia. What happened to Holt?' "Tell you what Pauline," Jim interjected in an effort to prevent a full blown row breaking out, which Simon would no doubt loose. "How about a mystery tour this morning and Holt in the afternoon." 'Well where's the mystery tour going to be?' 'If we told you that my love it wouldn't be a mystery.' 'Thank you Simon I was just saying.... ..', Kym stepped in with 'Go on, we're up for it. What say you Emma?' 'If it's all boys stuff, steam engines and things I'd rather stay on the beach and look for more seals.' Simon laughed. 'Promise it's not and if you don't like it you can throw me in the sea!' An hour later all fed washed and watered with the tents closed against a threatening shower they set off. Kym and Emma sharing Bowler with Jim while Simon and Pauline had the four boys squeezed in the back. Along the winding coast road to Norton Quay we will stop for a cup of coffee at the pub.

A few groans were uttered in each car. It wasn't really time for a stop they'd only been going just over half an hour but the dads were driving and they both turned in. It was a lovely little pub that also served as a tea rooms. Quaint and old fashioned but clean and friendly. 'Oh! look Jim they do boat trips to see the seals. That would be nice to do at some time.' 'Thank you Mr Daily you're on the twelve o'clock sailing. Bit of a squeeze but its changeover day so we got you all in.'

Kym did a double take looking first at Jim, then the landlord then back at Jim. 'You bugger!', she said, through a wide beaming smile her eyes closing as if to hide a tear of joy. 'You two had this organised all along. Are we really going to see the seals?'

"I can't tell you. It's a surprise. Do you want to tell Pauline or shall I?"

'Let's leave that to Simon, see how long he can last.'

"Right, steam museum it is then. Follow me."

The two cars set off again through the little villages of cobblestone and thatch with a huge great church in each, past inviting pubs, tea rooms and wondrous windmills everyone wanted to stop at some other time. A turning to the right along a single track lane led to Morston Quay. A dirt and shingle spit head where inshore fishermen tied their boats and lonely windswept seagulls strutted their stuff as if dancing to music unheard by the human ear. The boats were mostly small wooden things open to all the elements about 16 to 20 foot long without even a cabin. All of pretty reds, whites, blues and yellows; some with inboard engines some with outboards. Some looking as though they were held together with years of paint on paint. Used mainly for crabbing or working the mussel beds of the Wash these were real fishermen's' crafts. A meagre living could be made but there was no way it would reap rich rewards. The men who fished in this way did it because they loved it. There were also a few larger vessels tied at the ends of rickety wooden piers. Similar in colour and style but larger, sturdier and less weather beaten. Equipped to take tourists the mile or so along the estuary out to the spit head where the seal colony nested, had their pups and basked in the sunshine of Norfolk.

'Oh Jim this is lovely. I forgive you.'

"Thanks Pauline but its Simon's idea. I don't know what's come over him in the last twenty four hours. It's either the camping or the sand dunes, I'm not sure which."

Pauline gave a look and a smile but said nothing.

166

It was two o'clock by the time they returned to their cars. It had been a great success there were more seals than they could ever have hoped for. They stopped counting at 200 and walking across the spit head allowed them to get up so close to them that it was better than being at the zoo. Having avoided the shower earlier it managed to catch them as they drove from Morston to Holt. Following instincts rather than agreed direction Jim turned into the Gresham School field where an antique and art sale was taking place. Without getting out of the cars but talking through lowered windows to avoid the rain they agreed a run to the large marquee was favourite. The afternoon was spent dodging the raindrops between the various tents. A game of "We've got one of those." was organised with the children recognising an item, they had to find out the price to work out how rich they would be if it were sold.

'Never did get to Holt. Have to do that another time, lovely day though despite the rain. Those seals were just amazing.' It was late evening, Pauline was sitting down relaxing with a hot chocolate while Jim and Simon were finishing off their good night story. Kym flopped into the chair next to her. 'Yes, been a lovely few days really, shame it's got to end.' Simon seems to have enjoyed it.'

'Oh don't you start. What with Jim and his comments.'

'Listen Sis, there's nothing wrong with looking at the stars. Norfolk's a magical place, you enjoy it while you can.'

'I could say the same for you.'

"Sorry girls, not interrupting anything are we? Simons just making sure the tents are secure. The seal team are all out for the count. We didn't even get half way through the story." 'I'm the same. I think me and Simon will have an early night tonight'. "We will have a quick walk on the beach and probably do the same eh kym?"

'Yes, I suppose so.'

Returning quietly from the beach hand in hand Jim placed his index finger on Kym's lips to signify quietness.

167

He looked into his tent shared by the five sleeping children. He listened outside Simon and Pauline's tent, they too were sound asleep. He poured two glasses of cider and quietly slipped into Kym's tent as she followed him. "It's not even ten o'clock it would be a shame to waste the evening. I thought we could discuss the merits of Basildon over Norfolk".

'Oh shut up you.' They fell backward onto the lilos, their bodies entwining as they kissed, each trying to fondle and pet as they lovingly removed the others clothing.

"Oh bollocks! What time is it?" It was dark. Jim realised he'd fallen asleep No, they'd fallen asleep. His mind was doing cartwheels. Fumbling for his watch and a light he realised he was naked. Covered only by an open sleeping bag. Next to him was Kym in the same state.

"Hey! wake up." 'No' a sultry half awake response. 'Oh okay then. Yes, go on'.

"No you twit." Half Shouting in a whispered tone. "We've overslept".

'Oh shit! Did you do the tent up?'

"No, did you? I left it open so we could hear the kids."

'Well I haven't heard them, have you?'

"No, I'll check." They unzipped the tent. With a sleeping bag and a towel wrapped around to hide their modesty. All the children were fast asleep. As was Simon. Simon? It struck them that he had gone to bed with Pauline and yet here he was sleeping with the children.

'What should we do? Its past twelve o'clock, shall we move them or let them sleep?'

'Let them sleep Kym.' It was Pauline's voice. Her head poked through the lower zip aperture of their tent. 'You two go back to bed, the kids are quite safe and Simon won't complain, trust me.' They looked at each other, and then at Pauline,

'Thanks Pauline. We owe you.' 'Shsh! You don't want to wake them, good night.' They returned to the lilos and slept like two spoons in a cutlery box, safely wrapped up in a loving embrace. Simon and his tent full of mischief woke last. Breakfast was well on its way, all the other adults were dressed and in the process of packing things away. Breaking camp always held a sadness for Jim but today was different. He felt whole again, filled with hope for a new chapter in his life. All those around him had enjoyed this break and had memories as he had that would last forever.

Chapter 10 Birds of a Feather

Having dropped the boys off with Betty, Jim made for home. It was 4.30 in the afternoon and he thought maybe he could give Peter a hand with getting the water tank installed in the loft space. Hornham was only a small village and usually very quiet, particularly on a Sunday afternoon. Today was different. There seemed a lot more people around, strangers, many of them with cameras and binoculars, dressed in dark green or brown, the classic look of a twitcher. May be the bird reserve were having an open day. The nearer he got to home the more there seemed to be. All looking towards the marshes. The field by the side of Peter's house was a sea of canvas and bird watchers. There was hardly a blade of grass to be seen. Cars were abandoned en route as if the world had suddenly stopped and the drivers just got out and left them. Jim was unable to even find a space and in frustration drove to the pub hoping to park there. He found a space just as someone left and he drove in. He didn't want to park there, next to a ford Capri that was owned by his wife's lover but there were no options. Getting out he thought it only fair that he call at the pub and inform Barry and Ann that he was leaving the car there. Rounding the corner under the canopy of hanging baskets he met the landlady collecting glasses. As he explained about the car he was interrupted by her saying 'No problem we are stacked out any way. But I suppose you would know that. If you and Pete want to come in for dinner later when it quietens down it's on me.' A call went out from behind the bar for more glasses and she was gone. Obviously something had happened while he was away for a few days, but what? "Peter!" They met at the entrance ditch leading to the field.

'Christ boyee, you choose the right time to goo away.'

"Obviously I did but what is going on? I left you with four campers on the field and now it's full. There must be fifty tents there."

'Forty two, can't get no more in so oim chargin entry fee for those on foot. Oil let you off though as you lives hair.'

"What are they all here for?"

'Seems like those twitchers we had saw a Bittern; first one for 30 years. They told Mike the RSPB chap, the press got hold of it and hair we are. The world and his woife has descended on us. Most of them leave today or tomarra but some are staying for a while.'

"Well the Wherry is doing a roaring trade. Ann said if we go down later the meal is on the house."

'An a foo bairs as well I ope. Scuse me there's a punter.' Peter dived to the gate like a fielder on the cricket pitch reaching for a wide ball, ready to take a ticket or fifty pence off the visitor who seemed more than happy to pay for the opportunity of seeing a Bittern.

'Well we had been watching the marsh harrier really and then there it was, large as life.... We thought it was a heron at first then we heard it!' The tubby little chap was being interviewed by Anglia Television from a point in Peter's field where the river and marsh could clearly be seen as a back drop. This was big news and all the press were there.

'The Bittern is a shy bird and is not happy around people that's why we have not heard it for a day or two. Too many people will scare it off.' The experts were lined up each doing their piece to camera. The respected Turkish author and ornithologist Janis Sarros suggested that the media circus was destroying the very thing they were all there to see. However as she was being paid for her view this seemed to Jim and many others, double standards.

It was nine o'clock before Jim and Peter got into the pub. A special table had been reserved for them. The usual seats made of old barrels had been replaced with the more comfortable arm chairs. Two plastic reserved signs were prominently displayed to signify that this table was reserved for dignitaries. They eventually took their seats after shoving their way through the throng of customers. There was only one topic of conversation on everyone's lips; The Bittern. The pub, the village, the whole of Norfolk seemed to be taking about it.

'Best thing that happened here for many a long while.' Ann herself served their meals and this Jim knew, was a rare treat. 'Thank you Peter we've done a year's trade in 4 days. Mr. Stones coming in with his mum later, they are going to moor up on the jetty so I'll leave the reserved sign till they arrive.'

Half way through the large "Sunday roast" Jim became aware of a commotion in front and to his left. Someone was pushing their way through the crowd of drinkers. It was Salter, Betty's loved one. It was obvious he had been drinking too much and for too long. His drunken bravado and deep seated hatred of Jim were the only things giving him momentum. He stood about four feet from Jim, a half filled pint glass in one hand and pool cue in the other.

'I'll punch your lights out I will, see if I don't.' A hush went out like a ripple from a stone dropped in a pool of water. The room quietened.

'See, I'll have you.' Pointing a finger menacingly Salter was accompanied by three other men who Jim recognised as regular drinkers and trouble makers.

'Hoi! I'll have none of that in my pub. Clear out NOW Salter. You are barred'. Taking no notice of the landlady's exclamation Salter slammed the heavy end of the pool cue down on the table narrowly missing Peter's shoulder and smashing a plate in the process. Salter looked behind for back up from his three friends but there was none. Two had left and the one remaining was for some reason on his knees clutching his groin. Peter remained seated leaning forward expectantly waiting for the snooker cue to strike from behind him again. Jim was opposite Peter but could only see the figure of Salter as it fell forward on to its knees as if felled by some invisible force. Salter's hands went out but with a glass in one and

172

a snooker cue in the other he fell as if crucified hitting his nose with a large thud on the edge of the heavy mahogany pub table which having broken his fall, rocked as the drunken fool collapsed underneath it. An arm reached out and grabbed Salter's shirt collar from behind hoisting him forwards and up, crashing his head into the underside of the table with such a force as to make all the crockery and glasses jump an inch or two into the air.

'Go home Son! You're pissed and that's my seat.' Leyton Stone had arrived at what appeared to be just the right moment.

'Sorry Mother,' pulling the chair out as if nothing had happened, 'mother hates violence.' The two friends who had disappeared crept from the back of the crowd, picked their friend up and carried him out to shouts of 'He's barred!' 'Don't come in here again.' Stay out, next time it will be the police'. An awkward murmuring built up with people trying to resume conversations as if nothing had happened but wanting to discuss the recent events

'What was that about then?'

"It's a long story Leyton but thanks for your help. I thought for one moment I was a gonner"

'Hey, I was at front of the queue.' They laughed and as Peter realised what he'd said he did too. Jim briefly explained the whole story about his marriage, Salter, losing his job, finding it difficult to get another, the dinner jacket episode and the little red car. Leyton and his mother found it amusing and also tragic. 'You should write a book son, you are settled now though, aren't you?' "Oh yes, I really enjoy the job at the Larkswood, the hours are just right. The people are nice and we have a good laugh,. It doesn't pay much but I enjoy it."

'Happiness is more important than money son.'. 'Thank you mother for your timely intervention'. 'Thass a pleasure Peter. It takes the wisdom of us old uns to educate these young uns. Now tell me what's all this about some bird? The Larkswood is packed **we** even had trouble getting a meal tonight.'

173

'apparently some birdwatchers were staying hair at our place when they saw a Bittern. They wus common int Norfolk before the war but's extremely rare now.'

'Have you seen it?'

"No, I was off camping at Waxham Sands so I missed it"

'And I was cleaning out the water tank for our loft, thars a job and half. Took me nearly all day what with acid descale and flushing it through and banging it out, so oi dint see nuffin neither.'

"Ow'd they know it's a bittern then? Couldn't it be a crow with a broken wing or something? "

'Oi dunt know boyee but there's Mr. Twitch he'll tell us.' The tubby and ebullient young birdwatcher had been recounting his tale all night and did not take too much persuading to continue.

'Well yes of course. I saw it first. I thought it was just a grey heron at first, they are very similar in flight you know, but then it landed and I heard the distinctive call. Like a bitoom! We waited a while and there it was again. Bitoom! It's their mating call you know they puff their chests out and it's like banging on a drum. We heard it again later in the day. So exciting; Since all the fuss started and the crowds arrived we have not heard it. They are very shy you know. Scuse me must go there is Helen McDermott. I'm on TV with her and BC tomorrow.' Jim looked across at Peter and as the look was reciprocated with a wry smile they both realised the reason the bittern had not been heard of again was because Peter had been too busy collecting money to bang the remaining scale from the large galvanised water tank.

'Dun;t blame me boy, I didn't know till you did, but it does explain why I never saw it'. Jim just shook his head and laughed. After all he thought, they had made a lot of money and no one had been hurt.

'Don't you dare come round here after what you did to him.' Betty was her usual cheerful self. "Well Betty I don't know what your drunken boyfriend has told you or what he can even remember but I didn't lay a finger on him. He approached me, I think for a game of pool, but as he was drunk he fell over and proceeded to head butt the table."

'I know what happened, It was you and three mates got him in the car park.'

"Betty, is that really my style. For God's sake we have known each other long enough. Have you ever known me be violent?"

'Well I don't care, he's gonna punch your lights out. Just see if he doesn't. You ain't getting me back so don't fink you will.'

"I have news for you Betty. I don't want you back. You are the mother of our boys but other than that you have nothing I need"

'Well I'll stop you seeing them I will. I'll tell them what a cruel father you've been.'

"Ok, so who is taking them to school now then?"

'Well you are, that's wot your here for ain't it.?'

"Just checking for one moment I thought you and lover boy were doing it."

'No, he's so bad after what you done I'm going to have to look after him today. Here they are, they're all yours'. The boys were very quiet as they were bundled out the door.

"Thanks Betty, see you later". He was right they were quiet. He thought it was because he and Betty had been arguing again, so determined himself not to do it in front of them in future. Jim dropped them at school and playschool respectively. He went into work to be greeted by a mountain of plates to wash. The talk everywhere was of the bittern and how much trade it had brought to the village. The Larkswood was packed. The press having block booked all the available rooms. All available staff

175

were recruited to assist with packed lunches for the various press personalities and their retinue.

'Sorry about the plates Jim 'Andy gestured towards he mountain of badly stacked crockery wallowing in the cold greasy water of the double bowled sink. 'We have been rammed the last few days. It's great for business but we have had to get agency staff in. Especially waiting staff, to help out. If you can't understand 'em let Dave know, he seems to be able to cope. Mind you how they cope with him and his R's and W's I'll never know.'

Lunch time was quiet as the press pack were mostly out trying to get sight of the camera shy Bittern. 'Phone call Jim, Jim! Phone call for you'. Who would ring him at work? Maybe something was wrong.

"Hello, James Daily."

'Hi Jim, I won't keep you. Just wanted to hear your voice. I won't see you till the weekend and I didn't really get a chance to say thank you for a lovely camping trip so, thank you'. "Kym, It's great to hear from you. I was worried something was wrong".

'Not on my part. I thought everything was wonderful!'

"So did I, thank you. I can't stop we are going crazy here. Some bird watchers have seen a rare Bittern. They are all camped out in our field but let me have your number. I'll ring you during the week." 'You should already have it' but numbers were exchanged, pleasantries shared and she was gone. He wished he'd said more, told her how he felt, told her how he missed her and wanted to be with her. So much he could have said and yet so little was said. Right, I'll make up for it on Saturday he thought.

'Jim, any chance you can work through today?'

"I can't Andy I've got to pick the boys up but I'll work a few extra hours now and be back at 5.30 if that helps?" It did. It was a case of all hands to the pump. Even Mr. Paul was recruited into helping restock the bars while the kitchen brigade did the prep for the evening and next day's breakfast.

After collecting the boys and delivering them to Betty he returned via Peter's cottage, to work. Stopping only to get a quick change of clothes and make sure Peter was ok with the fact that he wouldn't be helping on the cottage. As it happened Peter was fine. Enjoying the limelight and taking the money. The small field was still full of tents, some having left as others took their place. 'Charging by the week now boyee.' Peter's smile lit his face up with those crow's feet wrinkles to his eyes showing clearly the pleasure he was getting from making a few extra pounds. Jim got into work just on time to help with the preparation for the evening meals.

'You are on Mise en place Jim if that's ok?'.

"Yes chef," Andy nodded his tall white hat accentuating the gesture, showing his approval at the correct response. He was a good chef and enjoyed a laugh but when the pressure was on he expected everyone to step up a gear and focus on the job. There was plenty of time to have a laugh at the end of service. He and Dave took their jobs seriously, wanting to do well for the customers and their own job satisfaction. Mise en place. From the French meaning, A place for everything and everything in its place. Jim knew the drill, lemons sliced, olives green and black drained and tossed in a little olive oil and garlic, melon boats cut, orange slices skewered with a cocktail stick and finished with a glace cherry ready to be popped on to the Melon at the last minute, parsley, some chopped, some picked and left in springs. Lettuce chiffonaded ready to fill glass coupes for the prawn cocktails; Basically prepare all the add-ons and garnishes which the chefs need in front of them to create the individual dishes.

'Jim can you cover starters and sweets.?'

"Yes chef, what about the wash up?". The thought flashed through Jims mind that he may have to do all three jobs which was almost impossible.

'Jon and Beano are in, they'll cover that.' The two students were hard working and always ready to join in with the banter. They seemed to have an answer for everything and usually it was an amusing one.

'Right you lot, listen up'. Andy called out to grab everyone's attention. 'It's going to be a slow start and then everyone will be in at once as soon as the sun goes down at about nine. We are full of wanabees and hasbeens and they'll all be showing off so expect the unexpected and don't worry. That's what I'm paid for. Ok?' The cry of "yes chef!" was universal, everyone knew it was going to be a long night. Carlos the head waiter had given the same talk to his team of waiters and waitresses odd bottles of strange vintage were warming in the restaurant rather than the cold cellar, bottles of champagne were being chilled in the base of the large ice machine.

Mr. Paul entered the kitchen from reception looked at the whole brigade and then at Andy before enquiring, 'Everything all right Andy? All prepared and ready? Good, give us a shout if you need me.' He left as quickly as he'd entered.

The few residents who were not part of the media circus and some people off the boats were served between six and eight. It was the lull before the storm. Then it hit, it was as if every table was occupied at once. Andy as always called the orders. He also served the vegetables into tureens and served up the roasts, sauces and soups. Dave was in his usual place managing steaks, fish and anything grilled as well as back up for Andy. Jim was tonight elevated from pot wash to starters and sweets.

'Table Four, 1 melon, 2 prawn, 2 turtle', Those were the starters that Jim was listening for,

"Yes Chef." Andy continued with the main course, '4 duck, 2 sole. Table 6, two whitebait, 1 pate.' The orders came in thick and fast. 'Table 4 away. Table 6 away.' After about an hour there was a lull. Andy roused the troops with a call of another 'lull before the storm hits again' speech.

'We will do double covers tonight.'

"What's double covers Dave?" 'That's where the westauwant seats only sixty but we welay the tables and we serve one hundwed and twenty'

'Table 19, Chef, there's a no veg'. Carlos was gesturing with his shoulders and arms as he stood by the hot place. He had been followed through the doors by Louigi and Italian casual waiter from the agency. Andy rounded on him straight away. 'No veg table 19. Did you take the peas?'

'No chef I respect you, I no takea da peas!'

'No,the green peas. Did you take the green peas?'

'Chef?' Louigi looked puzzled and became indignant.

'I not even in da union. Roberto from Portugal, He is in Union and he in Green Peace.' The kitchen erupted into laughter as Andy quickly prepared a tureen of petit pois, turned carrots and celery hearts. 'Table 19 veg away' Green Peace, I'don't know where do we get 'em?

Louigi looked first at one chef then another and shrugged his shoulders clearly not knowing what he had said or done.

The second wave hit a few moments later the earlier tables having been re-laid for a further sitting.

'Chef, put in hot water.' Carlos was gesturing this time towards Jim waving two red wine bottles. One empty, one full. 'Chef! Please, quick!'

'Jim, he's talking to you,' Jim looked one way then the other 'Yes you, you pwatt you're chef!'

Filled with a sense of pride Jim took the two bottles and rinsed them in Beano's wash up water while Carlos hurried back to the customers in the restaurant. Five minutes later he was back. 'Quick chef, quick, the bottles.' Carlos proceeded to remove the label of the full one and replace it with the label of the empty one. He saw Jim's puzzled look, shrugged his shoulders saying 'They'll never know, they already pissed. If they notice they must be expert.' Carlos was right. He was also right when he filled up the champagne bottles with dry cider. 'Twicks of the twade mate. The customa doesn't want to know if you've wun out. They just want to enjoy the night out.' Dave was right and most of the customers in the restaurant were press reporters. Media hangers-on and egos wanting to impress. It was nearly midnight when the last dessert was served. People were still drinking and it looked as though they would be for some time but Jim's duties were over for the night. He was pleased to leave it to Beano and his friend Jon to clean up. He said his thanks to them and goodnight as they continued washing dishes and mopping floors while whistling excerpts from Italian operas.

During the week the media furore died down. There had been no further sign of the now infamous bittern. The Larkswood and Peter's field were still fully booked but the queues of expectant visitors had gone.

'still gotta clear that tank out Jim, so that Bittern may return'

"No it won't, I'll take it over my Dads at the weekend and get it cleaned up there."

'All right boyee. I suppose you are right. It has set us up though so I can't complain'

Finishing work at lunchtime on Friday Jim loaded the water tank into the little red fiat before collecting the boys. They drove with the tank securely fastened to the front passenger seat by the seat belt and wedged in by the plastic shelf that formed the dash board. There was little conversation on the way to Jim's parents. It was as if they boys didn't want to talk about anything. There was some mention of the previous weekends camping trip but little else.

'Dad?' it was an enquiring Dad. A requesting Dad, a thoughtful and deliberate Dad most unlike Thomas. "Yes Tom."

'Why can't you come home and live with us?'

"I can't son. I wish I could but your mum and me have decided that although we love you and Matt and we both want to be with you, we don't love each other anymore and besides she has Bill Salter now and he looks after her."

'Why does he shout at her then?' There was hardly a pause as Thomas unloaded his feelings. 'We don't like him, he's nasty. He's a bully and you always said we shouldn't do what bullies say and we shouldn't be friends with them'. Jim found his owns words coming back to haunt him. He listened intently while Thomas told him how miserable they were at home when Bill Salter was there. "I tell you what I'll do. I can't promise anything but I'll have a word with Mummy and see if we can't work out something so you can stay with me more often."

'Daddy do you want lemonade?' Matthew interrupted at just the right moment skipping down the garden with his Grandma two or three paces behind carrying a tray of drinks and what looked like homemade carrot cake.

'It's all right Jimmy, it's real lemonade not your Dad's homemade. But if you'd rather...?'

"No mum, real lemonades fine. I'm working tonight and besides, I'm driving." Elizabeth set the tray down as Matthew and Thomas kicked and chased a football. 'Working? What's happening with the boys?

"They'll have to be at home with Betty."

'Oh dear, they won't like that. Matt's been telling me how they don't like that Salter bloke Betty's taken up with and that you got in a fight with him. That's not like you. Do you think that's a good example?'

"Mum, have you ever known me fight?"

'Well not since infants school, no.'

"Thank you, and I didn't fight this time either. Betty's bloke tried to have a go at me in the pub but he was too drunk and tripped up. I think he broke his nose on a table when he fell. I never touched him.'"

'Well they think you did; you're quite the hero.'

"Oh dear, I'll have to put them straight. Thomas has just been telling me too about how they are unhappy at home when Salter is there. I'm gonna have a word with Betty and see if I can't have them more often."

'Good idea. Here, have your lemonade while I go and get that washing I did for you last week.' "Morning Dad." John was dressed in customary old cardigan and loose fitting trousers that had seen better days. He loved his garden and was never happier than when he was pottering around in it. He was now as usual, dressed for the occasion. 'Got some produce for you son. Some cauli's, spring onions, taters and beets. I put them by the front gate. There's a couple of bottles of my mangle wurzel wine and one of apple. That should see you right for the weekend. Last year's cider is about ready too. I'll bottle some up during the week.'

"Dad you are very kind but you don't have to."

'I know Son but as I've said before it's my way of helping. I haven't got a lot but what I have I'm quite happy to share. And what's this I hear about you going three rounds with Cassius Clay.?' "I think he's Mohamed Ali now Dad and I didn't go three rounds with anyone. Betty's boyfriend fell over that's all. He was drunk and for some reason he thinks I hit him, but I didn't even touch him before or after he broke his nose." ' I don't mind if you did or didn't but Mothers not so keen. You know what these women are like. And what's this I hear about a bittern? I've never heard one or seen one. What's it like?'

"I don't know Dad but Peter tells me it tastes like chicken."

'Well he'd know if anybody would. Give him my best when you see him Jim.'

"I'm back there later and I'll tell him what you said. We are hoping to run in some cables. For the electrics now we have a roof on." 'It's coming on then that little cottage?'.

"Yea, but the bittern episode is slowing us down a bit, although there are mixed blessings as the money we are making from people camping has helped. I've never known the village so busy. That's why I'm working tonight. They are packed beyond capacity and need us all in."

'You're not seeing that mate of yours Simon and his sister then?'

"It's sister in law and I was hoping to see them yes, Why?"

'Nothing, just something your mother said.' The phrase "just something your mother said" conveyed a lot more than a short sentence. It meant they had been talking about Jim, Simon, Pauline and Kym. What had they made of her he wondered and should he be concerned or seek their approval of his friendships.

"They are a nice couple Dad and the children all get on together. God knows the boys need some friends to share a few laughs with at the moment."

'Yes, and that Kym's a nice girl too. What did her husband do?'

"He was a fireman Dad. He died falling off a ladder."

'It's hard to replace a hero son, you'll always be second best.'

"I don't intend to replace him we are just friends." The thought flashed through Jim's mind that he could tell his father the truth of Kym's husband's death but it would have served little use so dismissed it. 'You two chatting? You haven't even touched my cake. Mrs Buckhurst made it, she's a lovely cook, go on tuck in.' Both Father and son followed the instructions. Mrs Buckhurst was well known for her pies pastries and cakes. Elizabeth herself was a good cook but Mrs Buckhurst had the edge and Jim's mum was happy to admit it.

'What's that tank you bought me Jim,? Is it for the garden or what,?' enquired John through a mouth full of cake. Thankful the subject had changed Jim explained it needed descaling and cleaning so it could be used in the cottage. He'd pick it up in a few weeks if that was ok?

'Not a problem. I'll get next door to give me a hand. How's the car going by the way?'

"It's great Dad. The boys love it. We get some funny looks but it gets us from A to B."

'Dad can we camp in your field tonight? we love camping.'

'Yes come on Dad, please.' "Not tonight boys I've got to work this evening and it's full anyway. You'll see tomorrow when you come over. There are still lots of campers coming up to see the Bittern. There are so many I think they have frightened it away."

'If Chris and Emma are coming up can't we stay with them tonight?'

"No boys, I'm sorry but you can't. We will see them this afternoon and tomorrow but not tonight. I promise that I'll pick you up early tomorrow though and if you are good we will have a bar-b-cue feast at the cottage and you can be in charge."

'Can we go on a boat again?'

"I'm not sure Matt, I'll see what I can do. If I can get a day boat then I will."

Jim and the boys parked Bowler in the small car park outside the Norwich Railway station. An impressive and imposing building dating back to a bygone age when steam trains were the main means of transport and people travelled from far and wide to visit the East Anglian Coastal towns of Lowestoft, Great Yarmouth, Sheringham and Cromer. An era long gone but still warmly remembered as a romantic age where service and civility were as much a part of the railway culture as the steam trains themselves. They had all been replaced with quicker diesel engines and it was as if tradition had been sacrificed to speed.

'There they are Dad.' Thomas was jumping up and down, his blond hair rising and falling wildly in time with his excitement. 'I can't see, I can't see,' Jim lifted Matt on to his shoulders to give him a bird's eye view of Kym, Emma and Chris as they strode along the platform toward them. There was an awkward pause as both Jim and Kym were not quite sure how to greet each other. Hold hands,

184

yes, a kiss yes but on the lips, the cheek the hand? Both settled for the cheek each wanting more but not wishing to be too forward or show too much emotion in front of the children. 'Great to see you' she placed an arm in his as if they were a long established couple. It felt natural and right as they exchanged pleasantries on their way to the car. The children naturally chatting like friends. Mostly talking of the bittern. 'Did you see it on the television. Did you see Hornham and the cottage?' They were still talking about it as they piled into Bowler. The four children squashed into the back for the short journey to the old cattle market car park outside of the castle. They parked up and went up the incline towards the burger van. Not just any burger van. This was Zaks. Upmarket burgers and chips, real American style. A favourite treat for Matthew and Thomas but a new experience for Emma and Chris. After much deliberation meals were ordered with an agreement that if they didn't like it they could have Jim's chips. A quietness settled over their table as four hungry children ate the mini chips and burgers.

"I'm sorry I have to work tonight. It won't be for long. I should be away by about 9.30 and as the children will be in bed, how about you and me nip down the pub for a quiet drink?"

'Yes I'd like that. I'm sure Pauline and Simon won't mind.' The afternoon was spent walking around the market, the children pacified with a kinder egg, a cake and a drink of squash in the large apartment store opposite. An obligatory stop off at the toilets and the toy department made the stroll around the shops bearable for the four little live wires. Discussions around the hiring of a day boat also helped ease the pain of shopping. Jim however was trying to work out how he would fit it all in. He'd promised Peter he would help run the cables in for the lights and sockets so that Peter could get on and start laying the floorboards. Maybe up early, cable laying in the morning and boat in the afternoon. That's if he could borrow one or maybe do a deal. He realised he was beginning to think like Peter and realised how a lack of money focussed the mind. He was still thinking about it when he dropped Kym and her two off at Simon and Pauline's. He would have liked to have stopped but had to get back to Hornham, drop his boys off, drop the washing and food off with Peter, get changed and get to work by six o'clock. He also wanted to have a word with Betty but maybe that would have to wait. He didn't have to ring the bell, the door opened quickly and quietly. Betty ushered her boys inside and closed it in the same fashion. Not a word was spoken between the two parents and as Salter's Capri was parked outside Jim thought it best not to hang about and inflame the situation.

Work went well that evening. Jim had made it by six but only just. He was straight on mise en place chopping, slicing, peeling, preparing and setting out all the garnishes and additions that make the meal special.

'Can you do the hors doeuvres Jim please?'. The question was rhetorical. Jim had not prepared hors doeuvres before but had seen them done. Set out into white earthenware dishes and placed on a large silver trolley which was wheeled into the restaurant where the waiters would turn a handle on a wheel at the end giving a carousel of colour and mouth-watering flavour for the guests to choose from as it revolved slowly over from top to bottom.

By 7.00 p.m. service was on. The restaurant was buzzing with excitement. Some of the media circus had left but the hangers on and wanabees were still there. The shouts in the kitchen now familiar to Jim, were steady and appeared unabating. 'Table 6 away: main please, table 4 away, table 9 party of 8 check on!' 'Drink Jim?'

"No I'd better not Andy but thanks; I'm out with Kym after service."

'Half each then Washerups?

'Yes Please, can't refuse a drink can we.' Andy passed the pint size dimple mug of beer to the young students

186

beavering away in the sinks trying to keep up with the constant flow of dirty dishes. 'Top man, thanks Jim, thanks Andy, And Dave, thanks to the wegglars, Mr S and M,' Beano raised his glass to them all. 'Now they have done it wc will get maw, just wait and see'.

He was right of course and as Jim wasn't drinking his liquid tips were passed to Jon and Beano who each time saluted by raising a glass announcing S and M at the tops of their voices. It was obviously some in Joke that only they seemed aware of but no one worried as their light hearted banter broke the monotony of washing dishes; a dirty and thankless task.

"Nine fifteen chef, can I go, I'm all done and its quietened down?" Jim was clearing his work area, 'Yes I think so, I'll just check the trolley. Carlos, how's the hors d' oeuvres?' Carlos went into the restaurant and reappeared in moments with the hors douvre trolley. 'It needs tidying chef and some more Greek salad but its good'. Jim did as required, added some extra garnish and went to leave. 'Where are you going?

"Home chef, you said I could."

'No I mean tonight, you're going out with Kym aren't you, where you taking her?'

"I don't know. A pub I suppose."

'Try the Globe, best fish and chips you'll get this side of Yarmouth. See my mate Mike Farrow tell him I sent you and to put it on my bill.' "Thanks Andy that's really good." 'Not a problem and get going or you'll be late.' He descended the rear steps of the kitchen to the sound of 'thanks Jim' from Dave and a chorus of S & M from the student washup brigade.

The Globe car park was crowded. It had recently changed hands and Jim had not been in since the new owner had finished the refurbishment. Bowler was only small and they had parked half on and half off the pavement at the front. Reputed to be haunted it was opposite the old court house where prisoners were tried and sentenced. Tales of a passage leading to the hanging post where the pub now stood had never been proved but it always made for a good discussion and occasionally brought in extra trade. As they squeezed their way towards the bar Jim recognised a lady heading towards the ladies. 'Hello' she said, 'Do you know her?'. Kym was more puzzled than jealous. "Yes I do but I'm not sure where from, maybe it's the school run?" They got a drink but there was no chance they would get a table or be able to get a meal. 'I'm sorry I can't get you a table or anything but as you can see we are absolutely packed. If you can wait an hour or so I'll see what we can do. Excuse me.' The landlord turned and spoke to one of his waitresses who scurried off. 'Where were we, yes sorry about that. Andy's a good mate, do give him my best. Tell him we are not as posh as the Larkswood but we are busier. That'll wind him up.' He shook their hands and was off to organise the staff turning briefly to say over his shoulder 'get another drink if you want one, I'll see you later.' As Mike Farrow passed through the double glass panelled doors to the restaurant Jim again glimpsed the lady he had seen before. He saw too the person she was with and remembered where he had seen her before. She was the one who had exited Bill Salters Capri when he spun it in a cloud of smoke from Jim's little car. The person she was with had two black eyes and a plaster on the bridge of his nose. There was no mistaking the features of Bill Salter. 'We are not going to get very far here, shall we go to the Wherry?' It was music to his ears, he looked at Kym and smiled. "If you are happy with that," she returned the smile stood on tiptoe and kissed him gently on the cheek. The gesture was just the answer he needed.

The Wherry too was packed but Jims height meant that Ann saw him as soon as he entered the bar. A few nods and hand signals between them and drinks were organised by the time they reached the bar. 'You're late,' Ann shot them a broad smile as she passed the drinks. 'I hope

Bacardi and cokes are ok, the others are in the restaurant area, they're not eating but it was easier to reserve you a table there than in the bar. We're stacked out again. God bless the twitchers'. They snaked their way through the throng of people towards the small area of a dozen tables that formed the restaurant. They pulled up 2 extra chairs and sat with Mr Stone, his mother, Peter and Jess. 'You're late where you bin?'

"Oh! don't you start. We've just had that from Ann." 'We went to the Globe, it's too crowded, we didn't stop.' "We did see Bill Salter though." 'Really what did he say?' " Nothing, we didn't give him the opportunity. Discretion is the better part of valour." 'I thought Peter said Betty had the kids?' "Yes Jess, but he wasn't with Betty. It was some other lady. I recognised her but I'm not sure where from. Anyway, that's his problem. Cheers all," he raised his glass and the conversation changed. A few drinks later, a plate of sandwiches given by Ann together with a plastic basket full of hot fried potatoes and it was nearly time to go.

"Can we start early tomorrow Peter, I want to work through till lunch and see if I can get a day boat or something. The boys are plaguing me."

'You can have our boat. We'll take you on a cruise around to Rockland. We'll meet here and cruise over there.' 'There's a lovely fish and chip shop.' "Well there's quite a few of us Mrs Stone. It's very nice of you to offer but...." 'Don't be silly son, if mother says it's ok then it's ok. Besides the dog loves company, especially youngsters. Game on! Here tomorrow at two.' 'There's nine of us Leyton are you really sure?' 'Kym we had twenty two once. It was a bit wobbly when everyone was on the same side but it's a British boat built right here on the broads. I'll borrow some extra life jackets just in case though.'

Sunday 3rd June

The alarm rang at six thirty forcing James from a short deep sleep having been up until two o'clock with Kym just chatting, kissing and cuddling like a pair of love struck teenagers. 'Teas there Jim,' Peter had done it again, beaten him to it. It seemed whatever time Jim got up, Peter had already beaten him to it but he didn't mind, wrapping his hands around the mug for warmth. Jim looked out on yet another beautiful Norfolk misty morning with the eastern sky a silver glow of early morning sunshine. The birds called good day to each other as they jostled for position in the pecking order... The noises of the twitchers up early to catch a glimpse of the elusive bittern or other birds, wafted through the open back door on a cool June breeze.

"I'm gonna start in the loft and work my way down using that drawing Mark did for us. What do you think?" 'You do the clambering about up top. I'll do the work at the lower level; you're younger than me an besides, I might need to take some money.' Armed with the first fix drawings and a few reels of cable Jim started up into the small almost non-existent loft space. It was more awkward than anything else, cables having to be run from the point where lights or sockets would eventually be to the place where the switch would be. All this around, through and along the joists. Always crouching, kneeling or bending the life of an electrician wasn't an easy one Jim mused. The money may not be good as a kitchen porter but it was easier on the body. As yet another cable reel fell in a controlled way from first floor to ground level Jim could smell bacon frying. It created a hunger in him that his work that day had suppressed. The familiar cry of 'teas up!' that quickly followed it sent him scurrying down the ladder.

"I've nearly done up stairs Peter. The cables need to be clipped in and the heavy stuff for the immersion has to be fitted but I think we are nearly there. So I'm going to have

190

this and go and get the boys if that's ok.?" 'Thars fine by me son, you goo get them boys, they can play hair in relative safety while we starts on the lower level. I feel like you do, the more you see 'em and the less Salter does, the better.' Jim and the boys arrived back just as Simon and the others did. With Pauline Kym and children despatched to the Mace market to get some provisions, Simon pitched in as usual to run cables, fit clips and do anything required so they could meet the boat by 2.00 p.m. as arranged.

'Well!,?'

"Well what?",

'Well how did it go?'

"It was great. I can't understand how he got twenty two people on his boat but it is like Dr Who's Tardis. There was eleven of us and the dog. We sailed over the Rockland broad and moored up in the shallows there watching the swans and herons fly around us as we fed the ducks. Mrs Stone was great, she provided afternoon tea, games for the children and everything. We were so full we didn't even bother with the chip shop".

'Well this is great boyee but I meant your weekend with Kym not just the boat trip.'

"Sorry Peter" chuckled Jim, quietly amused that everyone seemed to have his relationship with Kym on their minds. "It was fine Peter. A bit awkward in a way, neither of us are new at this but in a way we are. It's not anything like my relationship with Betty was." ' Well thas a good thing!.'

"Yes but its, I don't know," Jim in a way was lost for words to describe his feelings he knew how he felt but couldn't quite put it into simple words, eventually saying "I feel like a teenager Peter." 'I'll see if I can get you one!'

"Ha ha! You know what I mean." 'I think I do son but it was a long time ago. You enjoy it while you can'

"Morning Andy."

'Hi ya Jim, a good few days off?'

"Yes great. How's things here? Still bonkers due to the elusive bittern?".

'No,' said with an air of deflation, 'seems it's been spotted at Salhouse so they've all gone over there. Just a few hangers on left.'

Jim smiled a knowing smile but thought it best not to say anything. He quietly thought to himself it had probably been heard but not seen. It was also a timely reminder that he needed to collect the water tank from his father.

'I think it will be quiet tonight. You and Dave are on. Beano will be on wash up and you'll do starters and sweets if that's ok?'

"Yes thanks Andy that's fine by me as long as you are ok with it."

'We're fine with it and I've told Mr Paul to increase your money when you are covering for one of the brigade so make sure you mark it on your time sheet.'

"More money, thanks Andy." He didn't even bother to ask how much more. Anything was welcome and he just trusted that Andy and Mr Paul would be fair.

"Mr Paul, you know those materials and the caravan, have you any idea how long we will need to hold on to them? It's just that if it's to be a while we may move them to the other side of the field so we can get some windows in." 'I don't know Jim. Let me check with the directors in London and I'll let you know; Are you ok for a day or two?'.

"No problem. We are ok for months it's just that the money we made letting the field out will pay for the windows." 'Ok leave it with me and while I've got you, did Andy tell you you're on staff now and will get enhancements when you cover. You'll also get a share of the tronk.

"Ok that's great thanks."

'Our pleasure, you earned it. We knew you were ok from the first day we met you. I said as much to your solicitor by the way... Nice lady. I don't know how you do it but you move in the right circles.' Jim was a little confused but didn't want to argue after all he'd just got a pay increase. "Andy, what's a trunk?" 'Anywhere between six and thirty pounds. It's the tips and just depends on how busy we have been, and it's Tronk, why?' "Well Mr Paul said I'd get a share that's all." 'Well it's not a great deal just treat it as an extra and don't rely on it. I put mine away for holidays.'

Jim had his day all planned; Home after lunch and run the last of the electrics ready for the electricians to do their bit, collect the boys and drop them off with Betty.

"What's this I hear your new bloke's bought them a telly for their room? Is that sensible? They could watch all sorts of stuff."

'Such as?' Betty sneered as she spoke. Her mood seemed to be a constantly bad one; her nose and mouth wrinkled into a permanent grimace.

"Well, I don't know, sex and violence that sort of thing. Who's going to monitor it? They're only young."

'Well we will won't we, me and Bill.'

"Oh! That's great, a lady of questionable morals and a drunkard watching over the innocence of my children. That's great that is."

'Well at least we are spending money on them and giving them treats rather than making them work doing your DIY'.

The customary slam of the door followed and it was off to work.

'Bloody Andy's stitched me up again.' Jim had only just stepped inside the door of the Larkswood Hotel and Country Club and Dave the chef was moaning albeit in a slightly half-hearted manner. 'It's the specials. He's put on Wavioli. John Dorwee, wissoles in a wed wussian sauce. And as a main he's got oven woasted wabbit. He does know how to wind me up.'

"What's John Dory? I thought it was a boat?"

'It's a fish isn't it. Bit like a Dover sole but fleshier and slightly stwonger flavour. Lovely fish and served with new potatoes, locally gwoan aspawagas and hollandaise sauce, you can't beat it.' "Hollandaise sauce?"

'Yes it's like hot mayonnaise with attitude. I'll show you when you've got your pwep done.' Jim changed into his chefs uniform of blue and grey checked trousers, white chefs jacket and a small paper hat. The tall ones being reserved for Andy and Dave. He felt a sense of pride at occasionally being elevated to the position of assistant chef. He was still happy being the plonjer but the added responsibility brought a greater job satisfaction at the end of a session. The evening was a quite one as far as the restaurant was concerned. Busy enough to create an atmosphere but quiet enough for the waiters to be more attentive. It also allowed the kitchen team to chat amongst themselves. A thing they could never do when it was busy. Dave showed both Beano and Jim how to make hollandaise sauce. He also allowed Jim to pipe duchess potato around the silver dish. It took a few goes but on the fourth attempt it was passable. Not good enough for service at the Larkswood but it was passable..

'Eh! Is not a'my fault! A misunderstanding.' Luigi was protesting as Carlos the wine waiter pushed him gently but purposefully through the swing door to the kitchen . If waiters are going to argue the golden rule is never in front of the customer. That generally means the kitchen or the servery. This was no exception.

'I say it's not a my fault chef.' 'Hey, don't get me involved, I don't even know what happened; '

Luigi went on despite Dave's protest.

'The lady was upset Chef and Roberto from Portugal overhear them. It's a my table he tell me. I say to her husband your wife she have a dry muff He want to know how I know. I say Roberto from Portugal tell me she have a dry muff. So the customer he start to get upset. I say a lot of ladies get a dry muff. She must drink Italian chinello.' Waving his hand as if fanning his cheek. 'Let it sit in the muff for a few moments. As she swallow dry muff go away.'

'Its mouth Luigi, Mouth! Not muff.'

'Ass wot I say, dry muff.' Carlos looked skywards and raised his hands in despair. As he left the kitchen to go and placate a confused customer it was left to Beano to explain the differences of language.

It was Friday morning and Sandy the duty receptionist, a tall slim girl with long legs and short blond hair cut in a boys style but left long at the back and by the side of the ears above a beautiful round face and deep blue eyes that all the waiters and the students found most attractive, was looking out for Jim. Seeing the little red car turn in and park at the back of the restaurant she ran out.

'Jim,! Mr Paul needs to see you right away. Before you even get changed. Can you go up?'

'Sorry to grab you Jim but a bit of an awkward situation and you may need to pop out when I've explained'. This was the third time Jim had been in Mr Paul's office. It always felt like visiting the headmasters study.. You didn't know if you were going to get a house point or a caning... Jim wasn't sure this time either. 'It's like this..' Mr Paul continued waving Jim into a seat opposite him. 'Those materials you are looking after for me do not appear on my books. I can't tell you where they came from or when they are likely to be needed here. I don't think they ever will be. In fact I've got some roof tiles coming in later today and I don't need them either or have anywhere to store them. These were all part of the original build and refurbishment. I've spoken to the directors and we are paying you to store the things so how about we cut our losses, stop paying you and you dispose of the materials as you see fit.?' Jim was silent, sitting there with mouth open. Trying to do the sums in his head.

On the one hand he was losing the income from the storage costs but on the other they could use the materials on the cottage.

'Well?'

"Yes, that's fine but are you sure?"

'I'll be honest with you. Look, this place has taken off better than we ever thought. I need to concentrate on running a hotel and country club not a builder's yard. We can always get building materials if we need them. The directors own a reclamation company in Chingford, near London so it's no problem. What I need now is to run this business.' The emphasis was on 'this business' and Jim could tell a deal was ready to be made.

"I hate to ask but it is all legitimate isn't it?"

'Yes of course, and just so no one can say anything I'll get the girls to type up a note on headed paper agreeing it.' He thrust his hand at Jim. A handshake and negotiations were over, or almost. "What about the caravan?" 'Oh! I forgot that. We own it. It will cost me two hundred pounds to move it. You give me one hundred and I'm three hundred pound better off. Ok?' The hand was outstretched again. "Why wasn't it this simple when I was selling" he thought.

'You're back early, thought you didn't finish till two?'

"I got off early Peter we need to have a chat"

'Blast me boyee what's up now?'

"Nothing I hope, but I need to agree it first before I go to the bank"

Jim recounted the conversation he had with Mr Paul earlier in the day.

'We've fallen on our feet boyee. I hope you didn't rip his hand off in your rush to shake on it.'

"No, I was worried it might be knocked off, but he's even put it in writing."

Jim passed the note over to Peter who studied first the letter and then the list. He looked puzzled and read the list again.

'It's got tiles down hair.. , We in't got no tiles. Certainly not two thousand.

"Well he mentioned them but I didn't realise he'd put them on the list. He said they were coming in today."

'Blast me boyee thars inuff to do the whole cottage there. 'If they turns up we'll have 'em.' Peter had a broad smile on his face, it was as if he'd won the lottery... You'd best go to the bank then boyee let's get the deal signed.'

Chapter 11 Building for the future

As he turned out of the village Jim passed a lorry with London Reclaim written on the side coming in the opposite direction. "Crikey! I wonder if that's our tiles. Well I can't stop now I have got to get to the bank before they close."

It was a chequeing account that Jim had opened so his wages could be paid in automatically without the need for cash to exchange. He had a cheque book but no cheque guarantee card so if he wanted any money he had to call at the Bank in person. Parking opposite the Pizza Restaurant in Norwich's Tombland he quickly ran the few hundred yards up the sloping street towards Bank Plain. Then across the street to the Co-op Bank.

"I need to write a cheque for one hundred pounds" smiling as he slid his card under the glass window ."but it needs to be authorised as I only have a checking account." 'That's not a problem Mr Daily, we can write a Managers Cheque for you. Who would you like it payable to?'

'Oh, Make it out to the Larkswood Hotel and Country Club will you?"

'Certainly, take a seat for a few minutes while I'll get it certified.'

He sat in one of the small tub chairs that were placed around a glass topped coffee table. Picking up a magazine on finance, shares and savings he hardly noticed the couple come in through the thick plate glass doors. They hurried towards the counter joining the queue for one of the service windows; each one segregated by a set of chrome posts and thick navy blue ropes.

Jim looked up from the boring magazine and realized the man was Bill Salter with the mystery woman in tow. He couldn't mistake that swagger. Jim finally put two and two together.

This was the woman who was in Salter's car when he spun it. This was the lady who said 'Hello' in the Globe.

This was the woman who works in the employment agency. Jim had met her while waiting for them to open. "Now" thought Jim "it becomes clear." She was obviously the one who ruined his chances of getting a sales job. In fact almost any job. His anger was beginning to boil inside as a call of 'Managers Cheque' interrupted his thought pattern. A small blind rose on a cashier's window at the end of the three queues as the announcement was made.

Rising from his seat Jim walked towards it pausing only to unclip a thick blue rope from its post and deftly attach it to the straps of small haversack. The one Salter was wearing.

Jim signed for the cheque, turned towards Salter and the mystery lady, flashed them a broad smile, his head elevated and slightly cocked to one side and gave the most cheerful of "Good afternoons" as he could while he passed them. It took a few moments for it to register in the mind of the well-known bully and would be thug but when it did it was like a red rag to a bull. Jim was passing through the heavy glass doors as Salter took it into his head to run after him. With nostrils of an already broken nose flaring like a donkey on heat, eyes wide in anger, Salter made for the door in pursuit of his quarry. Three four foot lengths of rope and three heavy based chrome posts followed him with an almighty crash and a clatter. Security alarms sounded and all the doors locked shut automatically assuming the commotion was a raid.

Weighed down by the train of items attached to his haversack Salter's progress was halted and the recoil propelled him backwards where he landed heavily on the edge of a fallen post making him cry out in pain and frustration.

He lay on the floor thumping the blue nylon carpet tiles shouting

'I'll have him. I'll bloody have him I will. You see if I don't.'

Meanwhile Jim, having been on the outside of the security doors as they closed, wandered back to his car wondering what Salter would tell Betty this time and also wondering if she knew she was not the only one?

Kym and her children were waiting at the Loke for Jim when he returned. They wanted to go with him and collect the boys from school and Jim wanted to Introduce Kym to Mrs Nash. Their relationship was moving forward and Jim wanted to share his new found happiness with those who knew him. Next he had to drop the boys off with Betty but knew it wasn't the right time to introduce the wife to the girlfriend. He had to prize the two sets of young friends apart with the promise of a weekend together even so they were late getting them back home to Betty.

'You been up to your bloody tricks again?'

'What Betty? I don't know what you mean."

'Yes you bloody do. Come on boys! Get in and get upstairs. My Bills only just been released by the police. You beat him up in the bank.'

"If I did why haven't they arrested me? All I said was good afternoon. Now what's wrong in that? Oh and who was the lady with him? I've seen them together a few times but don't know her name. Bye boys. See you in the morning." He left the question hanging not needing an answer. It was now Jim's turn to leave with the upper hand having given Betty something to think about.

They walked the short walk back to the Loke hand in hand with Emma and Mickey skipping in front of them.

'I've sold a couple of paintings this month Jim. I have a new agent and he seems to have buyers who like my stuff. If it continues I'm going to have to spend more time in the studio.' Jim's heart sank, this would mean less time together and he was just getting to like the closeness of the relationship. "Oh that's a shame, do you have to work in Basildon?" 'No, funnily enough I was talking it over with Pauline and she has said I could use their garage. I do acrylics, modern art stuff and it's not like I need anything special. Just somewhere warm and dry where I can paint.'

His silence spoke for itself. He broke the awkward silence. "You going back tomorrow still?"

'Yes, I have a bit of an open ticket with regards to the kids' education but can't abuse it so I'm thinking that we will come up at weekends for a while and see how things go. What do you think?' "You want the truth?" They stopped; he looked her straight in the eye saying 'The more I see you the happier I am. When I'm with you I feel like I am the cat that's got the cream. Just thinking of you sets my heart pounding but I don't want to rush things. I never thought I'd ever feel like this. I'm like a teenager again but I know we have both been hurt so I'm frightened. Scared. Scared it will all come crashing down like a house of cards. Shit! There it is, I've said it. The simple answer is if I can only have weekends then weekends it is."

'You silly sod, I feel exactly the same I was so worried that i was pushing you too fast to soon and we were rushing into a relationship out of convenience..'

'Mum!' children have a way of bringing you back down to earth with a bump.

'Yes Emma?'. 'Can we stop at the Mace and get something for the journey tomorrow?'

The grownups minds were still on their previous conversation but both knew that here and now was not the time or place to continue it. A look and a smile between them as their eyes met, said it all.

Jim ran Kym and the children over to Pauline and Simon's home before going into work. Both were quiet on the journey reflecting on what each had said earlier.

"Pick you up at 9.30? for an hour or so tonight?"

'Yes please, don't care where we go as I said earlier.' She blew him a kiss and the children waved as he drove away.

"What am I tonight chef?"

'We're still busy with the press and foreign TV coz of that bloody bittern so can you do starters and sweets? Paddy's in with Jon. They'll do wash up.'

Jim worked hard to make sure the hors d'oeuvres trolley was kept filled and looking good, The prawn cocktails were prepped. Small Ogen melons were cut and ready on a tray and the mis-en-place was there with all garnishes and accompaniments.

"Can you spare me for five minutes chef? I have to see Mr Stone and pay him a cheque."

'Shouldn't he be paying you?'

"No this is for his caravan. We bought it, mind you what we will do with it I don't know but Peters got an idea or two so it's staying on our plot or rather his plot for now."

"Hi Daisy, can I go up and see the boss?" The deep brown eyes set in the coffee coloured skin of the young receptionist opened wide and an alluring smile underlined the warmth of Daisy's personality. It was easy to see why she had been selected as the first and last person you saw at the Larkswood.

'He's got someone with him right now , can you give him five. I'll give you a call if you like?'

"Ugh, yes, thanks. But I'm really busy in the kitchen tonight can you give him this cheque and say thanks from me?"

'Well ok, I'll let him know'

Service was as Andy predicted, busy. Although the illusive bittern had moved from Hornham to Salhouse it appeared that the press entourage preferred the comfort of the Larkswood to other establishments and after all it was on expenses for most of them. A few had left but only to be replaced by serious ornithologists and as Anglia TV boasted the best wildlife department in the UK they had to maintain a presence. There were various comings and goings by the waiting staff who all congregated in the kitchen to vent their frustrations at the chefs regarding customers and staff alike. The mix of nationalities made it difficult to handle sometimes. The Greeks disliked the Turks, the French distrusted the Italians and Dave being a

Jewish chef was seen as an outsider by all. However the cosmopolitan mix seemed to work.

'Jim, I got your cheque thanks. I've asked Daisy to write you a receipt but she's busy just now so it may be a day or two.'

"Thanks Mr Paul. I appreciate it. Roberto table four starters away please. Sorry Mr Paul, rather busy. Gloria you got table sixteen's sweet order?" Mr Paul waved as he left the kitchen entering into the restaurant thinking to himself that his judge of character had been confirmed in Jim's appointment and promotions and hoped they could hold on to him.

It was nearly 10.00 p.m. when Jim called at Pauline and Simon's rented home to be warmly greeted by Pauline looking a picture in a smart navy blue and red spotted dress above knee length dark suede boots and wearing full make up.

'Glad you're here, we are off to the Wherry. You and Kym are babysitting, ok?'

"Yes fine, you go out and have a good time."

'We will, there's beer in the fridge and some left over pork from dinner if you're hungry. See you at 11.30 p.m. or maybe 12.00 p.m. Have a good one.' Dragging an equally smart Simon by the hand they were gone. Jim closed the front door turning around to be greeted by the outstretched arms of Kym. A long lingering kiss was followed by Kym placing her finger to her lips 'shoosh' be quiet, we have an hour and a half to ourselves, let's make the most of it.'

Guiding him to the settee she began to undress him kneeling down to release his belt and loosen his trousers he reached down and began to remove her blouse.......

"I suppose we had better get dressed. Your sister will be back in half an hour."

'Do we have to? can't we just stay like this and tell them to go straight to bed?'

"I wish we could but I think Simon would have a fit."

'No he's alright, ever since they went out looking at stars he's been a different man. Pauline's noticed and I think it's done them both the world of good.' They kissed again arousing within them the passion they felt for each other. They somehow fought the temptation to renew their coupling and with Jim trying to dress and Kym playfully attempting to stop him they eventually got to a state of attire that would be reasonable if interrupted.

'Oh Jim I wish I didn't want you as much as i do. I've just been so irresponsible. What would have happened if the kids had woken up?'

"We would have put them back to bed. You would probably have had to say you were having a bath but we'd have managed. It's not as if what we are doing is wrong and oh! That reminds me, I need to tell you what happened today. I went in to work and Mr Paul," a key turned in the lock and a very noisy Pauline came through the front door with an equally quiet Simon pleading with her not to wake the children. They paused for what seemed an age then giggling like two school children proceeded to enter the lounge where Jim and Kym were cuddling on the settee.

'I'll make a coffee then you can finish telling me about what happened today' said Kym rising from the settee and straightening her skirt with both hands as she did so. as if to show them she was properly dressed.

'Well go on then tell us all.' Jim sighed, took a slurp of his tea, a deep breath and then proceeded to recount his experiences of the day and the fact that Betty said Bill Salter had been arrested but Jim wasn't sure exactly why.

Having said his farewell to Kym the night before Jim called in to collect the boys ready for school. He was wary of what Bill Salter might do or say to him but he knew he had to brave it out and appear as though nothing had happened. He rang the doorbell and Betty opened it ushering the boys through without looking directly at Jim, head turned and bowed towards the floor.

'Hope you feel better mummy' Tom hugged his mother.

'Thanks Tom, now go, go on' she sniffed. It was obvious she had been crying. Despite their difference Jim felt concerned.

"You alrigh?t", he enquired with genuine concern in his voice.

'I fell over that's all. Now take them boys to school.' Looking up as she said it Jim could see a black eye, a bruised cheek and a split lip.

"Oh Betty, I'm sorry; I think this is my fault. I didn't realise he'd take it out on you."

'This ain't your fault its mine for trusting the bastard. Anyway he can't take it out on you he's been bound over to keep the peace.'

"Look I'll drop the boys at school and come back." He did just that and was ushered in with a friendliness he hadn't seen for a long while.

'Oh Jim, I've made a terrible mistake.'

"You only just realised that?"

'No I have. I know I have. Can't you come back and we can start again? I'll sling him out and you move back in.' She tried to open her eyes like a puppy that had been whipped and was talking soft and low. Jim smiled at her as he took both her hands in his and looked down at her bruised and battered face.

"Betty, I'd love to. To live with the boys again in this house as a happy family unit? I'd love to;"

She sighed and tried to smile despite the cracked lips

"but there is no way I can live with you again. I'm sorry love, but as man and wife we are over. I have a new life now and you're not part of it. You caused it, but you're not part of it."

Betty started to cry showing a weakness that had been hidden for the past few months.

Jim hugged her as if comforting a sister or maiden aunt who had lost someone dear to them.

There was no love but there was pity and after all, she was the mother of his children.

'Well I suggest we press on with the divorce. Whatever state your wife's relationship is in with her cohabiter, it matters not to you and your desire to make a clean break with open access to your children.' Mrs Lamb had it right and Jim readily agreed. Betty's problems were her own and Jim didn't need to get involved unless they affected his children.

'Whilst we continue with that one; What about the claim for unfair dismissal?'

"I don't know if we can, can we?"

'Yes I believe so; I am reliably informed that your previous employer colluded with your wife's cohabiter to restrict your employment. I believe we can prove that the breakup of your marriage, which took place over a weekend, was in no way related to your activities at work and should have had no bearing on any disciplinary procedure the company was entitled to carry out. You were not warned and or given any opportunity to be represented at any discussion or hearing.'

"No, that's true. I was just sacked, but I was told it was gross misconduct so they could do that." 'Gross incompetence more like. I believe we have a strong case and with your permission I will write to The Company Secretary of Graham Wilkins Wire Works in London and inform them of our intention to proceed with a claim.'

Mrs Lamb was a fiery little thing thought Jim. I'm glad she is on my side. He could see she was fired up and ready to fight what she saw as an injustice.

'I'll need to write to your current employer if that's ok. I know they won't have a problem as I have already spoken to them but I'm letting you know just in case you do.'

"No, I'm fine with it but I'll warn them out of courtesy".

Jim informed Mr Paul who seemed remarkably unflustered by the fact that a solicitor was going to be contacting him. He appeared to take it as just a matter of course. He was more interested in the fact that Salter had been bound over to keep the peace.

'You know he's barred from here don't you?'

"No! I didn't know, I hope it's not because of me."

'Him, his family and your ex-boss, what's his name, Dixon?, He's barred too.'

"Why?,"

'We don't need their sort. We don't like being told what to do and when they phoned up telling us not to employ you the directors saw red and barred the lot.'

"So that's why there was a delay. One minute I have a job, then I haven't, then I have."

'Yes, sorry about that. I didn't say anything because I wanted to make my own mind up and I have. You're alright, and aren't you supposed to be working?'

"Err yes."

'Well get on with it then.' Mr Paul smiled and gave a friendly nod as if to say I'm still the boss but there is a friendship there too. Jim wanted to know more. What Salter and Dixon had said? Why they said it, what was their motive? These questions would have to wait, work had to come first. Another busy night in the kitchen loomed. Andy should have been off, but had come in to make sure all was covered and to lend an extra hand. Jim was again acting as chef and enjoying the role.

"How do you know when a steaks done Dave?" Jim was fascinated, he had watched for weeks and seen Dave cooking all manner of foods, from half a duck, through to gammon to Sole and of course steaks. All cooked under a red hot grill with a cast iron ribbed plate that gave charred lines to whatever was being cooked while also allowing the juices and fat to run off.

'You poke 'em. Well its easy Jim.'

"Poke them?"

'Yes, you'll soon get used to it.'

"But even if I poke them and I've seen you do it, how do I know what I'm poking?"

'I don't know' Dave thought for a moment. 'Listen, with yaw left hand put the thumb and index finga togetha in an ok shape like the scuba divsa do. See the fleshy bit of your palm by yaw thumb, well pwess that with your wight hand index finga.' Dave demonstrated as Jim copied.

'Well that's ware,'

"Whats where?"

'No not where, ware! as in well done, medium, and ware. Almost what we call blue.'

"Yes ok," Jim understood but was puzzled.

'Now take the next finga on the left hand and do the same.' Again Jim copied. As he pressed it with his right index finger, he noticed it was different.

'That's medium. Now take your wing finga and do the same That's well done.

Jim did and was pleased he could see and feel the difference.

'Hey you two, check on!' Andy interrupted the discussion calling the order for table twelve. 'Two hors d'oeuvres from the trolley, one gammon and pineapple, one duck A l'Orange. Beano get us a pineapple. The call to the kitchen porter was acknowledged as Beano left the pot wash sink and headed into the stores.

'None fresh, only tinned chef.'

'Well open it and give it to Dave quick.'

'It's Chunks, bloody chunks'. The Larkswood prided itself on presentation; a gammon steak was always accompanied with a ring of fresh pineapple, sprinkled with brown sugar and a pinch of cinnamon and glazed under the grill to caramelise it. At the worst a ring of tinned pineapple would do but not chunks. That was the stuff of other restaurants.

'Do what you can Dave. Jim, help him will you.' Jim could see the predicament and quickly drained the tin of juice, turned a silver serving dish upside down and

208

working as quick as he could neatly arranged some of the segments into a circle. A sprinkle of sugar and cinnamon and they were ready for grilling. Having turned the silver dish upside down the caramelised ring slid easily off onto the grilled gammon as it was served.

'Well done Jim. Put the rest of the pineapple in the fridge with the chicken.'

"Yes chef." Service continued and Andy announced that it would probably be double covers again. 'Bloody Bittern! I wish they'd shot the bloody thing.' Andy didn't mean it and Jim was pleased they hadn't. The last thing he needed was pellet holes in his water tank.

'Jim you bloody twat! When I said put the pineapple with the chicken, I meant on the same shelf, not together. What am I gonna do now?'

"Sorry chef," he almost said, I only followed orders but though better of it.

"I'll use it up chef. I've got to refresh the hors d'oeuvres trolley." His brain was racing. Two poached chicken breasts and half a tin of pineapple. Suddenly from nowhere inspiration hit him, Chopping both the chicken and pineapple into small chunks about the size of the fingernail on his smallest finger he mixed the two with just enough mayonnaise to bind them together. Laying this on a bed of shredded lettuce and garnishing with a pinch of Cayenne pepper in a line to add a rich red colour, he served up two trays of hors d'oeuvres.

'Go on then clever dick what do we tell the waiters?' Andy's frustration at a possible waste of food had dissipated into an almost resigned respect. His quick taste of the finished item using the teaspoon he kept tucked into the top of his chefs uniform had not gone unnoticed by Jim. "Hawaiian Chicken chef."

'Well flipping heck! He's even got a name for it. Go on then.' nodding to the waiter whose job it was that evening to wheel the trolley. As Andy passed Jim on his way to place some empty soup tureens in the wash up the words 'A pinch more white pepper next time' were uttered letting Jim know his work was appreciated but Andy was still the master.

'Cup of tea boyee?' Jim was woken by Peter bringing him a cup of tea. A service that Peter had dropped gradually over the weeks. "Thanks Peter, what's this in aid of.?"

'Well, we needs to talk boyee and plan out how we are gunna make this place habitable for others.. Its ok fur you 'n me, we're blokes, we can rough it, but you may want to bring Kym and her kids and your lads hair too at some toime. Howe we gunna ccommodate that?'

"I don't know Peter, I'm just pleased to have a roof over my head, and I'm pleased to be sharing it with you but at the end of the day this is your home. I really appreciate what you have done and I can't ever repay the service you have given me or the friendship you have shown so you just say what you want and I'll do it."

'You silly sod! I int lookin fur praise, wot we dun hair we dun together.' Peter sat himself down on the end of Jim's bed, I was gooin nowhere till you shooed up. Then I got a purpose. A reason. You kicks started me into doing something and what I'm saying is we needs to continue. An this bird thing has made me realise we hav a footture hair. This is a business I can cope with; campers. they're like me, drifters making the most of it, prepared to rough it a bit and not askin too much. But if we got to do it we got to do it roight. We needs to finish this cottage while we ha the money.' Jim sat back in his bed and thought for a few moments. It was the most he had ever heard Peter say in one session. "OK Peter," thinking on his feet and realising that the old man needed to let this off his chest but also needed answers and directions that could only come from discussion. "How about we have a chat this afternoon? I'm off from two and don't pick the boys up till three thirty."

'Sounds good to me boyee, enjoy the cuppa.'

All day Jim was thinking of what needed to be done to make the cottage properly habitable. Finish the plumbing, complete the electrics, plaster the walls and ceilings, finish the roof, fit two fire places, fit a kitchen. There was so much to do just to get the small house ready for decorating let alone occupation. Windows would help. In fact thought Jim that was probably the first thing. It would make the property fully watertight and a decent front and back door would make it secure. The current arrangements of an old ill-fitting door closed shut by a piece of blue nylon cord scavenged from someone's boat, was hardly ideal. But there again what's the rush? He mused to himself. It was home for the pair of them and they had moved it on considerably from where it was when Jim first moved in.

"How about we make a list of jobs we need to do and what materials we need and go and get them from the reclaim place in Oak Street?"

'We can't afford them all boyee but it would be worth a look.' "

At lease we'll have a target. That stuff from the Larkswood will help."

'Upstairs floor boards is the big one.'

"Yes, that and plasterboard. But if we can get it we can fit it ourselves. We can't do the plumbing and electrics but we know people who can so that's not too much of a problem."

Within an hour they had hatched a plan and agreed to go on Saturday to the reclaim centre where all sorts of building materials are bought and sold at knock down prices. Peter had said he would go to Acle market on Thursday to see if he could get some bargains. It was a busy local auction and vegetable market where everything from eggs and live poultry to bikes, furniture and household goods were traded. Occasionally local companies and businesses would auction surplus stock. Jim felt confident they now had a plan to work to so before collecting the boys he took time to phone Kym and let her know that he was occupied on Saturday that they had a plan if not a timetable, to crack on with the renovation of the cottage. Kym was upset that the weekend was to be cut short but she understood. The one who didn't was Betty. Still battered and bruised from as she called it 'falling down a step and hitting a door' she was irritated and aggressive when Jim told her he wouldn't be picking up the boys until lunch time on Saturday.

'That's your day. You said it was! You can't mess me about. I've got plans and I ain't gonna change 'em for you, see if I will? These boys will be ready for you at eight o'clock on Saturday waiting out here and if you're late that's between you and them. They'll be in the garden come rain or shine.' He looked at her and sighed.

"You know Betty you asked me the other day if I'd come back and live with you as man and wife and from what you have just said is there any wonder I said no? I'll pick the boys up first thing on Saturday and I'll bring them back at six on Sunday so you and lover boy can have a whole weekend together. May be he will let you go a couple of more rounds this time." As soon as he had said it, almost as he was saying it, he regretted it but what was said was said, he couldn't take it back. The door slammed in the customary manner shaking the glass panes and making the knocker bounce loudly.

'Young man!' The voice was behind him, old and croaky with a demand in its tone. Jim turned to see old Mr Hillingsworth standing in the opposite door way on the other side of the shared drive way. Jim didn't care much for the old boy. He had found him rude, ignorant and very self-centred. As a neighbour he was very demanding. His wife though was quite the opposite and was always apologising for the cantankerous nature of her husband. 'You are going to have to have words with your friends and your wife. I can't have them blocking up the driveway with that big black car like they do.'

"I'm sorry Mr Hillingsworth but you will have to speak to them yourself. I don't live here anymore and they are no friends of mine."

'What? I mean what about them two?' Hillingsworth lifted his walking stick using it as an extension to his index finger, and pointed to two characters loitering in the small alleyway nearly opposite Mr Hillingsworth's houses that led as a passageway to the next close.. 'They keep parking their flash car over my driveway and have only just moved it before you turned up.'

"Its a shared drive Mr Hillingsworth and as I said they are no friends of mine. I think they are casing the joint for a burglary. I suggest you call the police."

'What! Do you mean it?'

"Yes I do and if you don't mind I will go and check my back door, you should do the same." Jim had recognised one of the men as one of the party who was supposed to back up Salter when he attacked with the snooker cue. The other he wasn't so sure about but from the look of him he was more muscle than brains. Jim walked towards the back garden and opened the small wooden gate slowly as if he had all the time in the world and he passed into the rear garden of his former home as if to go in the backdoor. He was now out of sight of the two thugs whom he suspected had been waiting to have words with him. He ran the short distance to the rear wall that separated the property from the local cricket ground vaulting it with one bound he ran as fast as he could across the pitch to the gate at the far side. Going through the heavy galvanised gate he slowed exiting nonchalantly on to the main road trying to catch his breath. As he did so he was passed by a police car with lights flashing and sirens blaring that swung round in the direction of Mr Hillingsworth's home. "Good old boy, he took the bait." Jim's thoughts were now with Peter and he rushed to the Loke to warn him. 'Oi saw them boyee but it int me there after, its you! I wondered what they was up to when Oi fust saw em they didn't look, like twitchers. Stuck out like a sore thumb. I never saw 'em last time. I had me back to 'em remember? You take it easy son. That bloody Salter is a mean bastard, mark my words.'

Jim was worried. Things were now becoming serious. His wife's lover unable to accost Jim directly because he was bound over to keep the peace, had obviously recruited friends to do it for him. Salter the thug, had obviously beaten up Jim's estranged wife and was living with her in Jim's home with Jim's two young children. "Hell! It couldn't get much worse." Jim considered his options. Speak to the police, Speak to Salter, Speak to his solicitor. He really didn't see any solution in any of them. The children were his main concern. "I must protect them above all" he thought. "Maybe Peter will have some more ideas. I'll speak to him after work tonight." Jim worked on but his mid wasn't really on it. All the possibilities and options were racing through his head.

"Chef, I'm done here is there any chance I can go early? I need to see Peter before I turn in tonight."

'Yes chef, you go and take it easy, see you in the morning.'

"Thanks chef."

Chef! the words hung in his memory for few moments, chef! He called me chef. Jim felt elated the word Chef to him from Andy meant more than thank you, more than well done; it was recognition, a salutation, an elevation from kitchen porter. It probably won't last, ending as soon as the bittern saga does but for now it was a high he needed, He jumped into bowler and started the little engine his pride at being called chef bringing a wide smile to his face. "Peter will probably be in the Wherry. I'll head there first." Out of the car park, along the country road around a few bends and a sharp left turn down the steep hill toward the pub. As he turned the sharp left, Jim noticed the car wasn't responding as it should. He had to press firmly on the break and he was only in second gear. He pressed again and his foot went to the floor easily. There was nothing there. No responding pressure. "Oh shit! The brakes have gone." He was heading down one of the steepest hills in Norfolk. He thought fast, luckily he was only in second gear still. He

214

pumped the clutch and with a grinding of the gears forced the gear lever into first. The little car jolted and slowed but was still going too fast for the hand brake to be effective. At that moment he saw the crossing gate keeper start to close the gates. He sounded the horn, flashed the lights. Two choices, slow down and crash into the gates or speed up and hopefully get through them. He felt the latter was his only choice. Shoving the leaver from first to third he pressed the accelerator and aimed at the gap between the gate and the post as it was narrowing. One hand on the horn the other on the steering wheel, he waited. The world to him was in slow motion. He could see the crossing keeper closing the gate an expression of fear as he realised Jim was not going to stop. His face changing from red to white as the blood drained from it. His change of mind as he calculated the distance was insufficient to avoid a collision, his rapid change of direction pushing the gate open rather than pulling it shut. He moved just in time as Jim and bower bumped across the lines missing the posts and the gate by inches. No time to waste. Jim now had to slow the car and quickly. It was a single track road with passing places either side. Meeting another vehicle could be fatal. Changing down from third to first with another crunching of gears to achieve a manoeuvre the little gear box was not designed for. A further jolt as the engine took the strain and acted as a break. Jim put the gears into neutral and applied the hand break gradually to bring the car to a halt some two hundred yards past the railway lines. He turned it around using the first gear only and hand break and gingerly drove it into the car park of the Wherry.

"Sorry mate my breaks have gone and it was either run into the gates or go through them. You ok?" The crossing keeper had still not recovered his face ashen in colour and lacking any expression. His eyes wide open as if in disbelief as to what had just happened. He took a deep breath and managed to utter 'No worries mate I'm alright. Just need to go and change my underwear'

Chapter 12 The Plan

'You alright Jim? You look like you've seen a ghost.'

"Yes I'm fine Ann but I have had a bit of a problem with the car. Is Peter in tonight?"

'Yes he's in the restaurant area with Me & Mrs Stone. Go through, I'll bring you a beer.'

'Let's have a look at your car then Jim.' Jim had recounted the issues of the day to Leyton, Peter, Leyton's Mum and Jessie who had joined half way through but seemed to know all about it anyway. "I'm not worried about the car I'm sure it's the servo and that's easily fixed, its Salter and his thugs I need do something with." '

All the same son without that little car you are buggered, Lets go and have a quick look.'

'Dunt look at me boyee, I know nuffin abut cars.' Peter was shrugging his shoulders and Jim knew he was right.

Jim reached in to release the rear engine cover but as he did so Leyton was already scrabbling about under the car.

'Don't bother Jim, I can see what it is. Your break lines have been cut. Good job too, just enough to let you get going but as soon as you apply full pressure whoosh! All the fluid comes pissing out. You've been set up mate. Someone wants you out of the way and we both know who.'

"Oh Shit! I need to tell the police."

'Not just yet, and what they gonna do? You got any proof?' Jim didn't answer. 'Thought not. Let's wait twenty four hours and see what transpires. We need to think of their next move and counter it before it happens.' Jim was silent but the thoughts were racing through his mind. Leyton closed the rear engine cover. He had assumed an air of superiority. With a calm but firm control as if this was his territory, an area of expertise he knew but kept hidden.

'Did you see any one following you? Any lights of cars or motor bikes behind you when you came down the hill?'

"No I don't think so. I was the only one coming down the hill and they certainly didn't follow me across the lines as I nearly took the gates out." 'Good, let's see the gate keeper then.' Jim was puzzled but followed as they went to speak to the crossing keeper. Leyton was relaxed and approached the hut as if he were a concerned friend worried about the health and wellbeing of the poor crossing keeper. 'Hello mate, how you feeling now? It must have been a terrible shock. I know you are not supposed to drink on duty but can I get you a brandy or something?'

'No I'm fine now, it was a shock but......' The crossing keeper had recovered his colour but Jim wasn't really listening. He wittered on then came the crunch question from Leyton that Jim hadn't thought about but Leyton obviously had. 'Anyone else come through after my mate? You see we may have to claim on the insurance against the garage that serviced it. and might need witnesses.'

'Well yes, one car did. It went down the lane.'

'It hasn't come back across then?'

'No it was a big black Merc. I'd have seen it if it had.'

'OK mate, you sure you don't want that drink?'

'Oh go on then, but just one. A brandy and lemonade'

'Ok mate, I'll bring it out. Any chance I can borrow your pen?'

Outside of the little crossing control box Leyton passed the pen to Jim.

'Hold on to that and make a note of any car registration that comes past either way. My thoughts are that they will be parked up somewhere down the lane and don't realize their plans to wreck you and your car have actually worked. They're still waiting for it to happen.

"Really?"

'Yes, I'll get this bloke his drink and let Mother know we may be a little while. You got any pliers? If so, get em; and a torch if you got one.'

A few moments later and Leyton and Jim walked slowly down the lane that led from the station towards the boat yards.

"There it is! That Mercedes. They've been watching the Pub from there. They will have seen us looking at the brakes."

'NO your car's just out of their line of sight.'

"Yes but they can see us now"

'Yes, but it's you they are looking for not me; Pretend to go into the next chalet and wave me goodnight. Give it five minutes and come back out as if you have left something at the pub and head back there. I'll be back in ten, Oh! And give me the pliers and torch.'

Jim did as instructed. He wasn't sure what Leyton had planned but trusted him and his assured manner. A cheery wave and loud good night were followed by Jim opening the gate to the garden of an empty holiday chalet. He stepped in as Leyton passed the Merc with its two occupants furtively trying to see but not be seen.

'Hoi! What's your game?' Lights went on as an annoyed tourist dressed only in a robe like dressing gown shouted at Jim.

"Sorry mate I was looking for Andy Lewis. I'm borrowing his boat tomorrow" 'Well he don't live here so bugger off.' 'More lights came on around the property and saying "Sorry, Sorry". Jim backed out through the gate. The occupants of the Merc sunk further down in their seats still trying to remain hidden from view. Jim strode purposefully towards the pub not looking back, hoping he was not being followed. He heard no footsteps or a car engine. The only sound was a long sigh of relief when he entered through the heavy wooden doors of the Wherry.

The others were anxious to know what was going on. Jim was still in the middle of explaining as Leyton joined them.

'I think we all need a drink after that. Well done Jim, Nice diversion. Here have your pliers back.'

"I didn't plan it. I thought there was no one home. I had to think of something quick as to why I was there. Did I sound convincing?"

'I don't know I was under their car. Letting one of their tyres down,. What with your ruckus they didn't hear a thing.'

"So what do we do now?"

'Well first thing you two' pointing his finger at Peter and Jim. 'are staying with me and Mother tonight on the boat. No arguments. I want you somewhere safe. Next thing is to act as though nothing has happened. And leave as normal. Can you drive that little car up the hill and pop it into Manor Garage?'

"Yes but can't I leave it here?"

'No I need them to follow it and you are the bait. I need them to think their evil little plan hasn't yet worked.'

"Yes OK. When do we do it? Now?"

'No. I need you to do it just before the last train at eleven twenty. You need to roar up that hill as fast as you can. They'll try and follow you. We will be waiting for you at the top. Mind you stop though. I don't want you crashing into my Jag.'

Peter and Mrs Stone were silent while all this was going on as if they didn't want to interrupt a carefully crafted plan. Exchanging glances with only the occasionally raised eyebrow to express concern or show a lack of understanding. It was evident they had moved into Leyton's area of expertise and no one felt qualified to question it. "I'm grateful for what you are doing Leyton, but I'm still worried about the boys and what Salter might do. Don't you think I should talk to the police?"

'We may have to but let's try it my way first. At the end of the day he works for the family business and I'm sure that if I speak to his parents they will see sense and stop all this bollocks.'

They drank up and left the pub along with the rest of the regulars Leyton, his Mother, Peter and Jessie, who had cadged a lift home, clambered into the dark blue Jaguar.

Jim made a great play of waving them goodbye and made sure he was last out of the car park. Again using the handbrake to slow the vehicle, he manoeuvred it into the road in front of the pub where it could and would be seen by Salter's thugs. He made ready for a quick getaway. He wound the driver's window down listening intently. There it was the bell! Ringing loudly from the gate keepers lodge indicating a train was coming.

As the crossing keeper approached the gate Jim's car accelerated aiming to do a quick sprint across the lines and up the hill. First Gear, into second and changing into third as he accelerated for all he was worth whilst bumping over the railway line. The little red car gave all the speed it could muster from it's little engine and sped up the steep incline like a rat up a drainpipe.

Should he look in the rear view mirror? No! No need he instinctively knew that he was being pursued by a large black Mercedes with two occupants who were anxious to witness his demise. Had he done so he would have seen the crossing keeper waving to him while closing the heavy crossing gates behind him.

He would have seen the driver of a Black Mercedes sounding his horn while the crossing Keeper oblivious to this, closed the second gate. The Mercedes was now up to sixty miles per hour and accelerating with less the forty feet to go between it and the gates. The driver had no option but to slam on the brakes and stop on the opposite side of the tracks to their quarry.

Pressing hard the driver realised it was in vain , as hard as he pumped and pressed there was no power in the brake system. He applied the hand brake but the car hardly slowed, it just slew to the side as if there was no air in the left hand tyre.

The Mercedes hit the heavy wooden post that held the crossing gate, with such a force that both car and gates were wrecked. Luckily no one was too badly hurt but it took over half an hour to release the two thugs and even then it was into the hands of the County and Railway

Police who wanted answers as to why these two idiots had rammed the gates.

Meanwhile at the top of the hill Jim allowed the little car to come to a slow speed and turned it into the customer car park of the Manor garage.

They heard the crash rather than saw it. Parking the little Fiat next to other cars for sale and repair, Jim hurriedly made his way to the waiting Jaguar. Stepping into the rear seat alongside Peter and Jessie he said what they had all been thinking, "That was a hell of a crash, I wonder what happened?"

'I think it's called karma Jim, they got what they intended for you. Strange how things like that can happen,'

Hardly another word was spoken until Jessie was dropped off. 'What's your take on all this Mother?' It was the first time Leyton had asked his Mother's opinion that Jim could remember.

'I think it's disgraceful son, can't you do something about it?, We can't have people going round threatening our friends it's just not right.'

'I'll have a word with Salter's family in the morning, businessman to businessman, I'm sure they'll see sense.'

"And if they won't?" Jim enquired with a tremble in his voice.

'Well we may have to involve the police but I doubt it. Let's try and keep them out of it for the kids sake.. We will try the diplomatic route first'. 'Yes good for you Leyton, go see 'em and talk some sense into them.' 'Thanks Mother'

"Do you want me to come with you?"'

"No, best you keep out of it Jim   It's known as deniability. A bit like that back there. We was nowhere near it, just been having a drink and left the pub as normal.'

Jim was relieved he didn't fancy a stand up argument with the abattoir's owners that were Salter's family. They had a mean reputation and Jim knew negotiations would not be easy.

A night afloat was not as bad as Peter had expected. He thought the rocking sensation would be greater than it was and anticipated a disturbed sleep. It was in fact quite the reverse, the gentle lapping of the water against the hull and a rhythmic sway helped him to sleep better than he usually did.

"Cup of tea here Peter."

'Makes a change boyee, you bringing me one. You sleep alright?'

"Not really the events of last night kept going round in my head what with that and your snoring I've had better nights. I've got to go and pick the kids up. Leyton's going to drop me off on his way to Salter's Abattoir. So I'll see you later."

'Good luck Jim. Remember just act normal as if nothing has happened. They will know now that we know what they are up to so we will just play it cool and keep the upper hand.'

"Yes, thanks Leyton, this is really good of you"

'That's all right son, I'm sure you will find a way of repaying me if we can't help a friend in time of difficulty then it's a sad old world. Play it cool, that's the motto of the day, just play it cool.' He was saying it over and over in his head. He could feel his heart pounding as he reached the door he was certain he would be faced by an angry Bill Salter. Instead it was Betty that opened the door. Still bruised and uncharacteristically quiet. "Bill not in then?"

'No, he got a call in the middle of the night and had to go out. His mate had a car accident.' Dropping the boys at their schools Jim called at the Manor Garage to arrange for them to repair the brake pipes on his little Fiat. It wasn't a standard part and it would take a day or two to get the bits delivered. 'Hopefully ready Friday afternoon if that's ok?' He couldn't argue and Friday would be ok. He hoped he could borrow Peter's bike until then to get to work and back. He walked down the Loke to get washed and changed ready for work, borrowed Peter's bike and left him a note. It was midway through the morning and Jim was helping Effel with the vegetable preparations for the lunch and evening service when Daisy the receptionist looked into the kitchen and announced there was a call for Jim.

'Jim? It's Leyton. The old man is having nothing to do with it. He says the sins of the son are nothing to do with the Father. He has agreed to stay out of it though and I'm sure he will coz he has a fiddle going on with dodgy meat that's not going through the books and I let it slip that I know.'

"Oh bloody hell, what do we do about Bill Salter?."

'I have got an appointment with him this afternoon at the abattoir. I'll let you know how it goes.'

"Thanks Leyton. I've got to go, I'm at work."

'I know, you twit, I rang you!' As he went to put the receiver down Jim noticed the call hadn't come through on the external phone it was an internal call re-routed from one of the offices. He wondered why or how Mr Stone had the office number rather than the customer number.

'Is that ok Jim?' The beautiful Daisy interrupted his thoughts. "Yes fine thank you." Starting to walk away he turned as a thought struck him. He needed to place the boys in a secure place for the next few nights. He didn't like to ask but it had to be his mum and dad's place in Salhouse. "Daisy, sorry to be a pain but can I use the phone?. 'Yes, sure.'

"Mum I'm in a pickle and I need your help .... " He quickly explained over the phone the predicament and the need to get the boys to a "safe house" for a few days. There was no question of a refusal. He would get a taxi and bring the boys over together with a change of clothes or two and Jim would collect them on Saturday morning.

'I know it's none of my business, but I overheard what you were saying. My boyfriend runs Barton's Taxis, he'll run you over there. He won't charge you' The beautiful Daisy had suddenly turned even more beautiful.

Thomas and Matthew loved being picked up in a taxi. Being collected by Dad in Bowler was good but a bright blue and yellow cab with Private Hire light on the roof with its own driver was an extra treat. A quick argument with Betty, a collection of clothes and a few toys and they were off to Salhouse. Jim had expected Betty to make more of a fuss. He thought there would be a stand up row and a refusal to let the boys stay with Jim's Parents but resistance seemed to have been a token with a reserved acceptance that it was for their safety. Jim's mother Elizabeth was delighted to have the boys for a couple of nights. She had arranged for them all to walk down to the Salhouse Broad and feed the ducks and if the weather was not good enough she was going to have them making cupcakes and helping Grandpa with a fire of garden rubbish. They may even get a chance to cook some marsh-mallows on sticks or do dough twists with homemade bread which they loved. Even better for them they had a day off school. They weren't sure why but a day off school is a day off school.

'You got problems then?' Enquired Len Barton as he drove Jim back towards Hornham. "Yeah, kind of. The ex-wife's new boyfriend has a bit of a grudge against me. It's got to such a point where I don't think the children are safe with him."

'Daisy said it's Salter.' "Yes it is. Him and a few of his thugs."

'Well I'm happy to help if needed; He bullied my brother at school and it seems as though time hasn't improved him so if you need a lift somewhere just give us a shout.'

"Thanks Len, I'm trying not to get too many people involved but I appreciate the support."

'You know, it's a funny thing, everywhere I go people tell me what a piece of detritus Salter is and how he has bullied this person or that and yet no one has stopped him or stood up to him. I think you are the first and good on you.'

"Thanks Len. I'll let you know if I need you."

It was nearly five o'clock when he returned to the Loke. "You heard anything Peter?"

'No not a thing boyee, I bin busy with the campers, How about you?'

"I dropped the boys off at my mums and came straight back. I've got to change for work and go there. If you hear from Leyton, can you let me know? If not I'll see you at the pub when I finish."

Work seemed to drag. The time just didn't go quick enough for Jim. Again he was Chef but as things were slack he filled his time with assisting Beano and John with the washing up.

'I saw your mate in the city today. I hardly recognized him.' Beano was making polite conversation while scrubbing a particularly burnt oval flat dish.

"Which mates that?"

'Well Peter course. The one with the camp site'

"He wasn't in the city today. He was on the site"

'No it was definitely him, I've known him for years. I was coming out of Pizza One and he was going in the solicitors next door. As I said I hardly recognized him, he had a jacket and tie on with a clean shirt. Must have been seeing the Bank Manager.'

Jim passed it off with a smile but behind Beano's flippant quip there was a story and he was concerned. Peter had said he had been looking after the campers so why had he lied.? And why was he seeing a solicitor? Jim's solicitor!

He would have to ask him later.

'Hello Son, Have you eaten?

"Yes, Thanks Barry, just a beer for me please I'm knackered from riding from the Larkswood. Peter's bike is alright but it certainly gets your knees."

'Helloo boyee, I couldn't ring ya. Oi dint ha a number but there's no news anyway.'

Peter turned a purposeful look towards Leyton as if to say over to you. Leyton responded quickly as he could see Jim was desperate for answers.

'He didn't show. It's a waiting game I'm afraid. He knows we know that he sent those two thugs to sort you out. He also knows we are prepared to fight dirty if necessary.'

"Shall we call the police? Let them sort it out.?"

'Problem is we haven't got any real evidence. I think our best bet is to see how the weekend goes. Although he didn't show I left a message with his Father and if he don't take notice, well, that's his lookout.

'What was the message Son?'

'I just said Mother, It ends now.'

"What? Was that it.?" Jim was surprised he had expected an explanation and a long ultimatum. "Sometimes, Jim less is more. It's now in his hands. His Father knows that and so will he if he tries anything. You've moved the kids out. They're safe. You and Peter can stay with us till we make your place secure at the weekend and if there is any more nonsense we will make sure the good guys win.'

"Thanks Leyton, I really am grateful for your help. You have been a good friend to Peter and I and I don't know if we can ever repay you."

'You will son, you will.' There was almost an undercurrent of a menacing threat as if Leyton had something in mind that Jim had to do, as yet unbeknown to him.

It was Friday. Jim had arranged to collect Bowler from Manor Garage as soon as he had finished his shift in the restaurant and Country Club. Cycling back on Peter's rickety old bike with little or no brakes, a well-used Brooks leather saddle and heavy rear carrier, he took in the beautiful scenery. Fields of bright yellow rape seed intersected with hedges of blackthorn, may, wild rose and gorse. Midday bird song indicating that birds were fledging and nests were to be protected by worried parents. Norfolk did indeed hold its own charm. Jim had lived in London, Essex and the West Country but Norfolk with the broads and coastline and the countryside was home, he couldn't imagine bringing the boys up anywhere else. Cycling up the long incline towards Manor Garage Jim wondered who it was that said Norfolk was flat.

'Sorry Jim we've had a problem with vandalism. Some idiots have been in and been slashing tyres. They also slashed your roof.'.

"What? When?".

'Last night. The police think they were disturbed because they only did your car.'

"Oh! Bloody hell, what's going to happen now?"

'Well we have to get a new roof. We've done the tyres but the roof will be a few days. I can't understand it, in thirty years we have never had this before. I've got a little black Austin allegro Estate I can lend you till we fix it. Is that ok?'

Jim drove to the campsite sounding the horn as he approached the entrance. Peter was surprised to see Jim in a black Allegro. Even more surprised to see his bike in the back.

'Somebody died boyee?'

A quick explanation and Peter was almost jumping with joy. Why the elation Peter. It's only an old Allegro that looks like a hearse."

'Yes boyee but you see that? it's got a tow bar. If'n I can borra a trailer were quids in tomarra when we collect the stuff from the reclaim.' He was right, yet again they had come up trumps and turned adversity into triumph, but there was still the nagging question of who had sabotaged his car. There was little doubt but again, no proof.

Bill Salter drove his treasured Ford Capri to the pub on the Halvergate marshes as usual on Friday afternoon. He met a young lady and stayed for a couple of pints. They left together around two thirty, hardly noticing the gentleman on the motorcycle that had followed him in. They drove some one hundred yards down the street. As he parked the car and went in to a house hand in hand with the young lady, the motorbike passed them. Unseen by the two lovers, it turned and returned to the pub where the rider used the phone box in the car park. Twenty five minutes later a cement lorry almost coasted down the street to where a motorcyclist had carefully opened the door of the Capri and lowered the window before deftly closing the heavy metal door. It took only a few minutes to fill the Capri with a ton of quick set cement. Not quite enough to fill it, just enough to come up to and cover, the seats, gear stick and foot pedals. An hour later Bill Salter left his young lady with a kiss and a farewell wave. He couldn't take it in at first. It was his car, but full of cement. Not only that he couldn't open the doors as the cement had filled the side pockets. Where there should have been a seat there was just a grey mass filling the car from front to back in a solid lump.

'Shit!' Now what did he do? He couldn't move the car, but he had to, the young lady's husband would want to know why it was there. If he called the police he would have some explaining to do. He was already bound over to keep the peace and what was worse there was a note left on the windscreen saying. I SAID IT ENDS NOW! How could Daily have arranged this? He fumed, 'He's broke. A washer up in a hotel, no friends except the bloke who runs the camping field. Nothing to his name, not even a car, I saw to that and yet he's done this. Bastard! I'll have him, I'll bloody well have him see if I don't. My car, my bloody car.' Salter wanted to cry. He almost did, the Capri was his pride and joy. His mind focused on his loss.

He paid no attention to his consort, the young lady from the employment agency who finished early on a Friday to spend time with him before her husband returned. It was a little ritual that until now had served them well.

'You can't leave that there, my Danny will be home at six and he'll want to know why your car is full of cement and parked outside his house when you are supposed to be at work.'

'Let me use your phone', returning to the house and picking up the receiver.

'Who did this? You don't think Danny knows about us do you.?'

'It's not him you silly cow, its Betty's husband.'

'I thought you'd done him over like you said and fixed him good and proper. That's what you said you was gonna do'

'Yea, well you just see if I don't this time. I'm gonna knock his block off! No not you mate, No, sorry I was talking to someone else. Is that the recovery? I've got a car needs collecting.......'

Jim and Peter were taking measurements of windows and door frames and room sizes ready for tomorrow when the scuttling of paws on the hard wooden floor boards was heard just in front of a friendly call from Leyton Stone. 'Are you two in?' Jim and Peter were attacked by the wagging tail and slobbering tongue of Polly, Leyton's golden retriever. She had always seen them as friends, part of her own pack ever since Jim saved her from drowning.

'I'm hair Leyton. We're in the main reception area off the west wing boyee, ya can't miss it. Just past the billiard room. If you gets to the swimming pool you've gone too far.' Peter hadn't even finished as Leyton walked in.

'You boys have certainly moved this on. It was a ruin last time I looked in. It's nearly what you'd call a house!'

'An arse? Thas charmin that is.?' As Peter took the Mickey out of Leyton's accent and cockney pronunciation of House, they each looked at the other and smiled.

'Hornham Hall and Campsite if you don't mind.'

'Good point Peter and well made. Listen I just came by to say make sure you have an alibi for today at 2.30 ish will you.'

"Oh Christ what's happened now?'

'The least you know the better it will be, let's just say Salter and I have cemented our relationship'. "You know him or one of his cronies slashed the tyres and roof on my little car last night."

'Yea, I did hear. I think he's regretting it now though.'

"Have you spoken to him?"

'No, not in so many words but he knows now the bar has been raised. I think he might have a go this weekend and if that is the case Jim I may need your help.'

"As long as it not illegal and no one gets harmed you can count me in."

'Now Jim how could you ever think I would do anything illegal?'

Leyton's wink and broad smile said more than any words could.

'Hello?'

"Missing you."

'Missing you too.' Their telephone calls were never long, or certainly never as long as they would like. and definitely never long enough. "You still coming up tomorrow?"

'Yes we sure are. The kids are looking forward to it'

"Good, So are we. There have been a few developments this end though. The boys are at my Mums and Peter and I will pick them up tomorrow. We are hoping to collect enough stuff from the reclaim yard to make the cottage secure this weekend and I was hoping you could help us?"

'Of course; You don't even need to ask you silly sausage. What's the weather supposed to do?'

"Fine I think but whatever happens we have to do it. This thing with Salter is getting serious and we need to make sure that the place can be secured. At the moment any Tom Dick or Harry could walk in."

'Where are you sleeping tonight then?'

"We're still on Leyton's boat. It's more comfortable than you would expect. And it has hot running water. Admittedly there is Carpet on the walls rather than on the floors but it's still carpeted"

'I know, it's a lovely boat and his mum keeps it so clean. I'm sure having you two as house guests put extra pressure on her though.'

"No. She loves it. I think she has a soft spot for Peter. So look, what time tomorrow and can you make your own way to Hornham?"

'Trains in at ten past ten so we will be with you at eleven as long as we can get a connection'

"OK; The pips are going and I have no more coins so see you then, love you.

'Do you still?'

"Course I do. You don't doubt it do you?"

'It's just so difficult when we are apart like this. I miss you so much'

"Me too. Let's put that right this weekend..." He wasn't sure she heard him as the final three loud pips went followed by the long continual tone to signify time had elapsed. Any more conversation would have to wait until the next day.

Jim drove over to his parent's home to let them know the arrangements for tomorrow, see the boys and read them a bed time story.

Sitting down with a hot cup of tea he recanted the previous day's events to his inquisitive parents. The boys had enjoyed their story, a Roald Dowal favourite of the Twits. They enjoyed too telling him of their two days holiday. They were full of fun and happy, such a change from midweek. He realised he had done the right thing in removing them from Bill Salter's influence. His parents too appeared more content and relaxed. They liked to be involved and feel useful as part of the family. They couldn't cope with the boys on a full time basis but occasionally they loved it. 'Stopping for dinner son?'

"No," Jim was reluctant but knew there were more pressing issues. "I'd love to but I have to go. We are expecting Salter may try something again tonight. Although two of his cronies are out of commission he no doubt has more. Anyway Leyton has a plan and wants to discuss and prepare it tonight."

'OK but before you go, two things; When are we going to meet her?' There was a major emphasis on the ''We' "I don't know what you mean?"

'Yes you do,. The boys have done nothing but talk about her and her kids. They hardly mentioned their Mum'

"OK, well she is coming up this weekend. If I get a chance we will pop over to see you or would you prefer to pop over to us and see Peter's cottage?"

'That would be good. Can you give us a ring on Sunday morning?'

"Yes of course and what was the second thing?"

'That television. I warned you about putting it in the boy's bedroom. I said it would lead to trouble. I caught them on Thursday talking about 'Love juice.' They are only little lads for heaven's sake. What have you been letting them watch?'

Jim thought for a moment a heavy frown resting on his forehead. Then realising, his eyes opened wide as he smiled and said "Wimbledon" All three burst into laughter as much from relief as humour.

'Jim, it may seem crazy but I want you to wash and polish that allegro and park it outside your old house when I say.' Leyton did indeed have things worked out. He had a plan

and if it worked all would be well. It was also agreed that
if it didn't work they would go to the police.

The phone at Jim's old home rang and Betty answered.
She didn't say the number as she normally would but
answered with an enquiring 'Yes?' slow and stretched out
as if unsure she should be answering it at all.

'Can I speak to Mr Salter please? It's inspector
Cambridge of Norfolk Constabulary. We met the other day
when he was bound over.'

'He aint in'

'Well is that Mrs. Daily? He gave your number as a
contact.'

'Well, what's it about?'

It's rather important we get hold of him as we have
reason to believe he may be in some kind of danger. We
can send a car for him if you wish'

'He's at the shoulder of Mutton tonight. You may get
him there.'

'Thank you Mrs. Daily. If you do see him please do tell
him of our concerns and if he is worried, to ring and ask
for me. If I'm not on station DCI Zac Lincoln may be able
to help'

The black Austin Allegro estate had been washed and
polished. It now sat parked outside the home of Mr
Hillingsworth. In it sat two shady looking characters
wearing leather jackets and trilby hats pulled down to give
a little protection from enquiring minds and afford some
form of a disguise.

It wasn't parked there for long before the Norfolk
Constabulary received a call from Mr Hillingsworth
worried that the two thieves who had been casing his
property intent on robbery, had returned.

It was only a few minutes after receiving the call from
Inspector Cambridge that the sound of a police car siren
alerted Betty to something happening outside. As she

looked out she saw a police car with head lights on and blue lights flashing pulled up behind a mysterious black Allegro which proceeded to drive off slowly along the road. The blue and white ford Anglia following a few feet behind.

"Sorry officer I didn't realise you were there for us. I thought I was in the way so I drove a little further on to give you room."

Jim explained that he lived there as he showed his driving licence.

"I'm in a different car and perhaps our neighbours hadn't recognised me. I think he's a bit paranoid since the recent burglary up the road." Jim had no idea if there had been one but it seemed like a good excuse.

'OK Sir, Sorry to have troubled you.'

Jim Drove off slowly in the direction of the Wherry public house. Looking in his rear view mirror he saw the policeman walking down the drive towards Mr Hillingsworth's House.

'Now we need your car at the shoulder of Mutton' Leyton was in charge and working his carefully constructed plan. 'I'll drive it and Peter, you can go as shotgun again.

Jim, you get a taxi to pick up Salter and take him home. Ring your mate, Daisy's bloke and tell him to make sure he tells Salter they are being followed'

An ashen faced Salter ran from the taxi into Betty's home. She had been watching out of the window, waiting for him. She ran to the door opening it just as he reached it.

'Christ Bill, where have you been? I've had the police round here and everything. They rang and said you was in danger. Two thugs turned up in a bloody hearse . The police scared 'em off but I'm sure they'll be back'

'I know woman don't go on. They was waiting for me up the pub and followed me home.' The ringing of the telephone made them both jump. It was obvious their nerves were on edge. Betty grabbed for it. 'Yes?' Quicker this time displaying an urgency and concern.

"Betty, Don't hang up it's me" She recognised Jim's voice in an instant.

'What do you want? I've got enough troubles without you wittering on.'

"That's why I'm ringing. There are two blokes looking for your bill. Apparently he has upset some Gangland boss from London and they are talking about him joining the foundations for the Orwell bridge. I don't like him but I don't want no part of that."

'Oh shit! Well we've had the police phoning up here and sent a car and all sorts. They even followed him home from the pub.'

"What the police? Oh good. At least he's safe"

'No! Not the police you idiot. The other blokes'

"Oh Crikey, They're not still there are they?"

All the while Bill Salter was trying to enquire who it was Betty was talking to on the other end of the line. He was gesturing that he wasn't there she hadn't seen him and not to say anything.

'It's Jim Bill. He says he won't have any part in it. Because some bloke you upset is out to top you and put you in the foundations of the Orwell Bridge. Have a look. See if they're out there.'

Switching the lounge light off first, he peered through the heavy draylon curtain. A sharp breath in was followed by 'Yes they're still there what do I do now?'

'Jim you hear that?'

"Yes. I did. Best bet is to get Bill to make himself scarce for a while. I'll get a taxi to meet him over the other side of the cricket Ground in fifteen minutes. Get him out the back way.

'Thanks Jim. We really owe you.' Still clutching the heavy red Bakelite telephone she replaced the receiver.

'Why should I do as he says?' feeling a little safer Salter's bravado was begging to return.

'Because he's right he's trying to save you. Whatever you think of him he's a good man. And he's more of a man than you'll ever be.'

Salter puffed his chest out, took a deep breath raising his right arm up to let loose a heavy slap as hard as he could to Betty's cheek. This time though she was ready for him. A slight side step and a full blow from a man twice her weight became but a glancing kiss from a gold sovereign ring; Enough to draw blood but not sufficient to knock her off her balance. Instinctively as her head went back away from the bully's blow she swung round with her arm, stretching out as if playing her best rounder's shot. Thwack! The heavy phone hit Salter full in the face. He went down and out like a light. An already broken nose and now with several front teeth missing, he hardly looked the lover she had once wanted to spend her days, and nights with.

As he awoke a few moments later coughing out teeth and spitting blood he was brought to his senses by an excruciating pain from his lower region. Not since his bicycle chain broke while pedalling hard up hill, had he encountered such pain. He felt sick, unable to stand, although desperate to repay Betty for the battering he had received at first to the face then obviously with a few deft kicks to his groin while he lay unconscious.

He hauled himself up using the armchair for support. She threw him a wet towel as another cough brought up more blood and sputum.

'Now Fuck off! and don't ever come back'

'You cow!' stumbling forward still wanting his revenge, he clenched his fists.

'Go on, you try it. She released the catch on the front door and began to open it. 'They're just waiting for you. Shall I call them?'

Realising his predicament he changed his mind from revenge to survival and made for the back door. He hobbled across the rear garden pausing only to spit out more blood; Betty's laughter ringing in his ears. As she closed it behind him the laughter turned to tears but he didn't know that. They were tears of relief, sorrow and hurt. She watched through the window as the pathetic figure of Bill Salter once again looking like the Hunch back of Notre Dame, limped and shuffled it's way across the cricket field. Gone from her life forever.

Chapter 13 The Debrief

"Thanks Len"

Don't thank me. It was an absolute pleasure. I dropped him off at Norwich Station for the London train. Apparently he's going away for a while. I even got to charge him double because he was bleeding from his injuries'

'Well me and Peter didn't touch him. We was out front all the time.'

"And I was waiting here in the pub with mother and Jessie for you two"

'Well he didn't look like that when I dropped him off so it must have been your Betty'

"She's not 'MY' Betty but I hope she has at last seen sense. I suppose we should check and make sure she is ok."

'You moved on then Jim?'

"Yes Jessie. I have. I like to think we will remain friends for the sake of the children but the love has gone from both of us. I couldn't go back to how it was." Changing the subject he rose and collected some of the empty glasses saying, "My round I think."

Leyton lent a hand to carry the drinks while Jim made a quick telephone call. On his return he took the opportunity to give Leyton thanks for a plan that worked better than any of them could have expected. "Where you got Inspector Cambridge from I'll never know."

That was Barry the landlord. He thought if any one queried it asking for Cambridge the plods would say we're not Cambridge were Norfolk.'

"Nice one, and Betty's OK by the way. Apparently she hit him with the phone"

'Oi 'ope he's got ringin in is airs then.' Quipped Peter.

'Take him home Jim. He's had too many' Mother's comment followed Peter's remark both of which relieved the tension and seemed to sum up the feelings of every one.

A dream of ice cream shared with a lady in a fur coat was interrupted by the realisation that his face was being licked by a friendly although somewhat smelly, golden retriever. This brought Jim quickly to his senses.

'Sorry Boy's, Kettles on and the engines fired up. There is plenty of hot water if you need a shower.'

"Thanks Mother" they said in unison as they realised where they were. Safe and well on Leyton's boat in the middle of Rockland Broad

Back to Normal

It was a cool damp and misty Norfolk morning. One of those where the early mist would hang just above the low lying fields and waterways until ten or eleven o'clock when the sun had hopefully risen sufficiently to burn off the excess moisture. The water was still with just a few mallards vying for the affection of a female. Peter's head arose from the cabin on to the stern deck where Jim was taking in the serenity of the moment.

"We're so lucky Peter to live where we live aren't we?"

'I don't really know boyee. I've only ever lived hair. I in't travelled like you, but I do know if I could paint. these are the pictures I'd paint. Them ducks flying overhead, the windmills, the reeds, the cattle fattening on the marshes, sail boats and small cruisers. People laughing and enjoying the simple pleasures; but as I can't I'll just have to enjoy it moiself.'

'Me an Mother are coming with you to the reclaim if that's ok.'

"That's fine but it's hardly a day out for you and we were going to load up the car as well as the trailer."

'We know that, we're bringing the jag. We'll go on from there. Mother wants to go to Jarolds and the market opposite the Castle'

They drove into the reclaim yard and a young lad ran out to move some cones and an old pallet that had been used to reserve a parking bay. Leyton swung the jaguar around and into the space. The allegro with old battered twin axle trailer followed. A few manoeuvres back and forth and they were in.

'Oi cun see you dun't do this every day,'

"Thanks Peter, at least I can drive!"

'As true boyee, I take it all back.'

"Do you see that?" Their attention had been drawn to the young lad, who having moved the cones, was opening the door not for Leyton but for Mother.

'You know them hair then Mother?'

'Yea, we dun a bit of business over the years. They tends to have what we ain't got and vice versa. Business is all about scratching backs and shaking hands, You just need to know when to do it and in which order.'

"Peter! What do you reckon to this?" Jim had found a good solid door with a lock and a key. Only one, but it was a key. They searched through racks of doors, windows and frames; Measuring this section and that. Oversized was ok as they could shave the sides to make the parts fit but undersized was useless as it was almost impossible to add without it looking odd. Some more panels to add to the existing ones on the ground floor, a toilet a low level flush system and their shopping trip was complete. All that was required was to pay. The young lad had a quick tot up.

'Windows, exterior doors, internal doors, pametes for the floor, toilet and wash basin. Two hundred pounds plus vat.' A little more than they hoped but it was worth it. Peter counted out two hundred and sixteen pounds. The boy was dispatched to pay the office manager who had not even bothered to rise and oversee the transaction. The lad returned as Jim and Peter assisted by Leyton, were loading up the car and trailer. He proceeded to hand Peter One hundred pounds back saying 'Trade discount'. Mother came out of the cabin with the office manager in tow, shook his hand warmly and with a smile said, 'scratching backs and shaking hands!' It was lost on Leyton and Jim but Peter knew exactly what she meant.

Peter clambered into the Allegro that was full to bursting as Jim announced "Listen guys, I hate to be rude but we are gonna have to rush coz I have to pick the boys up from my mums and I'm gonna be late.

'Why don't you and Mother take my car Jim, I'll go back with Peter'

"Yes that's great but I though mother wanted to go to Jarrolds?"

'Yes but we're up here most of next week so she can go Monday. She won't mind. Anyway give her a chance to meet your mum and dad before next weekend.'

"Next weekend? What's next weekend.?"

'Peter's hoping to have a barbecue on his field didn't he tell you.?'

"No, I expect the events of the past few days have made it slip his mind."

Jim's Mother looked out as the Midnight Blue Mark Six Jaguar pulled up outside her home.

'John! Jim's here in a posh new car with his new lady'

'Christ Elizabeth! She looks older than you. What's come over him? Can't he get a younger girl than that?'

"Hi Mum, Dad, this is Dorris. Leyton's Mum. He's lent us the car to collect the boys as we were running late."

'How do you do?' Mother or Doris as she had just been introduced, offered a smile as she held out a hand ready to shake the hand of Elizabeth who for some reason, had turned pale and looked as though she was recovering from shock.

As the relief overtook and the shock subsided, Jim's Mum Elizabeth and Leyton's mother Doris, got on like a house on fire. Having told his parents of the departure of

Bill Salter over a cup of tea, while the boys played in the garden with the Polly. The conversation centred around Highams Park, Leytonstone and Chingford. Each of the ladies having their own memories to tell and places to recall. Jim however was anxious to get back to Hornham. All Jim's father seemed interested in though was the jaguar. To own one was always one of his dreams and now here was his boy driving one. Tinted windows, electric ones at that, air conditioning, walnut and leather interior, wing mirrors you position from inside.

'Oh! Jim it's a dream. What's it like to drive?'

"Dead easy dad it's automatic."

'Yea if you don't fill it up with petrol it automatically stops.' interjected mother. The pride twinged with a little embarrassment from owing such a luxury showed.

'Come on Jim let's get these boys back and see if we can't get that stuff you bought unloaded.'

"You giving us a hand then mother?"

'No not me Son, I'm taking the dog for a walk through the village. The kids can come with me if they like and may be get an ice cream.' They were all clambering into the jaguar as they chatted the two boys in the back with Polly. Mrs Leyton and Jim in the front.

"Thanks Mum and you Dad for looking after the boys. We will phone you later and let you know what time we will be over."

'Bye Granma, bye Granddad, love you,' was their cry while waving enthusiastically as the dark blue jaguar rounded the corner on its way back to Hornham.

Kym was already there with Emma and Mickey. She was making tea while Peter and Leyton were unloading the doors. It was nearly two o'clock before they all stopped to eat the sandwiches and cakes Kym and Mother prepared following their walk to the bakery and village store. Crisps and chocolate biscuits completed the picnic washed down with lemonade for the children and cider for the men.

'A penny for them.' enquired Kym of a thoughtful looking Jim.

"I was just thinking how idyllic this is. All of us working together on Pete's cottage, the children playing together and you being here just adds to it." His arm stretched out around her shoulders pulling her close to him.

"I know it has only been a short while but I've realised over the past few weeks just what you mean to me. I hate being parted from you. I just want us to be a family together, you and your kids, me and mine."

'So do I Jim, So do I.' She snuggled her head deeper into the crook of Jim's arm as she wistfully replied.

'You know it's only been a few months since we first met at Happisburgh but it feels like I've known you a lifetime and feels so right. We only have a few weeks till the kids break up then we will move up here permanently. I'm not sure where we will stay or how we will manage it but I'm determined we do it. I've talked it through with the kids and Pauline. Essex doesn't hold anything for us now. This is where we belong.'

"You have just given me an idea. Let's get Peters cottage finished first." Continuing to hold her hand he pulled her towards the back door where Peter was struggling to come to terms with an old fashioned brace and bit, drilling a hole in the wooden support that framed the doorway. They laboured on through the day stopping only for cups of tea. They were joined by Pauline, Simon and the freckle faced Mickey at three o'clock. The children were given the task of rubbish for ice creams. As campers left, the children scoured the site for bits of paper, discarded tent pegs and bits of guy rope. The site was not as busy now but still bringing in a steady amount of ready cash and Peter was conscious of the fact that if he were to attract campers he needed to make sure the place was clean and looked like a camp site. Simon was a Godsend. It takes a quarter of the time to hang a door if there are two people rather than one, especially if it's not your usual

243

trade. One holding, one screwing. Exterior doors first then internals. Peter and Leyton were fitting the last of the windows that needed replacing while Jim and Simon hung the doors.

'Me and Mother's off in a while. We are at the Larkswood for dinner but maybe see you down the pub later. You staying at ours or what?'

"Leyton it's been great staying on the boat but we've promised the kids we will camp here tonight. And besides, we've got some more campers coming in later. We need to be on hand to get their cash."

'I think we'll take dinner out of the takings tonight boyee, what do ya think?'

"I'm ok with that but we will have to get the kids back for bed so can't stay too long. You buy the food I'll buy the beer and lemonade."

'Noo you wunt. Smoi treat. We saved a hundred on the materials s'mornun. Ow about we wash up, Clair up and goo at six? There's not much more we can do hair.'

"Ok Peter, Simon and Pauline are coming too so I'll pay for them."

'Noo you wunt! He's worked all arternoon, least oi cun do is buy him dinner. S'only the Wherry remember, none of yur fancy food and prices frum Larkswood.'

"Ok Peter, you win. The girls are putting the tents up. I'll let them know."

After the cool start to the morning the sun had quickly burnt off the overnight moisture and the day had become hot and sticky with only a slight wind to chill those toiling under the sun. 'Could be thunderstorm tonight boyee. I hope you're prepared to get wet.'

"That's half the fun of it Peter."

'You say that now, we in't got the glass in yet so if'n its bad I'll be in the caravan.'

It did indeed rain, not just rain, a thunderstorm as Peter had predicted. A real belter with fork lightning brightening up the whole campsite, a crashing and bashing of thunder. Having left Peter in the pub playing dominoes with Leyton, Mother and Jessie they had gathered together under the awning of Simons and Pauline's tent. They knew there was little hope of getting the children to sleep until the storm had passed so it was story time again interrupted by the odd rumble of thunder and lightning flash as the rain and wind passed eastwards towards Great Yarmouth and out to sea. It was followed some hours later by another less intense storm that seemed to skirt around the North Norfolk coast rather than follow the river as the previous one had. Having been woken by the rumbling of thunder and the sound of rain on the fly sheet Jim stood in the porch way of his tent looking out as the water ran in rivulets down the heavy canvas of Pauline and Simon's tent opposite. Only visible now and again, lit for a few seconds by each flash of lightening. The children had opted to share a tent together leaving the grownups one tent each. A situation everyone was happy with. Two small soft hands snaked around Jim's tall slim torso. Kym rested her head on his back. As she pulled herself in towards him she lovingly kissed his back between his shoulder blades. He could feel she was naked except for a small pair of bikini briefs as her pert breasts rubbed against him. 'Come back to bed,' she asked almost pleading. 'What you thinking anyway?'

"I **was** thinking how strange and secretive Peter's been lately but **now**, I'm thinking we are both awake, alone and nearly naked, it would be a shame to waste it...."

The ground was still wet from the past nights thunder storm. There was a thorough freshness in the air as if it had been cleansed by the heavy rain. A bright sun was rising the birds were singing and campers were inspecting tents ropes and awnings as Peter toured the site to make sure all was well and none of his eight or so paying groups of campers had been flooded out. Only one family had really suffered from the storm. They had left their ground sheet outside of the tent allowing the rain to run through and soak everything in its path.

'You know what you need here, a proper toilet block.'

"Pauline you are right, one toilet between all these people is not enough. If Peter's going to continue with this he will need another loo and a washing station. Most of these people are experienced campers and prepared to rough it a bit but he will need to attract others too. What's your view Kym?"

'Sorry, I was miles away. Yea I agree. Getting the kids up and dressed this morning was a nightmare. Thank heavens it's not still raining.'

"That's a point, I'd better inspect the cottage." Jim and Peter met at the rear door both having had the same thought. The rain had come through almost every window. Only those few that had glazing had escaped the ingress of water.

"Peter it may be a week or so before we can get these glazed. Why don't I cut up some of that clear plastic sheeting and close the windows on to it?"

'It won't look pretty, boyee but it'll keep us dry. Lets goo fur it.' An hour later and it was done.

'You know boyee, oi cum on more in four months with you than I did in forty years on my own. We've nairly got us a hum.'

"There's still a lot to do though Peter"

'Yes boyee but winters a way off and by the time it gets hair we will be warm and dry and measuring for curtains. An besides we also have our mobile hum. I stayed in it last night and oi likes it. I could happily live there boyee. Get rid of this place and move out there.' They closed the back door with a definite click as the heavy hard wood shut against a secure wooden surround. Both men proud of what had already been achieved.

"Mum, Dad, this is Emma and Christopher and this is Kym." Emma handed over a posy of freshly picked wild flowers interspersed with some pinks, a few roses and some laurel.

'I picked these especially for you Mrs Daily, I hope you like them.'

'Yes I do. Thank you and you must call me Grandma, everyone else does.'

"Thank God for that. First hurdle over." thought Jim.

'Thanks for that Mrs Daily the children have been so looking forward to meeting you both. They have heard so much from the boys. You have a great reputation to look up to.'

'Oh thank you dear, how sweet. If it makes it easier you can call me Grandma too.'

'And you can call me Pop.' John shot out his hand to welcome Kym into their humble home. The visit went better than Jim could have hoped. They'd agreed on afternoon tea in the end, easier and less formal than Sunday lunch or dinner and easier to cut short if things hadn't gone well.

"The children are quiet mum, what they up to?"

'They're all right, they have made a den with an old sheet draped over the dining room table and they are having a picnic there.'

"As long as they're not drinking Dads home brew then that's okay."

'That reminds me Son, I told Peter I'd bring some over next weekend for the barbecue. Has he decided if it is Saturday or Sunday yet?'

"He hasn't said anything. Everyone else seems to know but me.'

'I didn't know either Jim, but you said he had been a little strange lately and may be the episode with Salter took his mind off things'

"No Kym, its more than that. I mean, he said this morning he was thinking of selling the cottage and living in the caravan. Well that's all very well for him but where does that leave me?"

'You knew it was only temporary son. Peter's been really good to you, putting you up when you had nowhere to live.'

"Yes I know Dad and I'm grateful, I really am. Him and Mr Stone and his mum they have all been great, but it's just the uncertainty of it all."

He couldn't get it out of his mind. He tried to. He made polite conversation with Kym and his parents. He laughed and joked on his way back to Hornham but it kept niggling away at him. He was unsettled. He had hoped to live in the cottage with Peter until he settled things with Betty. Now he was unsure. Peter obviously saw the potential in the cottage and understandably wanted to capitalise on its value. It was probably worth Seven or eight thousand pounds and to someone who had nothing, that was a considerable sum. However, Jim and his friends had all put in a lot of unpaid work to make it habitable.

"As much as I love the old boy I still feel hurt. It's as if Salter's out the way so I can just move back with Betty but that's not what I want."

'That's not what I want either. Why don't you speak with him?'

"Yes I will Kym but I'll have to choose my moment. I'd hate for him to think I'm ungrateful. He saved me when I was at my lowest ebb. Maybe he can put off the sale until I've settled with Betty. I need to make sure the boys are safe and secure."

As the campsite loomed ahead Jim adjusted the rear view mirror to see four children fast asleep on the bench seat of the little Austin allegro estate. Jim had phoned Betty and agreed to keep the boys overnight again. He would pop round in the early morning to collect some school clothes for them. She seemed happy and cheerful to the surprise of Jim, to let the boys stay with him for yet another night when Jim happened to mention that Salter had gone to London she happily exclaimed 'Well as far as I'm concerned it's good riddance to bad rubbish. I hope the bastard rots in hell. He's never coming back here. What with his I'll knock his block off, see if I don't. The only block he ever knocked off was mine.'

The boys at school and Jim at work, Kym and her two children were preparing to break camp. The tents were to be left up ready for next weekend but the bedding and items that needed to be tidied away were to be stored in the caravan.

'Mr Mason about?'

A smart gentleman in a beige corduroy pair of trousers beneath a dog tooth tweed jacket with leather patches on the elbows was enquiring of Kym.

'He's not. I think he's gone to the shops. Can I help?'

'Yes probably, are you related?'

'No just friends'.

'Well tell him I called will you.' He handed her a card and turned to go pausing briefly to ask, 'What is the extent of the property?'

'I couldn't say' She could, but there was no way she was going to give that information to a stranger. Watching him exit across the ditch she read the card. Logan and Reid, Valuers and Estate Agents.

'Thanks Kym, Oi didn't expect him to be so quick. Don't say anything to anyone though please. I dunt want too many people knowing just yet.'

'OK, your secrets safe with me. Can I tell Jim?'

'Oi dunt want you two having secrets between you but just tell im to be discreet.'

She did just that and it worried Jim even more. He needed to progress the divorce as soon as possible. If he was going to be homeless he needed to secure the boys future as soon as he could.

Chapter 14 The Necessary Legal Eagles

'Mrs Lamb will see you now.' The pretty blond receptionist and legal secretary flashed a broad smile at Jim.

"Thanks Eileen." the smile was returned, she was pleased he had taken the time to read her name badge so many people never did. She made a mental note to take extra care over any correspondence she typed for him. Jim took only a few minutes to explain that he wanted to proceed as fast as possible with the divorce. He started to explain why and express his concerns over the fact that Peter was selling the house. She stopped him.

'I'm sorry Mr Daily but Mr Mason came to see me and I explained that I could not act for him as I already act for you and there could be a conflict of interest issue. His discussion with me is still privileged so can I suggest you speak with him direct?'

"Sorry, what does privileged mean?'

'It means confidential between the solicitor and client. Although I said I could not act for him as I was acting for you, at that time he was my client so anything he had said prior to my refusal to accept his brief is privileged and I am unable to discuss it with you. I directed him to Cudby and Littlechild in the Cloisters. Now can we discuss your unfair dismissal?'

Jim was somewhat taken aback by mrs Lambs reluctance to share information as she continued. 'You certainly have a claim and Wilkinson Wire works in London have accepted their local manager acted outside of their policies and procedures. They are taking that matter up separately with the individual and I feel we must leave them to do so. I have though agreed full disclosure on all we have discovered to date such as his personal vendetta against you, his relationships with your estranged wife's cohabiter. Yes, I'm sorry to say at this moment she is still your wife. Relationships that went beyond normal business and we believe may have had a financial implication for both parties. They have offered to reinstate you with full pay back dated to your dismissal. That is quite a sum but I believe from previous discussions you feel they have made your position untenable. I therefore intend to write subject to your approval; that we are not prepared to settle so cheaply and will proceed to tribunal. I believe they will come back with a second offer particularly when they realise your manager colluded with the employment agency and your estranged wife's cohabiter, to prevent your obtaining gainful employment. Basically Mr Daily we have them over a barrel and I intend to take them for all we can and I'm not adverse to threatening further legal action.' Jim was speechless. He was still trying to take it in whilst drinking a cup of tea delivered by the hand of Eileen, who Jim felt would certainly have some typing to do.

"How much do you think we will get?"

'I don't know, it's hard to say. At least a year's salary and costs. I expect it may even be a little more. But don't spend it yet. They may pull something out of the woodwork which we have not counted on. The speed of their response may show their hand. If you are in agreement I will draft a letter along the lines we have said. Can you pop in on Wednesday to go through it for accuracy of dates, times, names etc?'

"Yes I'll be pleased to."

'Good, see Eileen on your way out and she will book you in. With regards to the divorce, we will proceed with all haste for you particularly in the light of your possible dismissal claim. We don't want that shared. Particularly as your estranged wife was no doubt aware of the shenanigans that went on.'

'Jim, where you been?' Dave was unusually irate.

"Sorry chef, I was with the solicitor and got delayed."

'Listen, you ain't got time for soliciting. Andy's come off his moped he's not hurt too badly but is shook up though. I'm stepping up and so are you.'

"Yes chef! What about wash up?"

'I've got Beano coming in, he'll cover wash up. Jons in too and as long as we can stop them fwom whistling bloody Italian opwas we will be ok.'

"How many booked chef?"

'Thirty covers but we keep gwowing so it could be neawer fawty'

"On a Monday night!?"

'Yes that's what's known as success.'

"Ok chef, what's on special?"

'Don't ask me, that's your job. I think Andy got some veal in. Have a look in the fwidge.'

Oh Christ, he thought, suddenly I am the chef. There's no hiding behind others, just doing a few hors-d'oeuvres and sweets. I now have to do specials, main courses , grills and oversee Jon and Beano the washer ups who will have to do sweets and salads. Oh Shit! Jim looked in the fridge, the veal was there all right, all sliced and waiting to be egg and bread crumbed ready for shallow frying served as veal escallops with spaghetti and a Milanese sauce of tomatoes, onions and pimento. All served with a ring of lemon and capers. Jim knew how to do it having seen it served many times but it took time. A luxury he did not have. The spaghetti was already prepared so no bother there. He also needed a special. He quickly assessed that if he cut each escalope into strips he could flour them and cook them with a little chopped onion and garlic in a small pan, without colouring them, add a little brandy and some cream serving them on a small silver flat garnished with a sprinkle of fresh chopped parsley and sliced button mushrooms.

'So what we got chef?'

"Veal a la Larkswood chef."

'On your head be it but if it isn't good enough it won't pass the pass.'

"Do you want me to knock you one up?"

'No, no time for that, I will just have to trust you.'

Jon arrived, assisted by Beano and under Jim's direction, they prepared the hors-d'oeuvres in the dishes ready to go into the trolley. Prawn cocktails were always a favourite so glass coupes were prepared with chopped lettuce.

'I do a mean chiffonade chef, just watch me,' was Jon's motto. On top was placed twelve prawns, no more, no less. When prepared these were left in the walk in fridge ready to be brought forward as called. A sauce of mayonnaise mixed with tomato and a pinch of Tabasco was then placed or knapped over to serve to the customer. The head chef adding the slice of lemon cut vertically not horizontally, and a pinch of chopped parsley before passing to the waiter. All had done their part. Melons were cut ready to shape into boats, the hors-d'oeuvres trolley was filled with all the usual items including the now obligatory Hawaiian chicken, prawn cocktails were prepared, what could possibly go wrong?

'Table five, check on. Starters fwom the twolley. Main is two chicken' chaiwy sauce and two standard veg with sauté. Table six two Larkswood specials, one wice and one spaghetti.'

"That's the last of the rice chef, got no more."

'Well put some on then, you twat! It's on the menu as spaghetti or wice.' Jim quickly put two pans on the small gas fired hobs. To save time he poured the same amount of rice in each, he added seasoning to one then as he added what he thought was pepper he was frustrated to note it was turmeric. The water went a bright yellow but as tables were being called he had no time to stop the cooking process. He decided to let it continue intending to discard the yellow rice later and use the white rice from the other pan,

'Two sole meuniere and one cutlet d'agneau for table seven. Starters from the twolley.'

Jim grabbed the sole, dipped them in seasoned flour, greased a flat silver platter with melted butter and with the fish sitting neatly on it placed it under the grill. Service was fast and furious with hardly a moment to catch breath.

"Jon, do me a favour and drain the rice will you.?"

'Yes chef'.

'Table nine check on. Two pwawn cocktail, one melon, one soup, one special with wice, one duck, two fillets medium.'

"Yes chef; you got the rice John?"

'In the colander chef.' Jim looked and saw bright yellow rice mixed with the white in equal proportions.

"Oh sod it! We've got a problem chef. Are you happy to serve the special on coloured rice?" 'Do it up, let's see what it looks like.' He did and served it to the hot plate or pass as Andy and Dave called it. Dave produced the tasting spoon from the button hole of his chefs white jacket and tasted the special.

'Looks good, tastes good, I like it. Well done chef. Let's have them all like that please. Now where's them steaks?' At about nine o'clock there was a lull. The kitchen brigade took the opportunity to clear down their stations and prepare for a further rush of late orders. The head waiter came in and introduced two new waiters. Javier a happy Cuban wine waiter with a robust laugh that sent his ample frame jiggling when something tickled him and Harold, a Norfolk born and bred waiter from Great Yarmouth.

'I lives in Yarmouth now but I've worked f' Coonard'

'You'll have to work hard here too mate' chipped in Dave without even a pause.

"I don't think he got that Dave, humour obviously bypassed his part of Yarmouth."

'Table thirty, check on two hors d'oeuvres from the twolley. Two lobster soup, two specials, two chicken Maewyland with Wice.' Dave was in full song. He prepared the chicken maryland with fried banana, sweetcorn pancake and lemon wedges served with a rasher of bacon over a bread crumbed breast of Norfolk chicken. Always a favourite with the customer and one of Dave's signature dishes.

'Table thirty away chef.'

"Yes chef."

'Table twenty six, check on!' And so it went for another hour. Last orders was at ten o'clock. They were just clearing up and preparing to go when Gloria the waitress came in with a late request. 'I've got a table of two any chance chef?'

'Oh Glawia its gone time. Kitchens closed.'

"I'll do it chef, you can go. Beano and Jon are still here. As long as the customers don't hang about I'll be happy to stay."

'Ok chef. Glawia tell em chef is doing them a big favour. Can you come in early tomorrow Jim just in case Andy's not in again?

"I'll try chef. Is eight forty five ok?"

'Yes fine, I'm off, see you in the morning.'

'Sorry chef but it's one hors d'oeuvres, one scallops, then one wild duck in cherry sauce and one special.'

"No worries, what's the hors-d'oeuvres trolley looking like?" 'It's not bad chef but it has had a hammering tonight.'

"Well, bring it in and we will do them a platter of mixed instead." Gloria did as instructed and even helped Beano and Jon to create a display of various foods in all shapes and colours. Meanwhile a scallop shell was filled to over flowing with a mornay sauce knapped over six scallops. The shell was edged with duchess mashed potatoes piped by Jim, not as expertly as Dave would do he thought, but as it browned under the grill the imperfections disappeared. Two springs of parsley and away. Now the main course. The duck was pre-roasted so only needed to be halved and blasted in a very hot oven. There was just enough rice for the special and Jim was preparing vegetables and sauté potatoes when he realised that there was not enough cherry sauce for the duck.

"Gloria, you got any gravy boats left in the restaurant? I need some for the duck."

'I'll have a look chef.' Three gravy boats each half full were brought in. The contents of which were poured into a saucepan and heated with a small can of maraschino cherries with a slug of cherry brandy and a slug of port just before service.

'You ready chef?'

"Yes Gloria, when you are." The duck came out of the oven sizzling on the silver flat as the sauce was poured over it.

'They asked if the duck is wild chef.'

"Wild! It's not just wild, it's bloody furious Gloria, it's been roasting in the oven for 20 minutes." He poured the brandy over and set light to it.

"Go Gloria before the bugger goes out." As Gloria left the kitchen clutching the flaming duck, Mr Paul entered.

'I'll take the rest of table nineteen chef.'

"Thanks boss." Mr Paul left with the special in one hand, a silver salver of vegetables in the other whilst balancing another full of sauté potatoes on his arm. As the door opened all the kitchen team could hear was clapping cheering and laughter. Mr Paul re-entered the kitchen closely followed by Gloria.

'You bloody twit.' He rounded on Jim wagging his finger at him as he did so. 'And you, you should know better.' This time it was Gloria's turn.

"What? What did I do?" was Jim's protestation.

'She only bloody well repeated what you said about the duck. Luckily they took it in good part. They're having sweets from the trolley so you can go chef. Thanks for standing in. It seems as though Andy maybe in tomorrow but come in early, just in case eh?'

"Already agreed it with Dave. See you then. Thanks Gloria. Taking off his apron he left to get changed stopping only to thank Jon and Beano the unsung heroes of the kitchen brigade.

It was eleven o'clock, too late for the pub but too early to go to sleep. He was desperate to tell someone about the claim for unfair dismissal but at the same time didn't want to get anyone's hopes up, especially his own. They had been dashed too often before. Kym and her children were staying with Pauline and Simon but she had hung on in the hope of seeing Jim to tell him about the estate agents visit. It was ten thirty when Simon picked her up. I'll have to tell him in the morning she thought.

It was early in the morning, very early, Kym had had a restless night thinking of Jim and what options there were for him. She knew he would be upset about the estate agents and it kept going over and over in her mind. She eventually fell asleep when someone ringing bells, was waking her up. She sat up realising where she was. The phone was ringing, someone had answered it.

'Kym! You awake? It's Jim on the line.'

Pauline didn't sound too amused or look it, As Kym hurried down the stairs dressed in only her nightie. She almost snatched the phone from her sister's hand in her desperation to talk. "Missed you last night."

'Missed you too what happened?'

"Oh Andy's come off his moped so I had to work late." He explained all he could and even told her some of what Mrs Lamb had said and how he could have his old job back if he wanted. 'Do you? want it, that is?' "No, no way. I couldn't go back to selling wire works. I've moved on. I see more of the boys now than I ever did. I've got a good job. It doesn't pay too well but I reckon I can get by and besides, I've got you, and your two of course."

'Yes we do come as a package. But I've got to tell you Peter had the estate agents round yesterday. He's obviously going to sell the place but he doesn't want anyone to know yet so he says we are to be discreet.'

"Yes I know, Mrs Lamb told me as much yesterday. Apparently she has put him in touch with another solicitor so there is not conflict of interest because I'm his tenant."

'Do you have rights then?'

"I don't know. The agreement was I'd pay no rent but would help him do the place up. I'll have to speak with him but I need to choose the right moment. Preferably when we are alone."

The boys safely at school and play school respectively and still driving the Black allegro, Jim set off for the Larkswood. All the time wondering what Peter was up to and why he hadn't discussed selling the little cottage at The Loke with him. He was wondering what it was worth and would he be able to buy it if he did actually get a pay-out from Wilkinson's wire company. And why the rush to sell it now? Was there something Jim didn't know?

Did Peter need the money? Where would Peter move to if he did sell it.? What about the camp site? It was only just taking off why get rid of it now? What would Peter do for money? How quickly would the sale go through? There were so many questions. Just as I get one thing sorted another problem comes up. Why Me? What have I done to deserve all this squit?

"Bugger!" Slamming on the brakes as hard as he could Jim brought the car to a sharp halt. "too late" thought Jim as a large bird disappeared under the bonnet. The last thing he wanted was to take part in road kill on the way to work. Remonstrating with himself for not paying attention and being too full of his own troubles to consider others; he was about to open the door in order to go and clear up the mess when from under the front bumper, where the car had stopped only inches from it, out popped a beautiful male pheasant.. It shook it's plump body, waddled a few feet from the car and cocked it's red and blackish blue head to one side. Looking at Jim as if to say 'You Twat' it cocked it's head on the other side took three paces to gather speed and flew off.

"Thank God for that"

The incident had brought Jim back to his senses with a bump and he realised that he should concentrate on the positives and not the negatives. He had a job he enjoyed, he had some close friends, he had a girlfriend and above all he had his two boys.

Peter might well be selling the cottage but Jim would find somewhere else to live if necessary. Maybe he could rent a boat and moor it by the Wherry?

"Morning Chef, Are you ok? Good to see you, Ooh!" looking at the two black eyes and battered face of Andy Jim winced and took a deep breath in. "You look a bit battered and bruised,' like you've gone ten rounds with Muhamed Ali.

'Morning; I'm fine. Just a bit fragile today that's all. But more to the point, Which door did you come in this morning?'

Jim looked quizzically at Andy as he answered "The usual one. Why?"

'Your head not too big then? 'didn't get stuck?'

"Sorry Chef I'm not sure what you are on about. Have I done something wrong?"

'You're in the Eastern Daily Press or Should I say we are.

"Oh Shit! What for?" he feared the worse. All the events of the past few days going through his mind.

Andy passed over the local paper opened on the page for entertainment and food critiques. The headline 'A Furious Duck' jumped out at him.

"Oh I'm sorry Chef. It had been a long day this party came in late and I offered to stay on. I didn't know Gloria was going to repeat what I'd said. but it was my fault not hers. I'm really sorry if we got a bad review. We didn't know who they were."

'You bloody twit. It was the second best thing that has happened to this restaurant.

We were getting good reviews and I think they tried to test us by coming in after last orders in the restaurant. You turned the tables on them. Read it. In fact I'll get a few extra copies and we can frame 'em.. Well done Chef and now get to bloody work. We are going to be busy and it's all your fault'

"Thanks Chef. I had some good teachers though and a good team with me"

'You can't get out of it that easy. Here read the paper and mind you don't slip over on that bull shit you've just been spreading'

Jim read the article and was pleased that the review had praised not only the main meal but the starters, staff attitude, the humour and friendliness of everyone at the Larkswood despite it being very late on a Monday night.

'Come on you. We need veg done. And what's this I hear about a do round yours on Sunday?'

"What do?"

'Bar b Q, so I hear and me and my missus is invited'

"News travels fast. I'm not having a do. I think Peter is having a Bar B Q but I haven't even been invited myself yet."

'Well, Me and Dave and our respective other halves will be there.'

"Let's hope the weather holds then coz there's nowhere to go if it rains."

'Aint you finished that house then?'

"Nearly Andy, Nearly"

"There is something going on Kym I'm sure of it" Jim was on the phone to Kym. His break was precious but this was more important.. "Look, I'm worried. Peter appears to be inviting all sorts of People to his bar b Q but hasn't discussed any of it with me. He's also selling the place and hasn't mentioned that either. Have I upset him or something? I mean, I've worked bloody hard on that place. I've got friends and colleagues to help out too. I mean, what have I done for him to do the dirty on me now?"

Kym let him ramble on and get his feelings off his chest. There was a pause and she took the opportunity to interject with

'I don't know Jim. Maybe the issues with Salter have got to him. It's been a harrowing few weeks, or months and I think the best bet is for you to discuss it with him face to face'

"Well, I want to do that but I haven't seen him to have that conversation. I was think....,"

'Jim, Boss wants to see you soon as you're finished. Sorry to interrupt but I think it's important' Daisy flashed her beautiful eyes and the smile that could melt a thousand hearts.

"Gota go the Boss wants me, Love you, see you later."

He didn't even wait to hear the 'Love you too' response. He hung up the phone and ascended the stairs leading to the office suite above. He knew it was important otherwise Daisy would never have interrupted.

'Come!' Mr Paul was brief and business like as ever as James knocked on the heavy panelled office door.

'Ah James, thanks for popping up.' James? Usually it was Jim. This is formal. 'Take a seat' the gesture of the outstretched hand and welcome in the voice told Jim this was not a. rollicking for a misdemeanour or if it were, it was well disguised but on the other hand it was more formal than usual.

"I can't stop long Boss I've already had my break" said James almost apologising as he seated himself into the comfortable leather easy chair to which he had been directed.

'Don't worry Jim, I just wanted to say 'Well Done' for last night. We got a good review. It was unexpected and what's more that makes it all the more special.

I just want to let you know that as far as I am concerned we are classing you as Chef 'd Partie from now on and you will be paid as such. Welcome to the team Jim. You have earned your promotion.' Mr Paul rose and shot out his hand as he spoke the words. Jim reciprocated and joined in the hand shake as vigorously as Mr Paul, if not quite as hard and firm.

'You all right Chef?' asked Andy as Jim returned to the Kitchen.

"Yes I think so; I have just been told I'm Chef D' Partie. I'm not sure what it means does it give me free entry to the Disco? Mr Paul tells me it's a promotion".

'Ah! It carries all the weight and responsibility of being a Chef but none of the financial reward. It means Chef of a section or part of the Kitchen but in a small brigade as we are it's only any good if you apply for another job and can put it on your CV. If not, Carry on rewardless'

"Surely you mean regardless?"

Andy just looked at Jim and gave a wry smile as if to say 'No! I meant what I said.'

The day went quietly and quickly by with much talk of the favourable review in the local press. As service finished Jim excused himself and made a swift exit with a view to seeing Kym

He drove straight to Pauline and Simon's home to meet with Kym. Sitting in their kitchen his hands around a strong hot cup of tea, he discussed his promotion and his new found fame as a chef with a sense of humour. The conversation turned to the Bar b Q

'Pauline and Simon have been invited too you know?'

Jim looked across at Kym and then at Pauline who was washing dishes in the sink.

"Have you Pauline? What did he say when he invited you?

'Just said if the weather was OK Sunday would Simon and I and the kids like to come over for a bar b Q at about two pm. You and he are providing the food; just bring a bottle or whatever we want to drink'

"Well I wish he'd bloody told me."

'Maybe it's a surprise?' Said Pauline as she tried to pour oil on obviously troubled water.

262

"Well if so it's not a very well kept one. Everyone else seems to know but me. I'm going to have to speak with him about it."

'Helloo boyee, you a roight? Oi herd you wus in the paypa. Yore almoost as famous as that bloody bittern.'

"Not quite Peter, more infamous than famous I think."

'Well good for you son. You two cummn down the pub for a bair tonight?

"Yes we will Peter but I need to talk to you first. I keep hearing we are having a bar b Q on Sunday but you hadn't mentioned it."

'Ooh! Sorry son. I natrally thought you'd be up for it as a way of thanking all those people who helped us with the cottage and the camp site. In fact I was hoopin you'd do the cooking, but now you are a chef oime not sure we can afford you.'

Peters smile through his white stubbly chin and the few teeth he had remaining, melted Jim's heart and the displeasure he had felt from not being involved, quickly dissipated.

"Of course I'll do the cooking" Jim felt Kym squeeze his hand as if to say well done for not getting too upset.

'Oive invited most of the people who have helped us including Barry and Ann frum the Wherry. They have kindly said they will provide a keg of bair, So that's me sorted. You'll ha to git yaself sumit ta drink'

"It sounds good Peter, Let's hope the weather holds. I'm going to have to go back to work now but I do need to discuss some other concerns I have. Can we have a chat later?"

'Ooh! That sounds formal. Yes of course boyee, Meet in the Yare after you finish?'

"Yes OK, See you at ten."

They were driving back to Pauline and Simon's home so Jim could drop Kym off before he went to work. Kym had been quiet but as they turned out of the Loke on to the main road she quietly suggested that the pub was not perhaps the best place for Jim to raise his concerns with Peter. "You're right but I do need to raise them. If he is selling the cottage underneath us after we have done so much work on it he needs to at least let us know." 'It's not we and us it's You. I'm only an add on.'

"Well I don't see it as that. As far as I'm concerned 'we' are an 'us'. But I do see what you mean. I'll not discuss it too deeply but I will let him know I am aware. You want me to pick you up when I finish?"

'Us,' she thought to herself. 'He said We are an Us. Oh God, when do I dare tell him how much I love him and what do I do if he doesn't tell me he loves me too? And what do I do if it scares him off?'

'No, not tonight, I'll have a night in with my sis and leave you to chat with Peter. If I was there it may look like we are ganging up on him and he is a lovely bloke so I don't want him to get the wrong impression.'

Jim left the Larkswood later than planned. It had been busier than usual for a Tuesday evening with everyone putting it down to the continued good press and enhanced reputation. This delayed his arrival at The Wherry having parked the loan car at the cottage he made his way along the river path to the pub.

"Quiet night tonight Ann?" he offered almost as a statement as much as a question.

'Yes just the bridge boys' four old regulars that played bridge and discussed politics and football, 'And a few of the ladies what do' Nobody really knew what the 'Ladies what do' actually did, School teachers, doctor's receptionists and Council employees was a good guess. They were always polite, well dressed and well mannered. Jim always noticed that they smelt of expensive perfume. The fragrance you get when entering Jarolds department store in the centre of Norwich.

He nodded politely to them as he walked through to join Peter, Leyton, Mother and Jessie who were all seated at the table by the open fire.

"Evening all, sorry I'm late. We've been busy again tonight."

'Seems to be the reputation of the Larkswood is growing Jim'

'Yea, an' it's his fault I hear Mother'

"Thanks Leyton, Your Mothers right but I'm not sure it's my fault. I just work there"

'Well I hear different. Chef now aint ya? Started out as Kitchen porter and now chef.'

"You make it sound very grand Mother but there is a very good team there and I have just been lucky" 'Yea, and the harder you work the luckier you get. Don't knock it son, enjoy it.'

Leyton raised his half empty glass towards Jim in salute of his achievements and seeing this, the others followed suit.

'Thanks guys, and girls," a little late with the 'and girls' but not too late for the ladies to take offence, "But less about me and more about the Bar B Q on Sunday. What do you want us to do to help Peter?" 'Well boyee, we jus bin discussn it, an as yure now Chef we wants you t' do the cookun. If an you 'n the ladies cun prepare some salad in the mornnun oil git the meat and breads. Hows that sound?. Maybe the children can help with setting out the tables and chairs?' "Sounds good to me. How many are we catering for?" 'About twenty plus or minus a foo as oim invitun the campers on the field to join us if they wish.' 'Well me an Leyton are looking forward to it, aren't we son?' Mother nodded in the direction of her son who responded with a confirmed nod and grunt of approval.

The evening wore on, Jim was itching to talk to Peter on his own but every time there was an opportunity someone would but in or just be there listening. Jim wanted a quiet conversation, a private conversation, between the two of them. He decided to wait until they got home.

'G'night boyee;'

"Hold on Peter, I think we need a chat" 'Why's that then?' "Well, I hear you are selling the field and the cottage and if so I'd like to know how much for? We both know I can't afford it but I've worked so hard on the thing I would at least like the opportunity of discussing it with you, may be renting it or something or whatever, I don't know, just discussing it between us."

Peter's look of wonder and surprise took Jim off guard and encouraged him to explain. "I have just had so much on my plate over the past few months what with losing my job losing Betty and losing my home. All I wanted was a bit of stability. I thought I had that here. And now I find you are selling me out too." Jim sighed, a sigh of someone who had shed the load that had been weighing on their mind.

Peter's face changed. He looked annoyed his whole face became a frown as he scratched nervously at what little grey hair he had. He adjusted the collar on his shirt and seemed to twitch as he stuttered to say

'I int sellin it, I dunno where yoo got the idea I wus? I int got no deeds so I needs to register it as moine. Specially as wair now usin the field fur camping. Slicitor sent the Land agents round to measure the plot soos oie cun make me claim. Fur Gods sake, you didn't think I'd sell you out did you? You an all your lot, Leyton an is Mum, are best thing thas appened to me in yares. Gime sumat t live for; Sumat ta be proud of.'

The frown was easing as Peter's animated speech reached home to Jim.

"Oh Peter I just wished you'd said." Through an exasperated sigh Jim went on.

"I didn't know what to think. One minute I'm thinking everything is fine and the next I'm told you are selling up and seeing solicitors."

'I did boyee but she said she couldn't act for both on us. She toll me what I hat t do and then sent me to a mate of hers. To do the registering and get the land agents in.'

"Oh Peter I feel such a fool I'm sorry. But surely if it's just a land registry thing she could do it for you?"

'She could but yure a sittin tenant. I wunt gonna tell ya. As I dint wanna worry you. I wus gonna wait till it was all settled. Sce Boyee, She could a dun it but she wanted to make shure no one could come back in years ta cum an say you an her stitched me up.'

"Oh Peter, I don't know what to say. „I should have had more trust, " Jim's embarrassment had him lost for words. "I feel so humbled. Please forgive me for doubting you." He held his arms outstretched and gave Peter a big 'man hug'. An experience Peter had not had since boy hood and one at first he was reluctant to allow, but realizing the warmth of the affection it showed, relaxed and returned the embrace.

'As all right son but next time dunt believe the gossip. An I think' Changing the subject and relieving the tension. 'before we turn in for the night we should ha a drop of moi special occasion.' Peter produced a small square bottle of amber liquid with pictures of Peaches on it and proceeded to pour a good measure into two cups. Handing one to Jim he smiled his familiar smile through broken teeth set in a whiskered jaw and raised his cup to clink with Jim's saying ' To good friends and business partners.'

"Yes!; Good friends and business partners. God bless you Peter!" with that he took a swig and as the amber liquid swilled around his pallet he was taken back to a holiday in Italy some years before where he had enjoyed an Amaretto after each evening meal. "That's beautiful Peter. Where did you get that?'

'Oi cant say Boyee. It's made looclly from peaches and wine grown hare int village. Ass good int it? Special occasions only though.' Peter smiled again and cocked his head to one side as he pointed a warning finger towards Jim. 'Special occasions only'

Jim slept well that night, Helped by the warmth of a couple of large swigs of home produced Amaretto and his chat with Peter, the concerns he had harboured had melted away allowing his brain to switch off and give him the sleep he needed.

The next day was a rush to drop the boys off as usual, phone Kym and get to work on time. He made it but only just.

'You OK Chef? You're looking hassled.'

"Yes Chef I'm fine. Need to get away on time though today. I have to see the solicitor about my unfair dismissal claim." 'No worries, let's get all the mise en place done that we can and sauces made for this evening. We have a busy weekend on too what with a wedding on Saturday and your do on Sunday. We need to be planning for that too.'

"Yes Chef" Jim had never been involved with planning the menus or the ordering and was pleased that Andy wanted to involve him. The morning tea break was one long discussion between Andy and Dave around what to order for what function. How much was needed for next week's menu, should they change it and if so what do they drop in favour of another item.

'It's important to keep the menu current and alive Jim. If we don't rotate it the customers notice and vote with their feet'

'No chance of that at the moment Andy, what with Mr Escoffier here and his Furious Duck' 'Yes we are doing well but we mustn't let it drop. Now; The order for Sunday.' "I'm not sure what arrangements Peter's made about food. He has asked me and Kym and the boys to help prepare some salad on Sunday Morning if the weather is OK. But other than that I'm not sure."

'Well the weathers looking good and my instructions are to get in a dozen chickens, we'll marinade and precook them here. Don't want anyone going down with a dodgy tummy. It's not my do but my reputation would be shot and the press would have a field day. We are also getting 48 steaks in on Friday. We'll fridge 'em and season them ready so all you have to do is pop 'em on the grill along with the Chix and sausages. They're in on Friday too.'

"This is really good of you but how are we paying and who do we pay?"

'Dunnow Son. Better see Mr Paul. He's the one who told me to order whatever you wanted but to keep it separate from the restaurant and book it as a function. That includes the salad. We will make potato salad, Mayonnaise, and a selection of hors'd ouvres here on Saturday and bring them over with us.'

"Will you have time Chef or do you want me to come in?" 'Jon and Beano are in Saturday so don't worry. I have also asked them to come over on Sunday to yours and help lay out and clear up. They are a bit weird but they're good lads. And as it's in a field can I bring Bee?' "Bee?" 'Yea it's the dog' "Bee? Strange name; what's it short for?"

'Well, it's only got little legs' Andy and Jim both looked puzzled neither realizing they were talking at cross purposes but Dave couldn't help but laugh to himself and kept chuckling as the discussions came to a close and they returned to the Kitchen.

Jim drove into Norwich and went straight to his solicitor's office. Mrs. Lamb was waiting and unusually for her, with a face filled with a warm and welcoming smile as she waved Jim to be seated. 'I think we have them,' So eager was she to impart the good news she had dispensed with the pleasantries of 'good afternoon etc.' and dived straight in with it.

'They have come back to us and are wanting to settle out of court. They know they are on a loser and want to avoid further costs and bad publicity. Want a cup of tea? Eileen!' She had asked the question while pressing the intercom giving Jim no time to answer. 'Two teas please and can you bring the letter I dictated earlier to Wilkinson Wire works? Thanks.'

Jim read the letter slowly between sips of tea he placed it down on Mrs. Lamb's desk. "Have I got this right? We are asking them to pay thirteen thousand pounds and they have agreed?"

'Well not exactly, there are costs to go on that but Yes, you would end up with thirteen thousand pounds being equivalent to eighteen months salary and commission' My question to you is, Are you willing to accept that? It's a settlement in lieu of notice so most of it should be exempt of tax. We could hold out for more but we would run the risk of a judge giving a lesser figure.'

"Mrs. Lamb, Thirteen thousand pounds would be brilliant. I suppose I have to share it with my estranged wife?"

'Not necessarily. She was instrumental in your getting unfairly dismissed in the first place, which we can prove and no judge in his right mind would want to reward her for her misdeeds. I suggest we place half of it in a trust fund for your children. And use that as our bargaining chip in future discussions. I take it she still has possession of the marital home and the children?'

"Yes but I do have open access now that her lover has left the scene"

'I did hear; And his being bound over to keep the peace after being arrested following an altercation in a local bank, will not have helped her cause either. I suggest we continue to file for divorce whilst these things are still fresh and keep the pressure on.'

Jim nodded, the word divorce ringing in his ears. It wasn't a thing he really wanted to do as it was so final but he knew it had to be. There was no way back for him and Betty. He had moved on and life had a new meaning for him now.

'Meanwhile, I have been looking at the tangled web your previous employer has woven. Not the London parent company, but the local manager. I believe we could have a case against him for slander that resulted in your not being able to secure employment. Would you like to proceed with that or do you just wish us to send a letter pointing out that we reserve the right to issue proceedings should there be any further slanderous or libellous remarks raised by him? I understand he has been demoted by his company and issued a final warning'

"I think a letter along those lines would be fine and a copy to the employment agency as well would be good. Also what about a reference in case I want to change jobs?"

'Leave it with me. I shall make all the necessary arrangements and let you know the outcome. Meanwhile I will see you on Sunday. I understand you are cooking'

"Yes; and I spoke with Peter last night and he explained why you were unable to act for him. He was very complimentary of the way in which you handled the matter so thank you."

'Well it certainly is your lucky week isn't it? But you have suffered for a while so I suppose it all evens out in the long run. I'll see you on Sunday.' She stood and warmly shook his hand like an old friend.

A quick stroll across the cobblestoned courtyard of the Pizza and Pancake parlour and Jim joined Kym who had been waiting patiently for him with her sister. 'Well how did you get on?' Both the ladies were anxious to find out what was said and what was going to happen. Their anxiousness showed on their faces as they leaned in over the top of their coffee cups to hear the answers from Jim. He was reluctant to tell them both everything. He was happy to share confidences with Kym as they had a special bond but with Pauline it was different. Not that he didn't trust her, he did, but there are things you only share with those closest to you and the details of last night's conversation with Peter and the intricacies of the financial arrangements between him and his former employers was something he felt could be touched on but not gone into in great detail. He did however put their minds at ease over the gossip about the imminent sale of the cottage and explained that Peter was registering the land and in order to do so needed a survey from a land agent.

"So all is looking good at the moment and as long as the weather holds you will meet Mrs. Lamb on Sunday"

They were surprised she had been invited but were none the less curious to meet this woman who had achieved so much for Jim.

Saturday was spent clearing up the camp site and making the cottage look more presentable. Tidying the last of the cables out of the way so no one fell over them. sweeping through, so it looked presentable to the guests who would no doubt want to have a good look at the transformation that had taken place. A renovation from an old run down ruin into a tidy little cottage. Still not finished but so nearly there.

Kym and all the children were busy helping to get things ready for the Sunday Bar B Q. Everyone seemed happy to help and each had a job to do. James stopped for a moment and was leaning against the long handled broom he had been using. He was suddenly conscious of Peter who had been collecting fees from the few resident campers, being at his side. He too was in relaxed mode as he leant back against the wall.

'What you thinking Boyee?'

"I was just thinking Peter, How nice it is here and as I have said so many times, how lucky we are. Six months ago I would never have dreamt that I could be so contented. Thank you mate, it's all down to you. I don't know how I can ever thank you enough?"

'You're an idiot! It was all down to Salter if un he adden't made a play for your missus you wunt be hair now. We wouldn't be as we are and I wouldn't be as happy as a pig in Shit. And I can tell you Boyee I am. I say it before an I say it now, is the best thing thars appened to me.'

"Yes Peter, It's a funny thing but maybe we have a lot to thank Salter for"

They looked at each other and laughed out loud. They were still laughing when they were interrupted by a deputation of children led by Matthew, 'Can we sleep in the tents tonight Dad?' The hazel brown eyes and blond hair mixed with a broad smile was enough to melt even the coldest heart.

"Yes I'm sure you can. You Mum says you are mine for the week end so if you want to spend the night in the tent rather than the caravan or cottage who am I to object? We'd better check with Kym first though if you are all intending to have a sleep over"

Turning to Peter he raised his hands and shrugged his shoulders. "See what I mean Peter? They love it and what better place to bring them up than a camp site in Norfolk"

Jim was pleased that the sleeping arrangements had been agreed with the children all wanting to share a tent together leaving Jim and Kym to share the other one next to them. Saturday night was sorted. However; he was a little concerned that Betty was expecting the boys back on Sunday evening and felt he may not be able to drive safely if he had had a drink so would have to walk them through the village.

"That's three times I have called her and I still haven't got an answer. I hope she's OK" 'She's probably out Jim. Give it until this evening.' Kym was right thought Jim. The events of the past few weeks have probably taken their toll and she always reverted to a bit of retail therapy when the going got tough. "May be I'll call tonight." Kym too had phoned home, or at least to Simon and Pauline's and let them know she and her children were staying over at the Loke.

Sunday morning arrived earlier than expected. The days were getting longer and a bright early morning sun rose over the marshes bouncing it's light off the river as it followed a dawn chorus loud enough to wake the children and send them scurrying into Jim and Kym's tent.

It took all of Jim's powers of persuasion to get them to return to their beds for a lie in leaving the grownups to do the same but it didn't last long. They were too excited. The prospect of what the children considered a party, was too great. An early breakfast kept them quiet for a while but

Jim knew it wouldn't last. "Come on you lot, lets stroll down to the river"

They skipped across the field towards the river their laughter startling a small group of Canada Geese that flew upwards from the reads in a flurry of feathers and loud alarm, landing some thirty yards away within the safety of the river. Nearly an hour was spent walking along the river's edge watching the herons, coots, mallard ducks, geese and swans Most of which had young in tow. Jim raised a chorus of "The ugly Duckling" when he felt they were far enough away not to disturb the campers that might still be sleeping.

The bank was boggy underfoot and undefined in places causing wet feet, socks and shoes. The whole party squelched back into camp. Jim was not popular with Kym who had the job of drying wet cold feet while grayish brown water was wrung out from the children's socks.

'You plonker Jim why did you let them get wet?'
'We were enjoying ourselves' explained the children in his defense.

'You can make a cup of tea as penance.' she said nodding in the direction of the cottage and it's little kitchen.
'The kettle was already on Peter having beaten him to it as usual.

"I have just been for a walk along the river's edge with the children. They all got wet feet as it is so marshy down there. What do you think if I got some pallets like we used for the rafters and made a walkway?"

'Good idea boyee we cun then let it out fur fishun or boat moorun. Chroist! We soon be milinaires' "I wouldn't hold your breath but it may help us to attract extra campers; Now where's that tea?"

It was one o'clock as Jim saw the dark blue Jaguar glide down the hill towards the Loke. He noticed Leyton step out and open the doors to allow the passengers to disembark. One golden retriever, Leyton's Mother and Jims parents too. They were a little early but he was delighted to see them. Particularly as they were together. A friendship had obviously been forged between the two women.

Jim was in the process of firing up the Bar b Q. An old forty gallon drum cut in half lengthways into which was placed a bed of charcoal. Above that was a wire mesh courtesy of Wilkins Wire Works some years earlier that Jim had acquired.

'You want a hand son?'

"Yes please Dad. Where's Mum?"

'She's chatting with Leyton's Mother. A strange conversation that is. The elder one's called Mother the younger of the two only answers to Grandma and if that don't confuse the kids nothing will. I've brought some home brew by the way. A few glasses of that should straighten out the whole affair.'

"Well whatever you do don't get Simon on it."

'I love this bar b Q it takes me back to the war'

"I know you were at Dunkirk Dad but you've never spoken about it."

'No Son, May be one day when the memories are less painful. I made some good friends and lost just as many but that's another story.'

Beano and Jon arrived in a taxi and proceeded to unload the food from the Larkswood. Placing it on the trestle tables that were set with sheets to act as table cloths, setting it up so it looked appetizing in a rustic yet professional manner.

'Is this alright Chef?' "Yes thanks lads. Get yourselves a drink and have a break for a while. You'll have your work cut out later when we have to clear up."

Drinks in hand they raised their glasses towards the crowd of guests that had started to gather and said in unison

'S and M'

"What's with the S and M lads?" 'Mr Stone and Mother' says Beano raising his glass again.

"I didn't realize you knew them. I was told off for fraternizing with the guests"

'They're not guests' was Jon's reply as he copied Beano's salutation. 'They're the owners.' "Owners? What owners?"

'Owners of the Larkswood of course. Didn't you know?

"No I didn't" Jim was shocked "Since when?"

'For ages. They bought it a couple of years ago and done it up. The word is they have a demolition company in London that makes lots of money but they love it up here in Norfolk so they bought the Larkswood to have somewhere to stay in winter if the boats too cold. How do you know them?' "I rescued their dog and we have been friends ever since but they never said they owned the Larkswood"

'You all right love you look as though you've seen a ghost?' "Yea, thanks Kym. I think I have. Did you know Leyton and his Mum owned the Larkswood?"

'No! You're kidding. I thought they had a business in London. Construction or something. Are you sure? Why didn't they say?'

"I don't know. I will ask them though. This changes everything. I thought I got my promotions on merit but it now appears it's because I'm friends with the owners."

'You think she's hot enough to get the stakes on boyee?' Peter held his hands over the graying coals and found it too hot to keep them there for more than a few moments

"I think so Peter. Shall I start with the chicken? "

'yea why not? I'll leave it to you. Boyee, Yure the chef.'

"But while we are on that subject did you know Leyton and his Mum owned the Larkswood?"

'No they dunt. Who toll you that?'

"The lads here. They've worked there even before they bought it"

'Well blast me boyee he's a rum un. Why dint he say?'

"That's what I want to know? I am think,,,"

Before he could finish he was interrupted by the friendly voice of Andy

'Hi Chef how's it going?'

"Fine Chef how is it with you? I see you brought the dog with the little legs"

'Yes, I said it was only little. I've got to keep it on a lead it tends to have a go at bigger dogs and it wouldn't do to upset the Governor. I didn't realize he was going to be here. You obviously know him.'

"Didn't you know I knew him?"

'No. I probably wouldn't have employed you if I had. Don't want a spy in the camp.'

"Thank heavens for that. I was thinking I'd only got my promotion because I was a friend of Leyton's. I only just found out from Beano and Jon that he owned the Larkswood."

'Well chef, I'll tell you something, you gained your promotion because you deserved it. You have great potential and as we grow the business I expect you to grow with it. We are a team and you are a part of that. If you know the boss all well and good but we mustn't let it interfere with the business in the Kitchen.'

'Here here!'

Andy leapt as he heard the voice of his boss, Mr Paul over his shoulder.

"Did you know?"

'Good afternoon to you too.'

"Sorry it's just come as a shock that's all"

'Yes! Well,,, I didn't know you were friends with but I did know you rescued their dog. Apart from him telling me to ignore the reference we got from the agency and your former employer as far as I was concerned that's the only favour you have received.

Everything else is down to me and Andy in response to your own efforts so I suggest you get on with the cooking. I'm starving.'

Jim did just that and assisted by Beano, Jon and Jim's Dad commenced cooking the food for what seemed like ages. Everyone there had come up to him and chatted except Leyton and his Mother. It was as though they were avoiding him.

One of the last to come up and get a plate of hot food was Mrs. Lamb. Jim took the opportunity to introduce her to Kym and Pauline and was pleased to see them chatting away like old friends.

"Oh! Mrs Lamb, I hate to talk shop but Peter has asked me to sign some papers later. I think it's about me being a sitting tenant. Do I need an agreement or something?"

'I do think you will need to sign some papers but have a word with Peter. I'm sure he will explain. Nice chicken legs by the way.'

"Thank you but I always stand like this"

A smile broke across the face of the usually staid lawyer, as she walked away shaking her head at such a poor joke.

Jim grabbed a drink and ambled across the field towards Leyton who was standing chatting to Peter and Simon while Mrs Stone played Grand ma's footsteps with the children.

"Leyton you are a bugger. Why didn't you tell me you owned the Larkswood?"

'Would it have made any difference?'

"Well, No but,,"

'So what's the problem then? We are friends because we like each other's company. You do me a favour and don't ask for anything in return and I do the same for you. Mother loves you like a son. The dog adores you. Heaven only knows why. You always buy your round and don't sponge off me and as far as I'm concerned you are a mate. The fact that you work in a building I own has no bearing on anything. We own lots of buildings. Your employment is down to Mr Paul and Andy not me. And they seem to think the sun shines out of your backside. Now how about a drop of your dads home brew I've heard so much about.?'

"Thanks Leyton" A wistful smile on his face Jim understood exactly what Leyton had been saying 'No worries mate' a nod of the head and a reciprocating smile sealed their understanding.

It was six o'clock and people were drifting off home. Leyton and his entourage clambered into a taxi but not before the promise of extra money had persuaded the driver to allow the dog to sit on the floor at Leyton's feet.

Jim had eventually got hold of Betty and it transpired that she had a new boyfriend who worked on the North Sea rigs. Having had only one beer, Jim drove over to his old home and dropped the children off. They were reticent at first. The memories of Bill Salter still fresh in their minds but assured by both parents that such episodes were over they went upstairs to change ready for a well earned bath. Betty wanted to discuss the possibility of Jim having the boys for longer periods when the new boyfriend was home but Jim insisted they discuss it when Betty's relationship had stood the test of time rather than rush into it. However; he was quietly calculating how long it would be before he and Kym could have a home together with all their children.

Returning to the cottage he parked the car and entered the field where Simon, kym and Pauline were clearing the area of discarded serviettes, the occasional plastic glasses and several paper plates.

'Peter wants you apparently Jim. He's in the cottage'

"OK I'll be out in a mo and give you a hand. Is there any booze left?"

'Yes but I think Peters got you one already'

Peter was sat on an old wooden orange box which served as a chair. Next to it was another and a stool with official looking papers upon it.

'Ha a drink Boyee. An if you dunt moind you cun sign these papers' The square bottle was thrust forward with a clean glass.

"I thought you were saving this for special occasions"

'This moit be one boyee. It's like this. I int cut out to live in a big house. What we got hair int hooge but it's too big fur me. It ud suit you an yure family. I'm gonna live in the caravan and yure gonna live hair. We got joint ownership of the campsite as a business. That includes the land and this property. If either one of us dies the other owns the lot. Wot you say boyee? You prepared to make this your Humm? Thars still lots to do but I'll still help. We will keep the business gooing. You can keep your job at Larkswood coz I guess we will need that to keep some money coming in during the winter and till we finish the cottage. Thas moi proposal what you say?'

"Peter I can't accept it. I'll gladly live here and I'll finish the work needed to make it habitable but I can't take your land and your house and everything you have got. It's just not fair"

'Listen Boyee if it weren't fur you oid still be living in a damp old ruin with no prospect of bettering m'self and hardly a pot to piss in. Oim sayin a fifty fifty partnership. We both deserve that. We will have a business and a bit of money coming in. Not enough to live on but certainly a little extra for the comforts in life and what's more I'll have a rufff over moi ead.'

"I'll tell you what Peter, As long as you let me put the spare money I get from my dismissal claim in to doing up the cottage and putting in a proper path for the caravan and may be the river boardwalk. I agree."

'Settled then Boyee. Sign there. Next to Leyton's signature. I got him to sign as witness.'

"You bugger you knew I'd agree"

'Course I did. I can read you like a book. Now ha that drink before it gets too warm.'

'Are you two OK?' The smiling face of Kym leant in through the doorway 'Simon's going to take my two back with him and Pauline. I'm going to stay over if that's Ok?

"Yes of course it is"

'And oim taking the west wing tonight as I got'a get used to it'

Jim answered Kym's puzzled look with "The caravan. I'll explain later it's all a bit complicated but basically Peter and I are partners. Peter wants to live in the caravan and he wants me to live here permanently."

'Wow! That's terrific. Your kids will be so pleased.'

With Peter going off to bed in the caravan for an early night clutching a half empty bottle of whisky, Kym and Jim settled down into their own bed. It was a double mattress on the wooden flooring with a quilt and a few extra blankets. Two sleeping bags formed pillows to add to the coziness of the room.

"What a Week, What a day. I have never known anything like it before. One minute I'm broke and have no home, no job and no prospects, the next I'm rich, own my own business and a cottage with some land around it. It'll take us a while to do it up though but do you think we could live in it while we finish it?"

'What me live here with you and the children?'

"Yes. Like a proper family. I'll have to share mine with Betty but she's already talking about giving me access for three weeks at a time."

'Oh Jim' She snuggled up to him so close and hugged him with all her might. 'Yes! Yes! Yes! Yes! Yes!. I can't think of anything I'd like better. When can we move in and how long do you think it will be before we have the cottage finished?'

"You can move in as soon as you want but I reckon it will take us a few months to complete the work. Then you have to decorate and furnish it so say Christmas."

'Let's aim for that then; To be in by Christmas. That will just be in time for us to help Pauline and Simon decorate their baby room.'

"What! She isn't pregnant?"

'She is and she's due in January but its early days yet so don't say anything.'

"I won't. But I do think it's lovely. They must be over the moon.."

'What Simon? Over the moon about being a parent again?'

"Yes, Simon. I'm sure he is. I know I would be."

'But you have already got two and so have I.'
"Yes but one of our own would be lovely."

'I'm glad you said that. You'd better get the room decorated them Daddy. Norfolk stargazing has a lot to answer for.'

~~THE END~~

THE BEGINNING!

Once Bittern By

R.E.Buckhurst

Lightning Source UK Ltd.
Milton Keynes UK
UKOW01f0036130416

272079UK00001B/7/P

9 781785 077067